Catesby's Birds of Colonial America

The Fred W. Morrison Series
in Southern Studies

Catesby's
Birds
of Colonial
America

Edited by Alan Feduccia

The University of North Carolina Press

Chapel Hill and London

© 1985 The University of North Carolina Press

All rights reserved

Manufactured in the United States of America

Library of Congress Cataloging in Publication Data

Main entry under title:

Catesby's birds of colonial America.

(The Fred W. Morrison series in Southern studies)

Includes text: The natural history of Carolina,
Florida, and the Bahama Islands / Mark Catesby.

Bibliography: p.

Includes index.

1. Birds—Atlantic States—History. 2. Birds—
Southern States—History. 3. Natural history—Atlantic
States—Pre-Linnaean works. 4. Natural history—Southern
States—Pre-Linnaean works. I. Catesby, Mark, 1683–1749.
II. Feduccia, J. Alan. III. Catesby, Mark, 1683–1749.
Natural history of Carolina, Florida, and the Bahama
Islands. IV. Series.

QL683.A87C38 1985   598.2975   85-1176

ISBN 0-8078-1661-2 (cloth: alk. paper)

ISBN 0-8078-4816-6 (pbk.: alk. paper)

03 02 01 00 99   6 5 4 3 2

To Dr. Carl W. Buchheister,

pioneer in conservation

Contents

List of Color Plates

Foreword

Mark Catesby's *Natural History of Carolina, Florida, and the Bahama Islands*, a celebrated work during the latter part of the eighteenth century, was eclipsed by Alexander Wilson's *American Ornithology*, which appeared between 1808 and 1814, and then by *Birds of America*, published between 1827 and 1838 by John James Audubon. These latter two monumental works were succeeded by a flood of books on North American birds and other wildlife, and Catesby's great contribution entered a long period of neglect. Only major libraries possessed copies of *The Natural History of Carolina*, and the average naturalist was wholly unfamiliar with the contribution to our knowledge made by this important pioneer.

One reason for Catesby's obscurity is the fact that when he wrote his great work on the plants and animals of the southeastern United States and the Bahamas, there was no standard system for naming newly discovered species; there was no way for scientists of the period to make any sense out of the bewildering variety of new plants and animals being described in increasing numbers from all parts of the world. For animals, this confusion ended in 1758, with the tenth edition of the *Systema Naturae*, by the Swedish naturalist Carolus Linnaeus. Under the system proposed by Linnaeus, each species was to bear a two-part name, like *Homo sapiens* for our own species; and no other species could have that particular two-part combination. Any describer who did not follow the Linnaean system was disqualified, and any other writer could coin the necessary two-part name, thereby acquiring credit as the discoverer or namer of the species. A classic example involves the ivory-billed woodpecker, a common bird of southern swamps in Catesby's day. Catesby, the first naturalist to describe the bird in detail, called it "The Largest White-bill Wood-pecker, *Picus maximus rostro albo.*" Linnaeus himself consulted Catesby's book, shortened the name to "*Picus principalis*"—a good, two-word name—and took credit as the namer of this species.

For Mark Catesby's birds, at least, the long period of neglect is over. It is a joy to see the appearance of *Catesby's Birds of Colonial America*, with editorial and interpretative comments by Alan Feduccia. At long last the public will have a chance to see what this pioneer observer saw, to read of the wild, almost Arcadian America that Catesby visited and described almost two and a half centuries ago. At that time, man's impact on the wildlife of the continent was almost negligible; in his accounts of the "Parrot of Carolina" and of the "Pigeon of Passage" there is no hint that both of these birds would one day become extinct, that generations of Americans would be born into a world where these two species had ceased to exist. We find familiar birds called by names that surprise us; what most birders know as the myrtle warbler is here called the "Yellow-rump," showing that the official, modern name, yellow-rumped warbler, is not so new after all, despite its many critics. There is no doubt about the identity of Catesby's "Towhe-bird," or "Baltimore Bird," and it takes only a little pondering to decide what the Cowpen Bird" must be. But I'll let the reader discover for himself what Catesby had in mind when he wrote of the "White Curlew," or the "Fox Coloured Thrush."

Whatever names he used, Mark Catesby had a sharp eye and an inquiring mind. He was years ahead of his time in suggesting that bobolinks disappear in winter because they migrate and not, as was the prevailing view of the day, because they hibernate in caves or in the mud at the bottom of ponds. His brief accounts of the habits of many birds were the first to be read by Europeans. Even as they coined names of their own for Mark Catesby's birds, they learned much from this most illustrious of eighteenth-century naturalists in North America.

Alan Feduccia and the University of North Carolina Press are to be congratulated on restoring Mark Catesby and his *Natural History* to the public eye, and giving this forerunner of Audubon and Wilson the credit he so richly deserves.

Russell W. Peterson
President, National Audubon Society

Preface

The impact of John James Audubon's *Birds of America* (1827–38) was so great that all who came before and most who came after were overshadowed and obscured. This is nowhere more true than in the case of Mark Catesby, the first to draw an extensive array of the plants and animals of America. Catesby was quite well known in the eighteenth century in both America and Europe, and his *Natural History of Carolina, Florida, and the Bahama Islands*, 1731–43 (cited in the text as *Natural History*) was truly a pioneering work in the field of scientific illustration. In fact, it remained until the time of Audubon, a century later, the best illustrative treatment of the flora and fauna of North America. With the advent of the Audubonian era, however, Catesby quickly fell into obscurity, and, remarkably, the first major biographical treatment of Catesby was that of Elsa Guerdrum Allen in 1951. Shortly thereafter, however, in 1961, G. F. Frick and R. P. Stearns wrote an extensive and rather exhaustive biography. Catesby's prints have been reproduced from time to time, primarily for framing, and in 1974 a beautiful (and expensive) facsimile edition of part of Catesby's work with all the natural history prints in miniature appeared from the Beehive Press (Savannah, Georgia). Unfortunately, that edition incorrectly identified many plant and animals.

The purpose of this book is to provide for the first time an account of Catesby's birds for readers who have an interest in natural history during the colonial period in North America. For each bird, Catesby's description is given in its entirety, lightly edited and set in modern type for easier reading, followed by my own account of the species, including, when appropriate, some account of the perception of the species during the colonial period, comments on its habits, and anecdotes and quotes from other early naturalists, especially John Lawson. I also refer frequently to Alexander Wilson's *American Ornithology* (1808–14), as that work provided the first truly comprehensive descriptions of American birds. Following the bird plates the complete text of Catesby's work, edited for readability, is reproduced, also for the first time.

In the introduction I have attempted to piece together the most important facts relating to Mark Catesby's life, as well as provide information on several other early figures in American ornithology, including John White and John Lawson. Catesby's life is a historical enigma, and the veracity of information gleaned from various sources seems at times a bit suspect. Nevertheless, by restricting ourselves to the more established facts of his life, a story emerges.

I am indebted to J. R. Massey for advice on common plant names and to E. A. McMahan for help on insects. J. L. Sharpe, Curator of Rare Books at Duke University's Perkins Library, kindly provided access to their first edition of Catesby's *Natural History*, from which volumes all of the plates for this book were shot. W. R. Burk and J. S. Beam of the Couch Library, Department of Biology, the University of North Carolina at Chapel Hill, provided me with frequent access to a third edition of *Natural History* under their care. I also thank J. B. Darling of the department's Wilson Hall library for frequent help with references and for providing access to a copy of Alexander Wilson's *American Ornithology* under his care, and for photographic assistance I am indebted to S. S. Whitfield of the department's photography lab.

My interest in Mark Catesby began when, as a young boy growing up in Mississippi, I put myself to the task of learning the scientific names of the fauna of the South. Among the first names that I encountered was *Rana catesbeiana*, the bullfrog, whose vibrant, bass bellowings filled the moonlit nights of spring and early summer. It was some time later that I learned that it was Mark Catesby who first brought this marvelous creature to the attention of the world through his beautiful painting of this species with the pink lady's slipper, *Cypripedium acaule*; and that the bullfrog was later, in 1802, named for him as a fitting and lasting memorial. Now, some thirty years after my initial encounter with "Catesby," it is with a great deal of pleasure that I bring to the public this enigmatic and forgotten figure in American natural history.

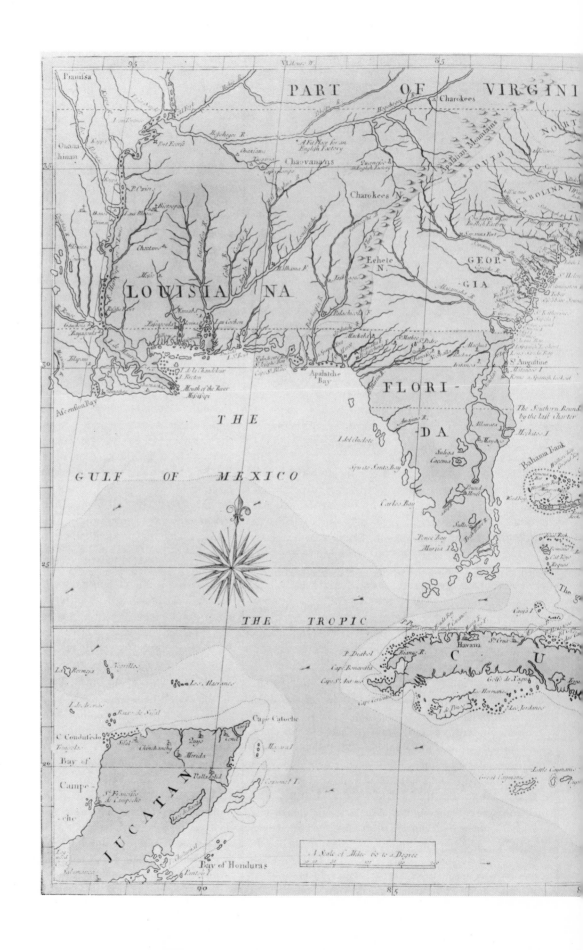

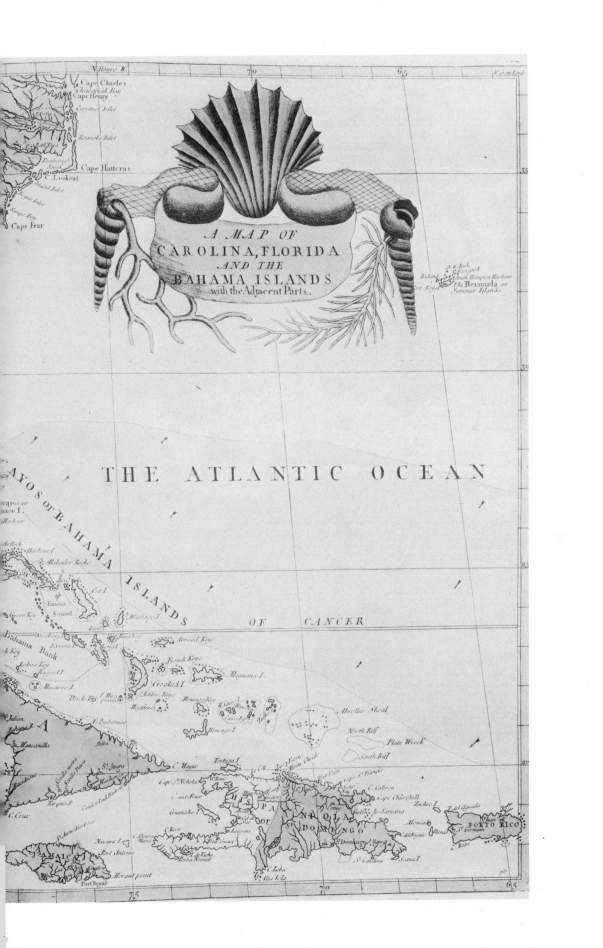

A MAP OF
CAROLINA, FLORIDA
AND THE
BAHAMA ISLANDS
with the Adjacent Parts.

THE ATLANTIC OCEAN

1. The Largest White-bill Wood-pecker (Ivory-billed Woodpecker)

2. The Purple Martin

3. The Mock-bird (Northern Mockingbird)

Magnolia Lauri folio, subtus albicante.
The Sweet Flowering Bay.

Coccothraustes cœrulea.
The Blew Grosbeak.

4. The Blew Gros-beak (Blue Grosbeak)

T. 24.

Turtur Caroliniensis.
The Turtle of Carolina.

Anapodophyllon Canadense &c.

5. The Turtle of Carolina (Mourning Dove)

Quercus folio non serrato, in Summitate quasi triangulo.
Water Oak.

Picus capite toto rubro
The red headed Woodpecker

6. *The Red-headed Wood-pecker*

7. The Blew Jay (Blue Jay)

8. The Pigeon of Passage (Passenger Pigeon)

Althea Floridana.

Avis Tricolor.
The Painted Finch.

9. The Painted Finch (Painted Bunting)

Ardea cærulea

10. *The Blue Heron (Little Blue Heron)*

11. The Fishing Hawk (Osprey)

12. The Ilathera Duck (White-cheeked Pintail)

13. The Chattering Plover (Killdeer)

14. The Parrot of Carolina (Carolina Parakeet)

Nux juglans Virginiana alba &c.
The Hiccory Tree.

The Pig-nut.

Coccothraustes ruber.
The red Bird.

15. The Red Bird (Northern Cardinal)

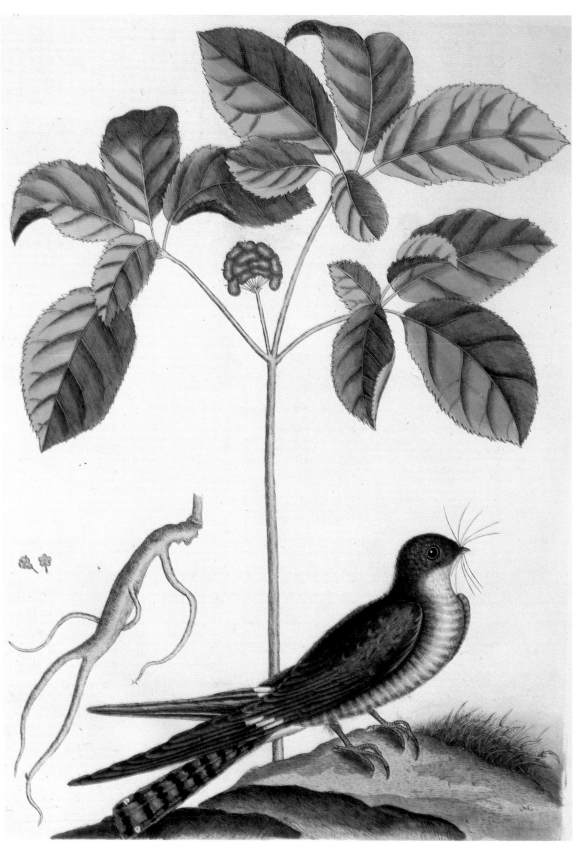

16. *The Whip-poor-will*

17. Urogallus Minor (Greater Prairie-Chicken)

18. *The Yellow and Black Pye (Troupial)*

T.82

Numenius albus.

19. The White Curlew (White Ibis)

20. *The Crested Bittern (Yellow-crowned Night-Heron)*

Catesby's Birds of Colonial America

Birds in America more beautiful than in Europe. —John Lawson, 1709

Introduction

... both volumes, ... containing in all 113 ... all the land birds I have ever seen, or could discover, in that part of North-America included between the 30th and 45th degrees of latitude.
—Mark Catesby, 1748

One beautiful day in late September of 1712 at Westover, the vast estate of William Byrd II on the James River, some twenty miles west of Williamsburg, Byrd was aroused from his usual afternoon session in his private library by a guest, Mark Catesby, a well-to-do thirty-year-old Englishman who was new to the Virginia colony. The visitor had sighted a bear. The New World career of the most important natural history illustrator of the American colonial period was off to a rousing start.

Mark Catesby (1682–1749) was born and educated in Essex, England, and from his early years had a keen interest in natural history, especially botany, an interest in which he had been encouraged by numerous individuals of prominence in England. Catesby came from a prominent English family; his father, John Catesby, was a magistrate in the town of Sudbury in Suffolk. John Catesby had also been mayor of the town several times and was a man of considerable means. He owned property in London as well as several farms and other holdings in Suffolk, some of which he left to Mark upon his death. Mark Catesby's mother, Elizabeth Jekyll, of Castle Hedingham, was also of prominent heritage; she was a descendant of a well-known antiquarian and historian, Thomas Jekyll (1570–1653). Mark was the youngest son of John and Elizabeth, the fourth of five children still alive when John Catesby's will was drawn up. Several children, including twin sons born in 1675, apparently did not survive their infancy.

Catesby's childhood and formative years pointed to a career in natural history. His mother's father, Nicholas Jekyll, was perhaps instrumental in turning young Mark in that direction. The Catesbys made frequent visits to Castle Hedingham, where they spent much of their time with their grandfather, who, like many prominent, wealthy Englishmen of the time, had his own botanical garden. John Ray, one of the founders of modern biological nomenclature, lived less than ten miles from Castle Hedingham and only about sixteen miles from Sudbury. Although the historical record is unclear on this point, it is hard to imagine that he would not have been an acquaintance of the Jekylls. Mark would have had ample opportunity to absorb much from Ray before the latter's death in 1705. No doubt through Nicholas Jekyll, and perhaps John Ray, young Catesby met Samuel Dale, the well-known Braintree apothecary and physician, who became widely known for his

Pharmacologia (1693). It is known that Dale visited the gardens of Nicholas Jekyll in 1711, only one year before Catesby sailed for America. Perhaps it was then that final arrangements were made for Mark to send botanical specimens back to Dale. Catesby's father died in 1705; he divided his property equitably among his children, leaving to Mark his houses in Sudbury, as well as properties in London, Chilton, and Suffolk. Thus the scene was set for young Mark to venture to the New World.

Catesby's most important sibling was his sister Elizabeth, who was born in either 1680 or 1681. She married William Cocke, without her parents' consent, and was subsequently termed by her father "my disobedient daughter." Elizabeth was to play a crucial role in Catesby's becoming a colonial naturalist because it was her move to Virginia that made it possible for Mark to venture to America.

"Virginia was the Place (I having Relations there) suited most with my Convenience to go," wrote Catesby (*Natural History* 1:v), speaking of his first voyage to the New World. Dr. William Cocke and Elizabeth had sailed for Virginia in the party of Lt. Governor Alexander Spotswood around or shortly after 1700. Cocke, who is buried in Bruton Parish Church in Williamsburg, was a success not only as a physician but also as a statesman. Under Spotswood's patronage, he was sworn in as secretary to the colony. Later, in 1713, Cocke would be elevated to become one of Her Majesty's Councilors, a very high position in the political life of the colony. Catesby was thus in an enviable position when he arrived in Williamsburg on 23 April 1712. Only a week or so after Catesby's arrival he met William Byrd II of Westover, a member of the Council of Virginia, who would entertain Catesby many times at his vast estate. At the time Byrd was still on very good terms with Dr. Cocke (they later came to odds over politics), and the relationship between Catesby and Byrd flourished. Beginning 24 May of the same year Catesby spent three weeks at Westover, where he took frequent walks with Byrd, an amateur naturalist, and helped him with his massive gardens. It can be debated just how much of Catesby and Byrd's time was spent on natural history, for the entertainment was apparently lavish. On one recorded occasion the two spent some time aboard a ship and, on the way home, "were so merry that Mr. Catesby sang" (Frick and Stearns 1961, 13).

Nevertheless, this close friendship with Byrd, which was to endure through later years in correspondence, brought Catesby into contact with the flora and fauna of Virginia and exposed him to many remote regions and their native inhabitants, the Indians. Almost a year after Catesby's arrival, Governor Spotswood himself sent seeds that had been collected by Catesby to the bishop of London. During this time Catesby apparently was primarily concerned with collecting plants, and he sent many specimens back to England to Castle Hedingham, and also to Samuel Dale and Thomas Fairchild. The shipments to Fairchild gained for Catesby much exposure in the elite natural history circles of London, and led James Petiver, the great promoter of botany, to call him "that curious Botanist Mark Catesby of Virginia."

Catesby was also becoming well known for his willingness to help those interested in gardening in Virginia, among whom was Thomas Jones, a well-to-do merchant and landowner who would later marry Catesby's niece Elizabeth Cocke. He also came to know John Custis, who was himself quite a knowledgeable botanist. Catesby traveled extensively, and on one trip in 1714 went westward to the Appalachian mountains. During the same year he made a voyage to Jamaica, an island that was of considerable interest to him because of Sir Hans Sloane's book *The Natural History of Jamaica* (1707), which had been widely acclaimed before Catesby's departure to America. His voyage apparently also included a glimpse of Bermuda, and during the voyage he collected specimens to supplement those of Sloane; he shipped many of these back to Samuel Dale, who shared them with William Sherard, a noted English botanist. These connections were to prove very important in later years when Catesby sought patronage for his second voyage. Catesby's first trip to the New World ended, after seven years, when he set sail for England in the autumn of 1719. In the same year he was to be introduced to such figures as Sherard and Sloane, members of the Temple House Coffee Club, the coterie of natural historians, and many other important figures in the Royal Society. Perhaps one of the most notable connections was his introduction to Col. Francis Nicholson, who was about to set sail in 1720 for South Carolina to assume his position as the royal governor of South Carolina. Nicholson agreed to sponsor Catesby during his term as governor (1720–25) and to give him an annual pension of twenty pounds so that he might "observe the rarities of that country." Nicholson's sponsorship, along with that of the Royal Society, was to open up many new avenues of patronage and support for the young naturalist. The complete list of patrons is given in the introduction to Catesby's text (*Natural History*, 1:vi; see p. 137 below).

John Lawson, the great American natural historian who preceded Catesby, had been corresponding with James Petiver, the most ambitious English promoter of plant collecting in the New World. Petiver had received numerous specimens of plants from Lawson, many of which are presently in the British Museum. Lawson was the author of *A New Voyage to Carolina*, which was published in London in 1709. At Petiver's urging, Lawson had agreed in 1710 to compile a complete natural history of America. Unfortunately, Lawson's untimely death at the hands of the Tuscarora Indians in 1711 prevented his undertaking this project. Interestingly, both Catesby and his friend William Byrd II would both later make extensive use of John Lawson's book; Catesby incorporated parts into the text of *Natural History* (especially the account of the Indians), and Byrd practically copied Lawson's book for his *Natural History of Virginia* (see p. 8).

Petiver died in 1718, but other members of the intimate circle of London natural historians, especially Sherard, were able to convince Catesby to take on the task that Lawson had left. By the time Catesby set sail for South Carolina he had gained enough subscriptions to be confident of success.

Catesby arrived in Charles Town, South Carolina, after a three-month voyage, on 3 May 1722. As his sponsors included some of the most influential members of the Royal Society, as well as Governor Nicholson, he was immediately introduced to some of the most influential families of the Charles Town area and extended their hospitality and cooperation.

Shortly after his arrival in South Carolina, Catesby made his first journey some forty miles into the interior, and he immediately relayed the news to Sherard on 22 June. He was thus off on his natural history mission, collecting specimens, taking notes, and presumably making drawings of the flora and fauna. As his work increased and more demands came from England for additional specimens, it became apparent that he would need assistance, and he wrote to Sherard asking if he could have twenty pounds to buy a "Negro Boy," which he later did. Catesby spent about three years in Carolina, making trips into the Piedmont, into parts of Florida, including the area of present-day Georgia, and to Fort Moore, a frontier garrison located on the Carolina side of the Savannah River opposite the present-day site of Augusta.

Catesby assembled an enormous collection of flora and fauna for his patrons. Some of them, especially Sloane and Sherard, were constantly at each other's throats concerning the disposition of Catesby's specimens. The logistics of transporting specimens and shipping them back to Europe were difficult. Seeds were stored and transported in gourds or small boxes. Snakes and other smaller animals were placed in jars filled with rum or other spirits; these were often pilfered by thirsty sailors on the way back to England.

Birds, too, were sometimes preserved in spirits, but more often Catesby baked them for a time in an oven and then stuffed them and covered them with tobacco dust.

Catesby wanted to make a trip to Mexico; he wrote to Sherard that this was the only way in which he could continue to get more varieties of organisms. He could not persuade his patrons to finance the trip, however. So instead, in 1725, Catesby sailed for Nassau (New Providence), Bahamas, where he stayèd as a guest of George Phenney, the governor, in a house on a steep hill overlooking the town. Catesby noted in his text that on two days in December 1725 it was so cold that to keep warm he had to make a fire in the kitchen of the mansion. Remaining in the Bahamas for the following year, Catesby visited the islands of Eleuthera, Andros, and Abaco.

It was perhaps on the islands that Catesby got some of his ideas for what is his most acclaimed paper, "Of Birds of Passage," which he read to the Royal Society and subsequently published in the *Philosophical Transactions* in 1747. Catesby writes of "lying upon the deck of a sloop at Andros Island" in September 1725 and for three nights listening to the sounds of the rice birds (bobolinks) passing overhead. The prevailing views of migration were still bound to the ideas that birds hibernated in caves or beneath ponds, but Catesby rejected this. He felt that migration of the rice birds was explained by their following the ripening of the rice fields from Carolina to Cuba.

Catesby also recorded perceptive views on variations in body size in plants and animals, stating that he had observed a diminution in their size in more northerly latitudes (see p. 167). In addition, his statements on p. 168 indicate that he had a clear view of the concept of tropical diversity.

Upon his return to England in 1726, Catesby faced financial problems because his former patrons, who were no longer receiving specimens, had terminated their contributions. He secured a loan without interest from his friend Peter Collinson and found some employment with certain nurserymen, among whom was Thomas Fairchild. Slowly he began to put together the text and illustrations for what would prove to be a monumental book, and by the spring of 1729 he had completed the first part. Money continued to be a problem through all the production stages, and in order to produce the book as inexpensively as possible Catesby had learned the engraving process and had actually done the coloring for most of the initial plates. He decided that in order properly to promote the book he would issue it in parts at a smaller price: eleven twenty-plate installments bound into volumes and sold at two guineas each. The first was presented to the Royal Society in May 1729, and subsequent parts were similarly presented; the fifth part, completing volume 1, was given in November 1732 (the date given on the title page, however, is 1731). Upon the completion of this volume, Peter Collinson presented Catesby for membership in the Royal Society, and he was elected a fellow on 3 May 1733.

The second volume of the *Natural History* proceeded much as had the first, but by this time Catesby was able to employ help in coloring the plates. The first twenty plates of volume 2 were presented in 1734–35. The last of the volume was not completed until 1743, however, and it was not until 1747 that the appendix to volume 2, also containing twenty plates, was completed. In a well-known letter from Collinson to Linnaeus, it was proclaimed that "Catesby's noble work is finished." The task of producing the two volumes had consumed some twenty years.

When finished, Catesby's *Natural History of Carolina, Florida, and the Bahama Islands* included 220 plates, illustrating 109 birds, 33 amphibians and reptiles, 46 fishes, 31 insects, 9 quadrupeds, and 171 plants. The text contained descriptions of the geography of the regions, including the climate, soil, agriculture, and so forth, and a rather lengthy essay on the Indians, a section Catesby admits owes much to John Lawson (1709). Although he does not seem to have copied any sections directly, Catesby's entire text is quite similar in both format and content to that of Lawson, even in many of his accounts of birds, fishes, and mammals. Of equal interest, Catesby directly copied at least seven of John White's drawings, which had been shown to him by Sir Hans Sloane (Hulton and Quinn 1964, 7, 27, 50–51).

Both John White and John Lawson stand apart in their contributions to early American ornithology. White was the first to draw American birds extensively; in all he depicted some thirty-two species, although some may be duplicates (List 1). Lawson founded the science of ornithology in America with his considerable observations in *A New Voyage to Carolina* (1709).

White made four voyages to the New World. On the second (1587) he went as governor of Sir Walter Raleigh's most ambitious attempt to found a colony on Roanoke Island, in what is now North Carolina, taking with him 150 settlers. There, his daughter and her husband would become the parents of Virginia Dare, the first English child born in British America. When supplies ran low, White returned to England with a number of disappointed colonists, but left most of the colonists behind, including his daughter and her family. Because of problems in England, White was unable to return until 1590. Upon his arrival he found little trace of the Roanoke Colony. The word *Croatoan* carved on a tree was the only clue, possibly indicating that the settlers had gone to live with friendly Indians, but others believe they were killed. We know little of White's subsequent life, except that he retired to Raleigh's estate in Kylmore, Ireland.

On an earlier voyage, in 1585, White had been in the company of the scientist Thomas Hariot, who published in London in 1588 a small volume, *A briefe and true report of the new found land of Virginia*. White's work as an illustrator of the inhabitants of America was to become quite well known through engravings done by Theodor de Bry, which de Bry published in 1590 along with Hariot's text. White's bird drawings, however, made no contribution at all to ornithology or ornithological illustration of the New World in the seventeenth century, as they came to light only much later. In 1709, Sir Hans Sloane discovered that one of White's descendants had a volume containing copies of 113 of the original drawings, which a member of White's family had made. At the time Sloane was not able to purchase the drawings, but had copies made. He later purchased the volume, and it passed to the British Museum at his death in 1753 (Hulton and Quinn 1964, 27). Long before that, however, he had reintroduced White's birds and fish to his elite circle of English natural historians through his copies. Sloane, a close friend and patron of Catesby, had shown the copies of White's drawings to him. Catesby was quick to use these to supplement his own drawings of American natural history, and directly plagiarized seven of the White drawings. In no case did he acknowledge the artist directly, but in one case, the "Swallow-tail" (*Papilio glaucus*), he acknowledged Raleigh and the Sloane volume.

The four fish that Catesby plagiarized are the catfish (Plate 23, vol. 2), the remora (Plate 26, vol. 2), the globe fish or puffer (Plate 28, vol. 2), and the gar (Plate 30, vol. 2). Also copied were the land crab (Plate 32, vol. 2), the Bahaman iguana (Plate 64, vol. 2), and the swallow-tail (Plate 97, vol. 2). In some, the plagiarism is apparent only upon close scrutiny; indeed, the swallow-tail is not an apparent copy and, except for the acknowledgment to the Sloane volume, would be thought to be original. In others, such as the gar and puffer, Catesby apparently made an attempt to conceal his source: he reversed the two so that his drawings illustrate the right side of the gar and the left side of the puffer; White's are the left side and right side, respectively. Both White's and Catesby's remoras show the right side, tilted to show the strange head. It would appear that the reversals of White's drawings are due to

LIST 1. *John White's Birds*

Note: Thirty-five drawings of thirty-two species. Current common names are given here; White's drawings were labeled with a combination of Indian and local names. The order is from Hulton and Quinn, 1964.

Caribbean and Oceanic:
Greater Flamingo
Magnificent Frigatebird
tropicbird (sp.)
Brown Booby
Brown Noddy

Sir Walter Raleigh's Virginia:
Brown Pelican (head)
Sandhill Crane
Common Loon (two versions)
Surf Scoter
Red-breasted Merganser
Bufflehead
Trumpeter Swan
gull (possibly herring)
Bald Eagle
Red-headed Woodpecker
Downy Woodpecker
Pileated Woodpecker
Common Grackle
Eastern Bluebird (?)
Rufous-sided Towhee (two versions?)
Blue-gray Gnatcatcher
Brown Thrasher (another version possibly thrasher)
Northern Oriole
Red-winged Blackbird
Barn Swallow
Northern Cardinal
Northern Flicker
Blue Jay
Yellow-billed Cuckoo (?)
Dark-eyed Junco (?)

European:
Hoopoe
Roller

Catesby's having traced the originals, which became naturally reversed when in the printing process the plates were pulled from the engravings, thus producing mirror images.

The catfish, land crab, and iguana are obvious plagiarisms. If one did not know that the catfish (Figure 1)

was a copy of a White drawing, it would stand alone as the most absurd of the Catesby fishes, and in fact is barely recognizable as a catfish except for the general shape and long barbels. It is a perfect caricature of a real catfish, and Frick and Stearns thought it was done from memory (1961, 77). Even though his illustration is a copy, Catesby describes the catfish (habits and all) in some detail in his text. Again, Catesby's catfish is reversed, his showing the right side, White's the left. Catesby's iguana is in a pose that would be difficult to invent, much less reproduce. The pose is identical to that of White's iguana, but Catesby's shows the left side; White's is the right side. Catesby's iguana is, however, placed on the pond-apple (*Annona glabra*), while White's is shown alone. The land crab is virtually identical to that of White's, but reversed. Five of the seven Catesby drawings that were plagiarized from White were cited by Linnaeus in the tenth edition of *Systema Naturae* (vol. 1, 1758) and two, the catfish and gar (Catesby's Plates 23 and 30 of vol. 2), were used by Linnaeus for the types of valid species. However, White's bird drawings were not very life-like, and none is known to have been plagiarized by any later artist.

John Lawson was among the most enigmatic of our famous early Americans. In the year 1700, Lawson met a gentleman who had been to America and assured him

FIGURE I.
John White's catfish, above, and Mark Catesby's plagiarized version of White's catfish, below (Catesby's print, vol. 2, plate 23).

that "Carolina was the best country he could go to." Lawson thus departed for the New World, landing in New York harbor, and subsequently sailed for Charleston, where in the same year he was appointed by the Lords Proprietors to explore and make a survey of the interior regions of "Carolina." In the fifty-nine days of his long trek, which Lawson claimed encompassed one thousand miles, he followed a horseshoe course from the coast of South Carolina through the piedmont of South Carolina and North Carolina, turning east at the area of present-day High Point, North Carolina, and ending up at the coast of North Carolina near the present site of Washington. During this arduous journey, on which he was assisted only by Indian guides, Lawson kept an extensive journal, making notes on all of the fauna and flora that he observed as well as on the natural history of the Indians he encountered. Lawson's journey is well documented by Lefler (1967), who calculated the actual distance to be nearer 550 miles.

Little is known of Lawson's early life. He is thought to have been from London, but even this is conjecture. Yet his accomplishments tell of a man of considerable education and knowledge of the world. Only five years after his arrival in the New World he was cofounder of Bath, North Carolina, oldest town in the state. Lawson remained in the colony a total of eight years, during which time he was engaged in writing his account of his explorations as well as surveying and encouraging settlements in the colony. He was appointed as surveyor-general of North Carolina by the Lords Proprietors. In 1709 Lawson was in London to oversee the publication of his book, *A New Voyage to Carolina*. At that time he was called upon by the Lords Proprietors to assist the Swiss adventurer Baron Christoph von Graffenried (de Graffenried) to settle a colony of 650 Palatines in the area of the Neuse River, where Lawson had already acquired 640 acres and had built a house for himself. On 4 August 1709, Graffenried paid fifty pounds for five thousand acres and a few days later was given a coat-of-arms and invested "in Robes of Scarlet interlaced with Gold, To be by [him] worne on all great and solemn occasions" (as quoted in Lefler and Powell 1973, 61). Thus, the deal was on, and in 1710 Lawson, along with the Palatine emigrants, the first settlers of New Bern, sailed for the New World.

Unfortunately, their venture was to have tragic consequences for Lawson and Graffenried. In 1711 the two men, in the company of two Negro slaves and two Indians, began an exploratory trip up the Neuse River. Their mission was to discover how far the Neuse was navigable and if there was a better route to Virginia. This was during the period preceding the great uprising of the Tuscarora Indians, who were quite angry with the whites' tyranny and with the usurpation of their land and the diminishing of their hunting rights. A large party of Tuscaroras captured the Lawson expedition and sentenced them to death. Von Graffenried, however, declaring himself under the particular care and protection of the Great White Queen, was turned loose, while Lawson was taken away for execution. In later accounts Graffenried blames the entire unfortunate incident on Lawson, stating that he had ruined their prospects by arguing with the King of the Corees. At any rate, it is thought that Lawson was executed in the manner he had first described in his own book, with pitch pine splinters stuck into his body and then lighted.

Lawson's *New Voyage to Carolina*, published in London in 1709, was one of the most important documents to come out of the Proprietary Period. In fact, it was the first major attempt at a natural history of the New World. It is unfortunate that the second edition of his book was entitled *History of North Carolina* because many subsequent writers have been quick to call Lawson North Carolina's first historian. Nothing could be further from the truth; his book is the account of his explorations and the natural history of the region.

A New Voyage to Carolina became very popular in Europe because of its vivid descriptions of the Indians and their customs, but, of more interest here, for the first time Europe also had a good description of the birds and other animals of the continent; Lawson's list of birds (List 2) included over a hundred species, and many of the descriptions were vivid (see McAtee 1955–56). In fact, his list of birds is, in reality, not particularly deficient when compared with Catesby's, and not only are many of his descriptions accurate (with a blend of folk legend) but some are similar to those of Catesby.

Lawson's book was so popular that it went through three English and two German editions between 1709 and 1722; his book was widely read and widely plagiarized. The plagiarisms of Lawson are given by Lefler (1967, lii–liv). The best-known is John Brickell's *The Natural History of North Carolina*, which is nearly a transcript. Another extensive plagiarism of Lawson's book was by William Byrd in his *Natural History of Virginia, or the Newly Discovered Eden*, published originally in German, by Samuel Jenner, in 1737. As Lefler wrote, "The 'real author' of the *Natural History of Virginia* was Lawson, certainly not William Byrd" (1967, liv).

Much less known, however, is Catesby's extensive use of Lawson. A good portion of Catesby's text of the *Natural History* is devoted to the habits and customs of Indians, and a major part of that essay is taken directly from Lawson's book. Catesby gave due credit for that

borrowing, but it is difficult to believe that he did not also make use of Lawson in the animal descriptions, especially when one considers the many similarities between Catesby's descriptions and those of Lawson (including some folk legends).

Examples are numerous, but one should suffice, that of the "devil-fish"—actually the manta ray—of which Lawson writes: "The devil-fish lies at some of our inlets, and as near as I can describe him, is shaped like a scate, or stingray; only he has on his head a pair of very thick strong horns, and is of a monstrous size, and strength; for this fish has been known to weigh a sloop's anchor, and run with the vessel a league or two, and bring her back, against tide, to almost the same place. Doubtless, they may afford good oil; but I have no experience of any profits which arise from them" (1709, 163).

Catesby writes of the "devil-fish": "It is a large fish, and of great strength, as will appear by the following circumstance. A sloop of 80 tons lying at anchor in the harbor of Charles-Town, was on a sudden observed to move and scud away at a great rate; this being in view of hundreds of spectators, and it being known that nobody was on board it, caused no small consternation. At length it appeared to be one of these fish, which had entangled its horns with the cable, and carried the sloop a course of some leagues before it could disentangle itself from it, which at length it did, and left the sloop at anchor again, not far from the place he moved it from" (see p. 160 of text).

Nor was he always scrupulously accurate and honest in his reporting. For example, he gives what one would take to be a first-person account of an extensive (actually unbelievable) flood at Fort Moore in September 1722 (see p. 143 of text); however, he could not possibly have witnessed the event, as he was an invalid at Charles Town at the time (Frick and Stearns 1961, 73).

Although Lawson had completed the first detailed ornithology for the New World twenty years before the publication of Catesby's first volume, the latter was without doubt the real founder of American ornithology. Lawson's work had very little impact in the long run, for people in Europe wanted to see vivid illustrations of the supposedly lavish and brightly colored birds, as well as the other fauna and flora, of the strange new continent. And it was Catesby who for the first time provided such a treatment. His *Natural History*, with its 220 color plates depicting a great variety of animals and plants, was a remarkable achievement. Catesby's art is of the primitive type, but the drawings are nonetheless lively portrayals of flora and fauna of North America, and, for the first time also, he com-

LIST 2. *John Lawson's 1709 List of Birds of Carolina*

Note: This was the first list of American birds. Lawson's actual names are given here. The total number of kinds of birds recognized by Lawson, including those only in the text of his book, such as mallard and woodcock, comes to 129. (See also McAtee, 1955–56.) This list comes directly from Lawson, 1709.

Eagle bald	Martins, two sorts	Water Fowl are,	Runners
Eagle gray	Diveling, or Swift	Water Fowl.	Ducks, as in England
Fishing Hawk	Swallow	Swans, called Trompeters	Ducks black, all Summer
Turkey Buzzard, or Vulture	Humming Bird	Swans, called Hoopers	Ducks pied, build on Trees
Herring-tail'd Hawk	Thrush	Geese, three sorts	Ducks whistling, at Sapona
Goshawk	Wood-Peckers, five sorts	Brant gray	Ducks scarlet-eye at Esaw
Falcon	Mocking-birds, two sorts	Brant white	Blue-wings
Merlin	Cat-Bird	Sea-pies or pied Curlues	Widgeon
Sparrow-hawk	Cuckoo	Will Willets	Teal, two sorts
Hobby	Blue-Bird	Great Gray Bulls	Shovelers
Jay	Bulfinch	Old Wives	Whisslers
Green Plover	Nightingale	Sea Cock	Black Flusterers,
Plover gray or whistling	Hedge-Sparrow	Curlues, three sorts	or bald Coot
Pigeon	Wren	Coots	Turkeys wild
Turtle Dove	Sparrows, two sorts	Kings-fisher	Fishermen
Parakeeto	Lark	Loons, two sorts	Divers
Ring-tail	The Tom-Tit, or Ox-Eye	Bitterns, three sorts	Raft Fowl
Raven	Owls, two sorts	Hern gray	Bull-necks
Crow	Scritch Owl	Hern white	Redheads
Black Birds, two sorts	Baltimore bird	Water Pheasant	Tropick-birds
Buntings, two sorts	Throstle, no Singer	Little gray Gull	Pellican
Pheasant	Wippoo Will	Little Fisher, or Dipper	Cormorant
Woodcock	Reed Sparrow	Gannet	Tutcocks
Snipe	Weet bird	Shear-water	Swaddle-bills
Partridge	Rice bird	Great black pied Gull	Men [mew]
Moorhen	Cranes and Storks	Marsh-hens	Sheldrakes
Red Bird	Snow-birds	Blue Peter's	Bald Faces
East-India Bat	Yellow-wings	Sand-birds	Water Witch, or Ware Coot

bined animals and plants in a meaningful manner on the same plates. Catesby was quite emphatic in stating that the animals and plants he depicted together had some true-life association, but this is not always the case: a number of plates exhibit animals and plants that would never occur together in nature. Many of the plants appear to have been drawn directly from herbarium sheets, but nevertheless most are rather accurate renditions, and the relationships between flora and fauna are for the most part reasonably accurate.

The timing of the publication of Catesby's *Natural History* was unfortunate in one sense: modern botanical nomenclature had its origins with the publication of *Species Plantarum* in Stockholm in 1753 and zoological nomenclature its beginnings with publication of the first volume of the tenth edition of *Systema Naturae* in

1758, both by the celebrated Swedish naturalist Linnaeus. So, Catesby's *Natural History* subsequently had no official standing for modern biological nomenclature; instead, many of his plates were later used by Linnaeus and others for formal descriptions and designations for species. If one excludes duplicates, Catesby treated 109 birds; of these, seventy-five North American and three Bahamian species were used for modern designations (see List 3). In addition to the birds, Catesby's treatments of many of the other animals as well as numerous plants formed the basis for subsequent designations. In the case of the catfish (Plate 23, vol. 2, see Figure 1) as well as others, the Catesby plate that formed the basis for the Linnaean designation was actually a plate Catesby had copied from White (see p. 7).

Aside from Catesby and Lawson, several other colonial naturalists dealt with American birds. Among the most notable was Thomas Hariot, who, with John White, was a member of the second of Sir Walter Raleigh's expeditions to America. His book, *A briefe and true report of the new found land of Virginia*, which was published in 1588, illustrates natural history writing of the period: "There are . . . Parats, Faulcons, & Marlin haukes, which although with us they bee not used for meate, yet for other causes I thought good to mention." Another was Thomas Morton, an Anglican trader who established the colony Merry Mount near Plymouth. Morton devoted ten pages to a chapter on birds in his *New English Canaan*, published in 1637; he tells of seeing "millions of turtledoves" and "pied ducks." Aside from Francisco Hernandes (1514–78), who dealt with Mexican natural history, perhaps the next figure of interest is John Josselyn, whose two books *New England Rarities Discovered* (1672) and *An Account of Two Voyages to New England* (1674) were the first attempts actually to make lists of the flora and fauna of America. John Clayton (1694–1773) also wrote about birds, but it was Lawson and Catesby who first put the natural history of the New World in its proper perspective and were able meaningly to document the fauna and flora. Indeed, after Lawson and Catesby it was not until the publication of William Bartram's *Travels Through North and South Carolina . . .* in 1791 that that study was advanced appreciably.

William Bartram (1739–1823) was the fifth son of John Bartram (1699–1777), a Pennsylvania farmer of Quaker descent who was America's first native botanist. William, who was both naturalist and artist, provided vivid descriptions of plants and scenery, as well as fauna. In his *Travels* he provided a catalogue of two hundred and fifteen birds, the first truly comprehensive list of American birds. Bartram's work can be said to have prepared the way for Alexander Wilson's *American Ornithology* (1808–14). Wilson, however, who is appropriately called the "Father of American Ornithology," completely overshadowed all previous work on birds when his *American Ornithology* appeared.

Mention should also be made of Thomas Jefferson, who in 1787 published a list of birds, with the Linnaean, Catesby, and popular names given in three columns, in his book *Notes on the State of Virginia* (printed for John Stockdale, Burlington-House, Piccadilly, pp. 113–18). Jefferson's list (List 4) has frequently been cited as a list of the birds of colonial Virginia, seventy-seven in number (E. Coues 1878–80, 588). In reality it is a list of Catesby's North American birds, along with thirty-three additional birds (given here) that Jefferson himself listed, many of which are duplicates of the ones in Catesby's list. Even the number seventy-seven was erroneous, as Coues counted only the left-hand column of Linnaean names in Jefferson's published list, and many of the birds had no such name. Thus Jefferson's list has little, if any, importance, and should simply be thought of as Catesby's list reproduced with an addendum of some additional species.

Catesby's final years were spent in the Parish of St. Luke, Old Street. There in October of 1747 he was married to Elizabeth Rowland, a widow with a grown daughter. At the time of Catesby's death on December 23, 1749, they had two children, Mark (who was about eight) and Ann. By that time Catesby's estate had dwindled and consisted of little more than the plates and some unsold copies of *Natural History*, which his widow was forced to sell.

After Catesby's death, George Edwards (1693–1773) took over the *Natural History* and published a revised edition in 1754. He made some minor revisions of the text, but the major difference in the new edition was the coloring of the plates. Edwards's colors were very bright and unnatural, and as a consequence the Edwards edition is easily distinguished from those done and supervised by Catesby. A third edition, published by Benjamin White, appeared in 1771 with the Linnaean names assigned to Catesby's animals and plants. Catesby's *Natural History* later appeared in numerous pirated editions in Latin, German, Dutch, and French.

Many of Catesby's collections now reside in the British Museum, along with many of his sketches and paintings, and the Sloane Manuscripts, also in the British Museum, include some unpublished paintings by Catesby of birds, plants, and insects. Catesby's *Natural History* remained the most authoritative work on the ornithology of America until the publication of Alexander Wilson's *American Ornithology* in 1808–14.

LIST 3. *Mark Catesby's Birds*

Note: The list of 109 species gives the current common name, followed by Catesby's name and the scientific name. Those species that were used by Linnaeus for his descriptions (71 in number) are indicated with an asterisk.

*1. Bald Eagle	Bald Eagle	*Haliaeetus leucocephalus*
*2. Osprey	Fishing Hawk	*Pandion haliaetus*
*3. Merlin	Pigeon-hawk	*Falco columbarius*
*4. American Swallow-tailed Kite	Swallow-tail Hawk	*Elanoides forficatus*
*5. American Kestrel	Little Hawk	*Falco sparverius*
6. Turkey Vulture	Turkey Buzzard	*Cathartes aura*
*7. Eastern Screech-Owl	Little Owl	*Otus asio*
*8. Chuck-will's-widow and		*Caprimulgus carolinensis*
Common Nighthawk	Goat-sucker of Carolina	*Chordeiles minor*
*9. Yellow-billed Cuckoo	Cuckow of Carolina	*Coccyzus americanus*
10. Cuban Parrot	Parrot of Paradise of Cuba	*Amazona leucocephala*
*11. Carolina Parakeet	Parrot of Carolina	*Conuropsis carolinensis*
*12. Common Grackle	Purple Jack Daw	*Quiscalus quiscula*
*13. Red-winged Blackbird	Red Wing'd Starling	*Agelaius phoeniceus*
*14. Bobolink	Rice-bird	*Dolichonyx oryzivorus*
*15. Blue Jay	Blew Jay	*Cyanocitta cristata*
*16. Ivory-billed Woodpecker	Largest White-bill Wood-pecker	*Campephilus principalis*
*17. Pileated Woodpecker	Larger Red-crested Wood-pecker	*Dryocopus pileatus*
*18. Northern Flicker	Gold-winged Wood-pecker	*Colaptes auratus*
*19. Red-bellied Woodpecker	Red-bellied Wood-pecker	*Melanerpes carolinus*
*19. Hairy Woodpecker	Hairy Wood-pecker	*Picoides villosus*
*20. Red-headed Woodpecker	Red-headed Wood-pecker	*Melanerpes erythrocephalus*
*21. Yellow-bellied Sapsucker	Yellow belly'd Wood-pecker	*Sphyrapicus varius*
*21. Downy Woodpecker	Smallest Spotted Wood-pecker	*Picoides pubescens*
22. White-breasted Nuthatch	Nuthatch	*Sitta carolinensis*
22. Brown-headed Nuthatch	Small Nuthatch	*Sitta pusilla*
*23. Passenger Pigeon	Pigeon of Passage	*Ectopistes migratorius*
*24. Mourning Dove	Turtle of Carolina	*Zenaida macroura*
*25. White-crowned Pigeon	White-crowned Pigeon	*Columba leucocephala*
*26. Common Ground-Dove	Ground Dove	*Columbina passerina*
*27. Northern Mockingbird	Mock-bird	*Mimus polyglottos*
*28. Brown Thrasher	Fox Coloured Thrush	*Toxostoma rufum*
*29. American Robin	Fieldfare of Carolina	*Turdus migratorius*
30. Red-legged Thrush	Red-leg'd Thrush	*Turdus plumbeus*
31. unknown thrush	Little Thrush	*Hylocichla* or *Catharus*, sp. ?
*32. Horned Lark	Lark	*Eremophila alpestris*
*33. Eastern Meadowlark	Large Lark	*Sturnella magna*
*34. Rufous-sided Towhee	Towhe-bird	*Pipilo erythrophthalmus*
34. Brown-headed Cowbird	Cowpen Bird	*Molothrus ater*
35. unknown sparrow	Little Sparrow	gen. & sp. ?
*36. Dark-eyed Junco	Snow-bird	*Junco hyemalis*
*37. Black-faced Grassquit	Bahama Sparrow	*Tiaris bicolor*
*38. Northern Cardinal	Red Bird	*Cardinalis cardinalis*
*39. Blue Grosbeak	Blew Gross-beak	*Guiraca caerulea*
40. Greater Antillean Bullfinch	Purple Gross-beak	*Loxigilla violacea*
*41. Purple Finch	Purple Finch	*Carpodacus purpureus*
42. Stripe-headed Tanager	Bahama Finch	*Spindalis zena*

*43. American Goldfinch	American Goldfinch	*Carduelis tristis*
*44. Painted Bunting	Painted Finch	*Passerina ciris*
*45. Indigo Bunting	Blew Linnet	*Passerina cyanea*
46. Cedar Waxwing	Chatterer	*Bombycilla cedrorum*
*47. Eastern Bluebird	Blew Bird	*Sialia sialis*
*48. Northern Oriole	Baltimore Bird	*Icterus galbula*
*49. Orchard Oriole	Bastard Baltimore	*Icterus spurius*
*50. Yellow-breasted Chat	Yellow Breasted Chat	*Icteria virens*
51. Purple Martin	Purple Martin	*Progne subis*
*52. Great Crested Flycatcher	Crested Fly-catcher	*Myiarchus crinitus*
53. Eastern Phoebe	Blackcap Fly-catcher	*Sayornis phoebe*
54. Eastern Wood-Pewee	Little brown Fly-catcher	*Contopus virens*
*54. Red-eyed Vireo	Red ey'd Fly-catcher	*Vireo olivaceus*
*55. Eastern Kingbird	Tyrant	*Tyrannus tyrannus*
*56. Summer Tanager	Summer Red-bird	*Piranga rubra*
*57. Tufted Titmouse	Crested Titmouse	*Parus bicolor*
58. Yellow-rumped Warbler	Yellow-rump	*Dendroica coronata*
59. Bananaquit	Bahama Titmouse	*Coereba flaveola*
60. Hooded Warbler	Hooded Titmouse	*Wilsonia citrina*
61. Pine Warbler	Pine-creeper	*Dendroica pinus*
62. Yellow-throated Warbler	Yellow-throated Creeper	*Dendroica dominica*
63. Yellow Warbler	Yellow Titmouse	*Dendroica petechia*
*64. Northern Parula	Finch-creeper	*Parula americana*
*65. Ruby-throated Hummingbird	Humming-bird	*Archilochus colubris*
*66. Gray Catbird	Cat-bird	*Dumetella carolinensis*
*67. American Redstart	Red-start	*Setophaga ruticilla*
68. Cuban Bullfinch	Little Black Bullfinch	*Melopyrrha nigra*
*69. Belted Kingfisher	King-fisher	*Ceryle alcyon*
70. Sora	Soree	*Porzana carolina*
*71. Kildeer	Chattering Plover	*Charadrius vociferus*
*72. Ruddy Turnstone	Turn-stone	*Arenaria interpres*
*73. Greated Flamingo	Flamingo	*Phoenicopterus ruber*
74. Greater Flamingo	Flamingo (head only)	*Phoenicopterus ruber*
*75. Whooping Crane	Hooping Crane	*Grus americana*
*76. Little Blue Heron	Blue Heron	*Egretta caerulea*
77. Little Blue Heron	Little White Heron	*Egretta caerulea*
78. Yellow-crowned Night-Heron	Brown Bittern	*Nycticorax violaceus*
*79. Yellow-crowned Night-Heron	Crested Bittern	*Nycticorax violaceus*
*80. Green-backed Heron	Small Bittern	*Butorides striatus*
81. Wood Stork	Wood Pelican	*Mycteria americana*
*82. White Ibis	White Curlew	*Eudocimus albus*
83. White Ibis	Brown Curlew	*Eudocimus albus*
*84. Scarlet Ibis	Red Curlew	*Eudocimus ruber*
85. American Oystercatcher	Oyster Catcher	*Haematopus palliatus*
86. Northern Gannet	Great Booby	*Sula bassanus*
87. Brown Booby	Booby	*Sula leucogaster*
*88. Brown Noddy	Noddy	*Anous stolidus*
*89. Laughing Gull	Laughing Gull	*Larus atricilla*
*90. Black Skimmer	Cut Water	*Rynchops niger*
*91. Pied-billed Grebe	Pied-Bill Dopchick	*Podilymbus podiceps*
*92. Canada Goose	Canada Goose	*Branta canadensis*
*93. White-cheeked Pintail	Ilathera Duck	*Anas bahamensis*
*94. Hooded Merganser	Round-crested Duck	*Lophodytes cucullatus*

95. Bufflehead	Buffel's Head Duck	*Bucephala albeola*
96. Northern Shoveler	Blue-wing Shoveler	*Anas clypeata*
*97. Wood Duck	Summer Duck	*Aix sponsa*
98. Bufflehead	Little Brown Duck	*Bucephala albeola*
99. Blue-winged Teal	Blue-wing Teal	*Anas discors*
*100. Blue-winged Teal	White-face Teal	*Anas discors*

Appendix

1. Greater Prairie-Chicken	Urogallus Minor	*Tympanuchus cupido*
3. Smooth-billed Ani	Razor-billed Black-bird of Jamaica	*Crotophaga ani*
5. Troupial	Yellow and Black Pye	*Icterus icterus*
8. Chimney Swift	American Swallow	*Chaetura pelagica*
10. Great Blue Heron	Largest Crested Heron	*Ardea herodias*
12. Northern Bobwhite	American Partridge	*Colinus virginianus*
13. Golden-crowned Kinglet	Regulus cristatus	*Regulus satrapa*
14. Red-billed Tropicbird	Tropick-bird	*Phaethon aethereus*
14. Wilson's Storm-Petrel	Storm-finck or Pittrel	*Oceanites oceanicus*
16. Whip-poor-will and	Whip-poor-will	*Caprimulgus vociferus*
Common Nighthawk combined		*Chordeiles minor*

LIST 4. *Thomas Jefferson's Birds*

Note: Jefferson's list was Mark Catesby's American birds with the addition of the 33 species listed here.

Royston crow
Crane
House swallow
Ground swallow
Greatest grey eagle
Smaller turkey buzzard, with a feathered head
Greatest owl, or night hawk
Wethawk, which feeds flying
Raven
Water pelican of the Mississippi, whose pouch holds a
   peck
Swan
Loon
Cormorant
Duck and Mallard
Widgeon
Sheldrach, or Canvas back

Black head
Bald Coot
Ballcoot
Sprigtail
Didapper, or Dopchick
Spoon billed duck
Water-witch
Water-pheasant
Mow-bird
Blue peter
Water wagtail
Yellow-legged snipe
Squatting snipe
Small plover
Whistling plover
Woodcock
Red bird, with black head, wings and tail

Editor's Note on the Plates

Catesby's bird plates appeared in volume 1 and the appendix to volume 2. The plates in the first volume begin with the bald eagle and end with the blue-winged teal, following no meaningful pattern. To conform to modern bird lists, but with no claim that these represent a "natural" arrangement, I have arranged the Catesby plates in the order that they appear in the latest checklist (6th edition) of the American Ornithologists' Union (1983). Species not included in the checklist (certain Bahamian species) have been inserted where most appropriate. Both common and scientific names of the birds conform strictly to the latest usage in the AOU checklist, although I personally would have preferred that some of the old names, such as "Baltimore oriole," be retained. I diverge from the AOU checklist in placing the flamingos and ducks after the shorebirds, from which both groups are clearly derived. In addition, common names are not capitalized within the text accounts because each species is referred to by many different names, ranging from Catesby's and Lawson's to modern usage.

The text from Catesby's *Natural History* accompanies each plate. These accounts have been lightly edited for readability. Only the lengthy (often several lines) Latin names of both plant and bird species used before each account have been omitted. These seemed to serve no useful purpose and represented incomprehensible and outmoded nomenclature. Catesby's original plate numbers are given in parentheses beside the Catesby bird names.

Common names have been substituted for the lengthy Latin plant names appearing as subtitles. In some cases, Catesby gave common names instead of the Latin, and these have been retained, with a modern common name in parentheses after the Catesby name. Where Catesby's plant name is the same as the modern usage, only the Catesby name appears; where Catesby gave no common name, the modern common name has been supplied in brackets.

The Catesby text from the *Natural History* is followed by my own analysis of the plate and the bird species in light of Catesby, certain of his predecessors, such as John Lawson, and his successors, such as Alexander Wilson, John James Audubon, and beyond. Scientific as well as common names are provided for all of Catesby's plants. The identification of and scientific nomenclature for the plants strictly follow Richard A. Howard and George W. Staples, "The Modern Names for Catesby's Plants" (1983, 511–46). Students of Catesby owe a great debt of gratitude to Howard and Staples for their fine work.

There are numerous quotes in the text from Alexander Wilson's *American Ornithology* (1808–14) and from John James Audubon's *Birds of America* (1827–44). Because these early editions are not accessible, however, the citations to Wilson's work are from the edition published between 1828 and 1829 in three volumes, and the citations to Audubon's work are from the first octavo edition, published between 1840 and 1844. Likewise, citations of John Lawson's *A New Voyage to Carolina* (1709) refer to pages in the latest reproduction of that book, that of Lefler, 1967. However, the date of the citations is given in the text as 1709.

As with any book involving species accounts, many references were used that are not specifically cited in the text. These general references are included in the bibliography, and include the following: A. C. Bent's *Life Histories of North American Birds* (21 vols., 1919–68); J. Bond, *Birds of the West Indies* (1974); N. L. Britton and C. F. Millspaugh, *The Bahama Flora* (1920); D. S. Correll and H. B. Correll, *Flora of the Bahama Archipelago* (1982); R. A. Howard and G. W. Staples, "The Modern Names for Catesby's Plants" (1983); E. L. Little, *The Audubon Field Guide to North American Trees, Eastern Region* (1980); W. L. McAtee, "Torpidity in Birds" (1947) and "Confusion of Eastern Caprimulgidae" (1948); D. McKinley, "Historical Review of the Carolina Parakeet in the Carolinas" (1979); H. S. Mosby and C. O. Handley, "The Wild Turkey in Virginia" (1943); W. A. Niering and N. C. Olmstead, *The Audubon Society Field Guide to North American Wildflowers, Eastern Region* (1979); A. Patterson, *Birds of the Bahamas* (1972); E. F. Potter et al., *Birds of the Carolinas* (1980); A. Sprunt, Jr., and E. B. Chamberlain, *South Carolina Bird Life* (1949); W. Stone, "Mark Catesby and the Nomenclature of North American Birds" (1929); and J. K. Terres, *The Audubon Society Encyclopedia of North American Birds* (1980).

The Parrot of Carolina.

Perroquet de la Caroline.

 HIS Bird is of the bigneſs, or rather leſs than a Black-bird, weighing three ounces and an half : the fore-part of the Head Orange-colour; the hind-part of the Head and Neck yellow. All the reſt of the Bird appears green; but upon nearer ſcrutiny the interior vanes of moſt of the wing-feathers are dark-brown : the upper-parts of the exterior vanes of the larger Wing-or Quill-feathers, are yellow, proceeding gradually deeper colour'd to the end, from yellow to green, and from green to blew : the edge of the Shoulder of the Wing, for about three inches down, is bright Orange-colour. The Wings are very long, as is the Tail; having the two middle-feathers longer than the others by an inch and half, and end in a point; the reſt are gradually ſhorter. The Legs and Feet are white : the ſmall Feathers covering the Thighs, are green, ending at the Knees with a verge of O-range-colour. They feed on Seeds and Kernels of Fruit; particularly thoſe of Cypreſs and Apples. The Orchards in Autumn are viſited by numerous flights of them; where they make great deſtruction for their Kernels only : for the ſame purpoſe they frequent *Virginia*; which is the furtheſt *North* I ever heard they have been ſeen. Their Guts is certain and ſpeedy poiſon to Cats. This is the only one of the Parrot kind in *Carolina*: ſome of them breed in in the Country ; but moſt of them retire more South.

 ET oiſeau eſt de la groſſeur d'un mer-le, ou même plus petit, & peſe trois onces & demi. Il a le devant de la tête & le col jaune. Tout le reſte de l'oiſeau paroit verd. Mais, après une recherche plus exacte, j'ai trou-vé, que les barbes interieures de la pluſpart des plumes de l'aile ſont d'un brun foncé, & le haut des barbes exterieures des plus grandes plumes de l'aile ſont jaunes, devenant par degrés plus foncées juſ-qu'au bout, tirant du jaune au verd, & du verd au bleu. Le bord du haut de l'aile eſt, à environ trois pouces en deſcendant, d'un beau couleur d'orange. Les ailes ſont fort longues, de même que la queüe, dont les deux plumes du milieu ſont un pouce & de-mi plus longues que les autres, & finiſſent en pointe : les autres ſont plus courtes, & cela par degrés. Les jambes & les piés ſont blancs. Les petites plumes, qui couvrent les cuiſſes juſqu'à la jointure de la jam-be, ſont vertes & bordées de couleur d'orange. Ils ſe nouriſſent des graines & des pepins des fruits, & ſurtout des graines de Cyprês & des pepins de pom-mes. Il vient en automne des volées innombrables de ces oiſeaux dans les vergers, où ils ſont un grand dégât; car ils ne mangent que les pepins. Ce ſont auſſi les pepins qui les attirent dans la Virginie, qui eſt l'endroit du Nord le plus éloigné où j'aye oüi dire qu'on ait vû de ces oiſeaux. Leurs boyaux ſont un poiſon prompt & aſſuré pour les chats. C'eſt la ſeule eſpece de perroquet qu'il y ait dans la Caroline. Quelques uns ſont leurs petits en ce païs; mais la pluſpart ſe retirent plus au Sud.

Cupreſſus Americana.

The CYPRESS of *America*.

Cyprês de l'Amerique.

THE Cypreſs (except the Tulip-tree) is the talleſt and largeſt in theſe parts of the world. Near the Ground ſome of 'em meaſure 30 foot in circumference, riſing pyramidally ſix foot, where it is about two thirds leſs; from which to the limbs, which is uſually 60 or 70 foot, it grows in like proportion of o-ther trees. Four or five foot round this Tree (in a ſingular man-ner) riſe many Stumps, ſome a little above ground, and others from one to four foot high, of various ſhape and ſize, their tops round, cover'd with a ſmooth red Bark. Theſe Stumps ſhoot from the Roots of the Tree, yet they produce neither leaf nor branch, the Tree increaſing only by ſeed, which in form are like the common Cypreſs, and contain a balſamic conſiſtence of a fragrant ſmell. The Timber this Tree affords, is excellent, particular-ly for covering Houſes with, it being light, of a free Grain, and reſiſting the injuries of the weather better than any other here. It is an Aquatic, and uſually grows from one, five and ſix foot deep in water ; which ſecure ſituation ſeems to invite a great number of different Birds to breed in its lofty branches ; amongſt which this Parrot delight to make their Neſts, and in *October* (at which Time the Seed is ripe) to feed on their Kernels.

CET arbre eſt le plus haut & le plus gros qu'il y ait dans cette partie du monde, excepté l'arbre qui porte des tulipes. Quelques uns ont trente piés de circonference près de terre. Ils s'élevent en di-minuant toûjours juſqu'à la hauteur de ſix piés, où reduits aux deux tiers de la groſſeur dont ils ſont au pied, ils continuent de croître ordinairement ſoixante où ſoixante & dix piés juſqu'à la tige, avec la même proportion que les autres arbres, Il ſort d'une maniere ſingu-liere, à quatre ou cinq piés autour de cet arbre, pluſieurs chicots de différente forme & de différente grandeur ; quelques uns un peu au deſſus de terre, & d'autres depuis un pié de haut juſqu'à quatre. Leur tête eſt couverte d'une écorce rouge & unie. Ces chicots ſortent des racines de l'arbre ; cependant ils ne produiſent ni feüilles ni branches; car l'arbre ne vient que du grain de ſemence, qui eſt de la même forme que celui des cyprês ordinaires, & qui contient une ſubſtance balſamique & odoriférante. Le bois de charpente qu'on fait de cet arbre eſt excellent, ſurtout pour couvrir les maiſons, à cauſe qu'il eſt leger, qu'il a le grain délié, & qu'il réſiſte aux inju-res du tems mieux que ne fait aucun autre que nous ayons dans ce païs ici. Il eſt aquatique, & croît ordinairement depuis un pié juſqu'à cinq & ſix de profondeur dans l'eau. Il ſemble que ſa ſi-tuation invite un grand nombre de différentes ſortes d'oiſeaux à ſe loger ſur ſes branches pour y multiplier leur eſpece. Ce perroquet en-tr'autres y fait volontiers ſon nid, & ſe nourrit des pepins en Octo-bre, qui eſt le tems de leur maturité.

FIGURE 2.
A page from the first edition of Mark Catesby's Natural History.

The Plates

PLATE 1

The Pied-bill Dopchick (91)

This bird weighs half a pound. The eyes are large, encompassed with a white circle; the throat has a black spot; a black list crosses the middle of the bill; the lower mandible, next the base, has a black spot. The head and neck are brown, particularly the crown of the head and back of the neck is darkest; the feathers of the breast are light brown, mixed with green; the belly is dusky white; the back and wings are brown.

These birds frequent fresh-water ponds in many of the inhabited parts of Carolina. This was a male.

Editor's Note / Pied-billed Grebe
(*Podilymbus podiceps*)

Commonly known as hell-divers and dabchicks, the grebes are ducklike diving birds occurring throughout the world. Unlike ducks, though, which have webbing over the entire foot, grebes have webbing on each individual toe, a condition known as lobate webbing. Of the three species that commonly occur in the coastal regions of the Carolinas, the pied-billed grebe is the common nesting species. In the summer a black ring appears on the white bill, giving the bird a "pied" appearance. This grebe is common in lakes, ponds, and marshes and during the winter can be found in salt bays. Its floating nest of marsh vegetation and debris is commonly anchored to a few rushes; it usually accommodates six to nine eggs. Grebes are well known for their diving abilities and their ability to simply sink beneath the surface of the water when danger approaches.

Lawson stated, "Of divers there are two sorts; the one pied, the other gray; both good meat" (1709, 153).

PLATE 2

The Storm-finck,
or Pittrel (appendix, 14)

This is about the size of a chaffinch. The whole bird, except the rump, which is white, is of a dusky brown color: the back being somewhat darker than the belly. The bill is half an inch long, slender, dark brown, and crooked at the end. By opening the head of one of these birds, I found that the nostrils consisted of two parallel tubes, proceeding from within the head, and running halfway along the upper mandible of the bill, forming thereon a protuberance. The wings extended an inch beyond the tail. The legs were slender. The feet were webbed with a very small claw on each heel, without a toe. They rove all over the Atlantic Ocean, and are seen on the coasts of America as well as on those of Europe, and many hundred leagues from each shore. Their appearance is generally believed by mariners to prognosticate a storm, or bad weather; and I must confess I never saw them but in a troubled sea. They use their wings and feet with surprising celerity. Their wings are long, and resemble those of swallows, with which they are equally swift, but without making such angles or short turns in their flight, as swallows do, but fly in a direct line. Though their feet are formed for swimming, they are likewise so for running, which use they seem most to put them to, being oftenest seen in the action of running swiftly on the surface of the waves in their greatest agitation, but with the assistance of their wings.

The storm-finck, in Hoier's Epistle to Clusius, is the bird here described; and though its nostrils give it so singular a characteristic, and that they are so numerous in all our adjacent seas, yet they have not been figured before, nor sufficiently described. As contrarily remarkable it is, that Mr. Edwards, in his *Ornithology*, lately published, has fortunately brought to light the knowledge of three more of this genus not known

before, which he has well described and figured. This bird, with the three beforementioned, seem to me apparently of the gull kind.

The Tropick-bird
(appendix, 14)

The tail of this bird is generally, though erroneously, reported by unobserving mariners, to consist of but one feather. Mr. Willughby's description of it, though very particular, was from a dried case of the bird, which, by being defective, seems to be the cause why his description differs somewhat from ours, which was made from the living bird. The legs in his, by long keeping, had lost their red color, which all that I have seen, while living, have. This bird is about the size of a partridge, and has very long wings. The bill is red, with an angle under the lower mandible, like those of the gull kind, of which it is a species. The eyes are encompassed with black, which ends in a point towards the back of the head. Three or four of the larger quill feathers, towards their ends, are black, tipped with white: all the rest of the bird is white, except the back, which is variegated with curved lines of black. The legs and feet are of a vermilion red. The toes are webbed. The tail consists of two long straight narrow feathers, almost of equal breadth from their quills to their points.

These birds are rarely seen but between the tropics, at the remotest distance from land. Their name seems to imply the limits of their abode; and though they are seldom seen but a few degrees north or south of either tropic, yet one of their breeding places is almost nine degrees from the northern tropic, viz. at Bermudas; where, from the high rocks that environ those islands, I have shot them at the time of their breeding: but those cliffs being inaccessible, prevented my seeing their nests and eggs. They breed also in great numbers on some little islands at the east end of Puerto Rico.

Editor's Note / Wilson's Storm-petrel (*Oceanites oceanicus*) and Red-billed Tropicbird (*Phaethon aethereus*)

The storm-petrel is a bird of many myths and superstitions, being particularly associated with the onset of storms, and it is true that they are often seen in windy weather at sea. The name petrel, a diminutive of St. Peter, is an allusion to the time when he walked on the water. These small seabirds are well known for their habit of pattering their feet along the water as they fly and hovering immediately above the surface in quest of small fishes and crustaceans.

All previous students of Catesby have identified his storm petrel as the British storm petrel (*Hydrobates pelagicus*), a bird never recorded in the areas of the New World visited by Catesby. It seems far more likely to be the only common storm petrel along the southern Atlantic coasts and the West Indies, Wilson's petrel (*Oceanites oceanicus*), even though a white rump is not shown. It is illustrated with the red-billed tropicbird.

Tropicbirds are ancient pelicanlike birds, represented by only three species today, that range throughout the tropical seas of the Atlantic, Pacific, and Indian oceans. Superficially they resemble large white terns with two extremely long central tail feathers. These pelagic birds dive headfirst into the water after their food, which consists primarily of squid and crustaceans. The family name Phaethontidae comes from Phaethon, son of Helios, the sun god, who drove his sun chariot across the skies.

The red-billed tropicbird is a widespread oceanic species of the Pacific and Indian oceans; in the West Indies, however, it is confined mainly to the Lesser Antilles and the Virgin Islands, although it is a casual visitor to Jamaica and Bermuda. Catesby's bird was thought to be the white-tailed tropicbird (*Phaethon lepturus*), which is widespread throughout the West Indies, and casual as far away as Florida and even South Carolina, but McAtee (1945, 137 39) has shown that the species illustrated by Catesby is the red-billed.

Anseri Raffano affinis fuscatus

PLATE 3

The Booby (87)

Is somewhat less than a goose. The base of the bill is yellow, and bare of feathers; in which the eyes are placed of a light gray color; the lower part of the bill is of a light brown. These birds vary so, that they are not to be distinguished by their colors only; in one of them the belly was white, and the back brown; in another the breast and belly was brown; in others all brown; nor could I perceive any outward difference in the cock and hen. Their wings are very long; their legs and feet pale yellow, and shaped like those of cormorants. They frequent the Bahama Islands, where they breed all months in the year. They lay one, two, and sometimes three eggs on the bare rocks. Dampier says, they breed on trees in an island called Bon-airy, in the West Indies, which he observes not to have seen elsewhere. While young, they are covered with a white down, and remain so until they are almost ready to fly. They subsist on fish only, which they catch by diving. This and the great booby are remarkable for having a joint in the upper mandible of the bill.

It is diverting to see the frequent contests between the booby and the man of war bird, which last lives on rapine and spoil of other sea birds, particularly the booby; which so soon as the man of war bird perceives he hath taken a fish, flies furiously at him, and obliges the booby for his security to dive under water. The man of war bird being incapable of following him, hovers over the place till the booby rises to breathe, and then attacks him again, and so repeats it at every opportunity, till the booby at length, tired and breathless, is necessitated to resign his fish; yet, not being discouraged, industriously goes to fishing again, and suffers repeated losses by fresh assaults from his rapacious enemy.

Having had no opportunity of seeing the man of war bird any otherwise than in the air, I cannot well describe it, nor say any thing more of it, except what has been related to me, which is this: While they are sitting and hatching their young, their heads changes from a brown to a scarlet color, which becomes brown again when they have done breeding. This was affirmed to me by many who have often seen them on their nests; for at that time they are very tame, and will suffer one to come near to them, though at other times very wild. These birds are numerous on most of the Bahama Islands.

PLATE 4

The Great Booby (86)

Its size is about that of a goose. The head and neck are remarkably thick. The bill large, and almost six inches in length, a channel or cranny extends from one end to the other of the upper mandible. The wings extended six feet, and, when closed, reach to the end of the tail. The middle feather of the tail was longest, the rest gradually decreasing in length, the eyes are large, of a hazel color, encompassed with a skin bare of feathers. These birds were of a dark brown color, elegantly spotted with white on their heads, the spots are thick and small, on the neck and breast they are thinner and broader, and on the back thinnest and broadest. The wings are likewise spotted, except the large quill feathers and the tail, which are brown. The belly is of a dusky white. The feet are black, and shaped like those of cormorant. That which is most remarkable in these birds is, that the upper mandible of the bill, two inches below the angle of the mouth, is jointed, by which it can raise it from the lower mandible two inches, without opening their mouths.

This bird so nearly resembles the booby (particularly in the singular structure of the bill) that I thought the name of great booby agreed best with it. It frequents large rivers, and plunges into them after fish, in like manner as the booby does at sea, continuing under water at a considerable time, and there pursuing the fish; and as I have several times found them disabled, and sometimes dead on the shore, probably they meet with sharks, and other large voracious fishes, that maim and sometimes devour them. They frequent the rivers and seacoast of Florida. The colors of the cock are brighter, and more beautiful than those of the hen.

Thymelaea
(white mangrove or bastard buttonwood)

This shrub riseth to the height of eight or ten feet, with a small trunk, covered with a whitish bark. The leaves are placed alternately on footstalks, one third of an inch long, narrow at the beginning, growing broader and rounding at the ends, two inches long, and one over, where broadest of a shining green, with one single rib. The flowers are tubulous, divided at top into four sections, they are white, except that within the cup there is a faint tincture of red, they grow in bunches at the ends of the branches.

These shrubs grow in many of the Bahama Islands, on the rocky shores amongst sedge.

Editor's Note / Brown Booby (*Sula leucogaster*) and Northern Gannet (*Sula bassanus*)

The gannets and boobies are large-sized sea birds closely allied with the pelicans and, like their cousins, have webbing connecting all four toes, a condition known as totipalmate. Both gannets and boobies feed in a similar fashion, plunging into the water from heights of forty to fifty feet with their wings folded to take fish of various sorts. Like the pelicans also, they have air sacs beneath their skin to cushion the fall.

Two species of boobies are common residents of the Bahama Islands: the brown and masked boobies (*Sula leucogaster* and *S. dactylatra*). These inhabitants of tropical seas are considerably smaller than their cousin the gannet, but in overall body form and habits they are quite similar. Boobies derive their name from their tame and stupid nature, which resulted in huge numbers being captured and killed by sailors. Vast colonies of both species of booby nest in the Bahamas, and in 1907 Frank Chapman estimated that Cay Verde had fifteen hundred breeding pairs.

Boobies are often the victims of piracy by the frigate-bird (*Fregata magnificens*), or man-o-war bird. Catesby described this scene from stories told to him and obviously had never observed it first-hand. Actually, the frigatebird simply harasses other seabirds, including gulls and boobies, into dropping their fish, which the frigatebird usually intercepts before it falls into the water. Even the osprey may fall victim to the piracy of the frigatebird. Catesby's description is far more dramatic—the frigatebird repeatedly attacks the booby as it rises to breathe from beneath the water, until at last it releases the fish. In fact, the frigatebird is helpless if it alights on the water.

Gannets, which are the size of geese, are the largest members of the booby family. Adults are white with black wing tips, and the first-year birds are brown with white streaks and white below. They nest on sea cliffs off the northern Atlantic coast of North America and spend the winter off the coast of the lower Atlantic states and the Gulf of Mexico.

Catesby's gannet is pictured with the white mangrove or bastard buttonwood of the Bahamas (*Laguncularia racemosa*).

Lawson stated of the gannet: "His fat or grease, is as yellow as saffron, and the best thing known, to preserve fire-arms, from rust" (1709, 154).

PLATE 5

The Largest Crested Heron
Fig. 1 (appendix, 10)

As I did not measure the length of this bird, I can only guess it to be not less than four feet and an half high, when erect. The bill measured almost eight inches from the angle of the mouth to the end of it; and was of a yellowish brown color behind the eyes; and under the throat of a light brownish yellow. The crest on its head was made up of long narrow brown feathers; the longest being five inches in length, which it could erect and let fall at pleasure. The neck and breast brown, but paler, and spotted on the under part. The rest of the body and legs brown, except the quill feathers, which are black. They feed not only on fish and frogs, but on lizards, efts, etc. They are natives of Virginia.

The Spotted Eft
Fig. 2 (spotted salamander, *Ambystoma maculatum*)

These are found in ditches, ponds, and standing waters, and are the food of herons and serpents. This was five inches long, having a large head. It had four toes on each of the fore-feet, and five on the hind-feet; a double row of white round spots extending from the crown of the head to the hind-legs, from which, to the end of the tail, they were single. They are as inoffensive as our common water-efts.

The Chegoe
Fig. 3 (chigoe, *Tunga penetrans*)

It is a very small kind of flea, that is found only in warm climates: it is a very troublesome insect, especially to Negroes and others that go barefoot, and are slovenly. They penetrate the skin, under which they lay a bunch or bag of eggs, which swell to the bigness of a small pea or tare, and give great pain till it is taken out; to perform which, great care is required for fear of breaking the bag, which endangers a mortification, and the loss of a leg, and sometimes life itself. This insect, in its natural size, is not above a fourth part so big as the common flea, but magnified by a microscope it appeared of the size of the figure here represented. From the mouth issued a hollow tube, like that of the common flea, between a pair of antennae. It had six jointed legs, and something resembling a tail, under which is represented one of its eggs, the size of which is so small that it can hardly be discerned by the naked eye; but magnified by a glass, appeared as here represented. These chegoes are a nuisance to most parts of

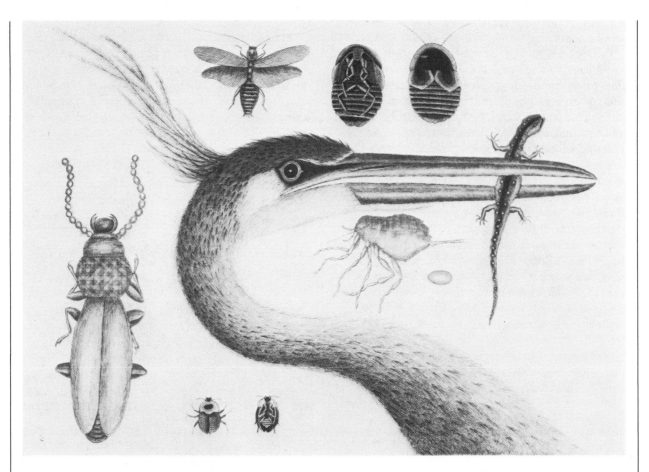

America between the tropics. See Sir Hans Sloane's *Hist. Jamaic.* Introd. p. CXXIV, and Vol. II p. 191, 192.

Scarabaeus capricornus minimus cutem penetrans
Fig. 4 (not identified)

In the year 1725, I being at the house of his Excellency Mr. Phinney, then Governor of the Bahama Islands, who, as he was searching of his feet for chegoes, at the time we were viewing them through a microscope, produced an odd insect on the point of his needle, as at Fig. 4. which he then picked out of his foot. I showed it to Negroes and others, and none of them had seen the like. The natural size of this insect was that of the spot over its head; but magnified, it appeared of the size and form here exhibited. I think it may be called as above.

The Cockroach
Fig. 5 *(Blatta Americana)*

These are very troublesome and destructive vermin, and are so numerous and voracious, that it is impossible to keep victuals of any kind from being devoured by them, without close covering. They are flat, and so thin, that few chests or boxes can exclude them. They eat not only leather, parchment, and woollen, but linen and paper. They disappear in winter, and appear most numerous in the hottest days in summer. It is at night they commit their depredations, and bite people in their beds, especially childrens fingers that are greasy. They lay innumerable eggs, creeping into the holes of old walls and rubbish, where they lie torpid all the winter. Some have wings, and others are without, perhaps of different sexes.

Blatta maxima fusca peltata
Fig. 6 (type of cockroach)

This is three times bigger than the common cockroach. The head and part of the thorax was covered with an hemispherical shining hard shield; from under which proceeded two other membranes of the like consistence, which covered part of the abdomen. The abdomen was crossed with eight annulli of a shining brown color. The face of it had somewhat the resemblance of a monkey. The antennae were about an inch long. It had six legs, each having three joints, the lowermost joint set with sharp prickles, and crooked claws at their ends. They are found in Carolina. What they subsist on, and in what manner they are propagated, I know not, having seen but this one of the kind.

Scarabaeus peltatus
Fig. 7 (possibly carrion beetle or silphid)

A membranous yellow shield, with a dark brown spot in the middle of it, covered part of the head and thorax; the wings covering the remaining part of the body, which were of a dusky purple, mottled with shining spots of the same color. It had six black legs, having two joints only. Each wing was strengthened withinside by a thin membranous yellow ridge extending the length of them. The remaining underpart of the wing of a shining green color. This insect was from Pennsylvania.

Editor's Note / Great Blue Heron
(*Ardea herodias*)

Also commonly known as the "blue crane," the great blue heron is easily distinguished from the other herons by its large size: a full-grown bird stands about four feet tall. This heron ranges from southern Canada to Mexico, and winters to northern South America. Great blue herons are common in Virginia and the Carolinas, but become rather rare inland during the summer months, when it commonly nests in undisturbed wooded swamps near the coast. These large herons are generally solitary during the winter, but become somewhat colonial during the breeding season, which begins in March. The nest is a platform of sticks placed in the top of a tall tree; dozens of nests have been found in the same tree, either all of this species or

in association with other herons. The nests, which may be three to four feet across, are repaired and used year after year. Four eggs are the normal clutch.

Great blue herons usually feed around dawn and just before dusk, although some night feeding has been observed. They feed primarily on fish, but their diet might also include frogs, salamanders, snakes, grasshoppers and aquatic insects, and even small mammals and birds.

Catesby's head of the "largest crested heron," with its exaggerated crest, is illustrated with the spotted salamander (*Ambystoma maculatum*), along with a number of insects.

PLATE 6
The Blue Heron (76)

This bird weighs fifteen ounces, and in size is somewhat less than a crow. The bill is blue; but darker towards the point. The irises of the eyes are yellow. The head and neck are of a changeable purple. All the rest of the body is blue. The legs and feet are green.

From the breast hang long narrow feathers, as there do likewise from the hind-part of the head; and likewise on the back are such like feathers, which are a foot in length, and extend four inches below the tail, which is a little shorter than the wings. These birds are not numerous in Carolina; and are rarely seen but in the spring of the year.

Whence they come, and where they breed, is to me unknown.

PLATE 7

The Little White Heron (77)

This bird is about the size of the preceding. The bill is red. The eyes have yellow irises. The legs and feet are green. The whole plumage is white. They feed on fish, frogs, etc. and frequent rivers, ponds and marshes, after the manner of other herons.

I believe they breed in Carolina; but I have never seen any of them in winter.

[Bahamian Phymosia]

This plant rises with several stems usually five feet high, producing broad serrated downy leaves, like the broad-leaved maple, divided by six sections. The flowers are in clusters, on the top of the stalk; of a pale red, and divided by five segments. The fruit is round and ribbed, about the bigness of a large hazel-nut, containing many small black seeds. They grow among the rocks of the Bahama Islands.

Editor's Note / Little Blue Heron (*Egretta caerulea*)

The little blue heron is one of the most common herons of the southern Atlantic states, where it occurs primarily along the coastal plain, but not very far inland. These birds nest in colonies, often with other species of herons, in swampy settings along the coast, where they build their stick platform nests in bushes or small trees; four eggs are the typical clutch. In the more southern parts of the breeding range, these rookeries may be infested with water moccasins and alligators that feed on the eggs and any young that happen to fall from the nest. Catesby's "blue heron" is an adult little blue heron in full nuptial plumage, and his "little white heron" appears to be a little blue heron in its immature plumage. As the bird molts into its adult blue plumage, it goes through a calico phase. By the molt that changes the bird into the adult blue plumage, a strange calico bird is produced during the interim of the molt period. The immature little blue heron (Plate 7) is depicted with the Bahamian phymosia (*Phymosia abutiloides*), an endemic Bahamian flowering plant.

PLATE 8

The Small Bittern (80)

The bill, from the angle of the mouth to the end, was a little more than six inches long, and black, except some part of the under mandible, which was yellow. The eyes yellow. A crest of long green feathers covers the crown of the head. The neck and breast of a dark muddy red. The back covered with long narrow pale green feathers. The large quill feathers of the wing of a very dark green, with a tincture of purple. All the rest of the wing feathers of a changeable shining green, having some

feathers edged with yellow. The legs and feet brown. They have a long neck, but usually sit with it contracted, on trees hanging over rivers, in a lonely manner waiting for their prey, which is frogs, crabs, and other small fish.

I don't remember to have seen any of them in winter; wherefore I believe, they retire from Virginia and Carolina more south.

[White Ash]

These trees are commonly of a mean size and height. The leaves are pointed at both ends. The seeds are winged, and hang in clusters. They grow in low moist places.

Editor's Note / Green-backed Heron (*Butorides striatus*)

The green-backed heron, called by Catesby the small bittern, is the smallest of the true herons in the Carolinas and Virginia, where it is also known as the "fly-up-the-creek" "shitepoke" or "Indian hen." This is no doubt the best-known heron in the United States, being a common inhabitant of ponds and streams, where it feeds on all sorts of small fish, frogs, and aquatic animal life. Unlike most other herons, the green-backed is not particularly gregarious; it is usually seen singly or in a pair. Typically, they nest in pairs, building a poorly constructed stick platform in trees or bushes near water; the usual clutch is three to six eggs. Catesby's green heron is illustrated with the white ash (*Fraxinus americana*).

PLATE 9

The Brown Bittern (78)

This is somewhat less than our English bittern. The bill is four inches long; the end and upper part of it black, the under part green. The eyes are large, having gold-colored irises, environed with a green skin. The whole body is brown, with a mixture of white feathers; the back being darker. The breast and belly more white. Most of the large wing feathers are white at the ends. The tail is short, and of a lead color. The legs and feet are of a yellowish green. The outer and middle toe are joined by a membrane. The interior side of the middle toe is serrated. These birds frequent fresh rivers and ponds in the upper parts of the country, remote from the sea.

PLATE 10

The Crested Bittern (79)

Weighs a pound and half. The bill is black and strong. The eyes very large and prominent, with red irises. The skin encompassing the eyes is green. The crown of the head, from the base of the bill, of a pale yellow, terminating in a peak; from which hang three or four long white feathers, the longest of which is six inches; which they erect, when irritated. From the angle of the mouth runs a broad white list. The rest of the head is of a blueish black. The neck, breast and belly dusky blue. The back is striped with black streaks, with a mixture of white. From the upper part of the back shoot many long narrow feathers, extending beyond the tail; some of which are seven inches long. The large feathers of the wing are brown, with a tincture of blue. The legs and feet are yellow. These birds are seen in Carolina in the rainy seasons; but in the Bahama Islands, they breed in bushes growing among the rocks in prodigious numbers, and are of great use to the inhabitants there; who, while these birds are young, and before they can fly, employ themselves in taking them, for the delicacy of their food. They are, in some of these rocky islands, so numerous, that in a few hours, two men will load one of their calapatches or little boats, taking them perching from off the rocks and bushes; they making no attempt to escape, though almost full grown. They are called, by the Bahamians, crab-catchers, crabs being what they mostly subsist on; yet they are well-tasted, and free from any rank or filthy savor.

[Inkberry or Black Soap]

This plant grows usually to the height of five or six feet. The leaves are, in thickness and form, not unlike purslain. At the end of a stalk, growing from the joint of a leaf, there are set three or four monopetalous white flowers, divided into five pointed sections, with a wreathed stamen hanging out. The flower here exhibited is slit down to the base and laid flat open. The flowers are succeeded by globular berries, of the size of black bullace, containing a stone, covered with a smooth black skin. These plants grow on the rocky shores of the Bahama Islands.

Editor's Note / Yellow-crowned Night-Heron (*Nycticorax violaceus*)

Plates 9 and 10 represent the yellow-crowned night heron, the immature in 9 and the adult in 10. Plate 9 could equally be that of an immature black-crowned night heron, as the two are quite similar and sufficient detail is lacking in the plate to make identification positive, but it seems more likely to be a yellow-crowned since the adult is shown in the following plate. Night herons are distinguished from other herons by their stocky appearance, shorter legs, and thick bills. As the name implies, night herons are denizens of the nocturnal and crepuscular hours; they leave their daytime roosts to venture to their feeding grounds, where they are often observed in early evening as silhouettes. Catesby incorrectly termed both of his night herons bitterns; the adult is pictured with the inkberry or black soap (*Scaevola plumieri*).

PLATE 11

The White Curlew (82)

This is about the size of a tame pigeon. The bill is six inches and a half long, of a pale red color, channeled from the base to the point; the iris of the eyes are gray; the fore part of the head, and round the eyes, is covered with a light red skin; four of the largest wing feathers have their ends dark green; all the rest of the bird is white, except the legs and feet, which are pale red. The flesh, particularly the fat, is very yellow, of a saffron color. When the great rains fall, which is usual at the latter end of summer, these birds arrive in Carolina in great numbers, and frequent the low watery lands.

The cock and hen are alike in appearance.

[Golden Club]

This plant grows by the sides of rivers, and in watery places; the root is tuberous, from which springs many broad oval leaves, eight or ten inches wide, on thick succulent round stalks, to the height of about four feet. From the root also shoot forth many of the like stalks, producing blue flowers at the end of every stalk; but as I had not an opportunity of observing them more critically while in blossom, I shall only take notice, that the flowers are succeeded by a bunch of green berries closely connected together, regularly, in the manner of a pineapple. These berries never harden, but drop off when ripe, being of the color, shape and consistency of capers.

PLATE 12

The Brown Curlew (83)

This is about the size of the white curlew. It has the same sort of bill, with red round the base of it, and eyes as the white curlew. The rest of the head and neck of a mixed gray. The upper part of the back, wings, and tail, are brown. The lower part of the back and rump are white, as it the under part of the body. The legs are

reddish, like those of the white, as is likewise its shape and size. This near resemblance in them made me suspect they differed only in sex, but by opening them, I found testicles in both the kinds. The flesh of this is dark, having not that yellow color which is in the white curlew. They both feed and associate in flocks, yet the white are twenty times more numerous than the brown kind. In the gizzard were crawfish. Both these kinds, accompanied with the wood pelicans, come annually about the middle of September, and frequent the watery savannas in numerous flights, continuing about six weeks, and then retire; and are not more seen until that time next year. In many of the hens of the white kind were clusters of eggs; from which I imagine they retire somewhere south to breed. Carolina, at that time of the year, would probably be too cold for that work of nature, it being much colder in the same latitude in that part of the world than in Europe. Very little or no difference appear in the feathers of the cock and hen.

[Arrow Arum]

This plant grows in ditches, and shallow water, to the height of three or four feet, with many arrow-headed leaves, on long succulent stalks springing from a tuberous root, from which also shoot forth large round stalks, at the end of each of which grows, in a hanging posture, a large roundish green seed vessel or capsule, containing many globular green berries of different bigness, some of the size of musket bullets, and others but half as big; this seed vessel (which is about the size of a hen's egg) when mature opens on both sides, and discloses the seeds, which are green and tender when ripe. I have seen the Indians boil them with their venison. They were excessive hot and astringent in my mouth, while green, but when boiled they lost those qualities, and were very palatable, and, as they said, wholesome. They are ripe in July.

Editor's Note / White Ibis (*Eudocimus albus*)

The family of ibises, which also includes the roseate spoonbill, is also confused with the herons. Unlike the latter, however, ibises fly with the neck extended and have narrow, thin, decurved bills. The white ibis is a fairly common bird in the coastal regions of the southern Atlantic states, where it shows a preference for coastal marshes and swamps, feeding to a large extent on insects, crayfish, fish, amphibians, and small snakes. They nest in large colonies, where they deposit three or four eggs in stick structures in small trees or even on the ground. The white ibis is a strikingly beautiful bird with a pure white body, black wing tips, and pink feet and decurved bill. It also has a characteristic pale red fleshy region surrounding the eyes and extending to the base of the bill. Catesby pictured his white curlew (Plate 11), a mature white ibis, with the golden club (*Orontium aquaticum*), a beautiful perennial of southern swamps.

Catesby's brown curlew (Plate 12) is an immature white ibis; it is brown on the head, neck, and back and has a white belly. It is figured with the arrow arum (*Peltandra virginica*).

PLATE 13

The Red Curlew (84)

Is a larger bird than the preceding, being about the bigness of a common crow. The bill is in form like that of other curlews, and of a pale red color. On the forepart of the head, and round the eyes, is a skin of the same color as the bill, and bare of feathers. The legs are likewise of a pale red color. About an inch of the end the wings are black. All the rest of the bird is red.

These birds frequent the coast of the Bahama Islands, and other parts of America between the tropics; and are seldom seen to the north or south of the tropics. The hens are of a dirtier red than the cocks.

Editor's Note / Scarlet Ibis (*Eudocimus ruber*)

This ibis, which Catesby called the red curlew, is one of the more enigmatic of the plates. It is the scarlet ibis (*Eudocimus ruber*), a tropical cousin of the white ibis now known to be simply a geographical color variant of the latter. The scarlet ibis is nearly identical to the white ibis in size, but the bird is a beautiful scarlet all over, with black wing tips and a bill of a more brownish color. The young are nearly indistinguishable from those of the white ibis. The scarlet ibis is strictly a tropical species; it is a resident of northern South America through Trinidad and has only been recorded as accidental in Texas, Florida, and Alabama. Reports of this species from Louisiana, Jamaica, Honduras, Costa Rica, and the Bahamas are still open to question.

In fact, the 1957 edition of the *Check-List of North American Birds* states of the species: "The type locality is usually restricted to 'Bahama Islands' from Catesby's account. Since no record is known from that island group this is incorrect" (p. 56). However, Catesby painted a bird that can only be the scarlet ibis and stated, "These birds frequent the coast of the Bahama Islands, and other parts of America between the tropics; and are seldom seen to the north or south of the tropics."

Obviously Catesby had knowledge of these birds. The simplest explanation is that during colonial times there was a great deal of boat traffic from tropical America and the West Indies to the United States and many exotic birds were taken along either alive or as skins to be traded or sold. The issue is complicated by Alexander Wilson's account of the species, however, which he terms common. "This beautiful bird is found in the most southern parts of Carolina; also in Georgia and Florida, chiefly about the seashore.... In most parts of America within the tropics, and in almost all the West India islands it is said to be common; also in the Bahamas. . . . The young . . . before they are able to fly white, continuing gradually assume their red color until the third year, when the scarlet plumage is complete. . . . They have frequently been domesticated" (1829, 3:92–93). Catesby and Wilson probably wrote of the scarlet ibis from what they had been told, and the species had been so commonly traded at the time that they were thought to be of common occurrence in the southernmost parts of the eastern United States and the Bahamas. However, it is certainly not beyond belief that the scarlet ibis, like a number of other species, could have occupied a broader range during colonial times, extending into the Bahamas and southern Florida, and has only subsequently retreated to its current range.

PLATE 14

The Wood Pelican (81)

This is about the bigness of a goose. The bill is nine inches and a half long, and curved towards the end; and next the head very big, being six inches and a half in circumference; the fore part of the head is covered with a dark bluish skin, bare of feathers; the back part of the head and neck are brown, the wings are large; all the lower part of them, from the shoulders to the ends, particularly the quill feathers, appear black at a distance, but are shaded with green; the upper part of the wing is white; the tail is black, very short and square at the end; all the rest of the body is white; the legs are black, and very long; the feet webbed, not so much as those of a duck, but are joined by a membrane reaching to the first joint of every toe, except the hindmost, which has no membrane, and is longer than common. That which demonstrates this bird to be of the pelican kin, is the pouch under the bill, though it is small, and contains not more than half a pint. In the latter end of summer there usually fall great rains in Carolina, at which time numerous flights of these birds frequent the open savannas, which are then under water, and they retire before November. They are very good eating fowls, though they feed on fish, and other water animals. It is a stupid bird, and void of fear, easily to be shot. They sit in great numbers on tall cypress and other trees, in an erect posture, resting their ponderous bills on their necks for their greater ease. I could not perceive any difference in the colors of the male and female.

Editor's Note / Wood Stork
(*Mycteria americana*)

Catesby's wood pelican, known today as the wood ibis, is in fact neither a pelican nor an ibis, but a true stork. Catesby thought that it belonged with the pelicans because of its partially webbed feet, and later the bird was thought to be an ibis because of its whitish color and slightly decurved bill. Structurally, though, it is no more than a stork; it shares with the other members of the family the absence of syringeal muscles, and the only noise it utters is a rattling of the bill. Like the cranes, and unlike the herons, the storks fly with the neck outstretched. In South Carolina the wood stork is a fairly common resident summer species in the coastal marshes, mudflats, and cypress swamps. The wood stork was apparently much more widespread in the past and no doubt occurred with some regularity either as a summer resident or a postbreeding wanderer as far north as North Carolina and Virginia. Wood storks walk along in shallow marsh waters in their pursuit of frogs, snakes, small turtles and alligators, and other small animal life. These birds frequently stir the water with one foot to frighten out fish and other aquatic life. The wood stork's nest is a huge stick structure placed in high trees in cypress swamps or other appropriate sites.

PLATE 15

The Turkey Buzzard (6)

This bird weighs four pounds and a half. The head, and part of the neck red, bald and fleshy, like that of a turkey, beset thinly with black hairs; the bill two inches and a half long, half covered with flesh, the end white, and hooked like that of a hawk; but without angles on the sides of the upper mandible. The nostrils are remarkably large and open, situate at an unusual distance from the eyes; the feathers of the whole body have a mixture of brown purple and green; the legs short, of a flesh color; their toes are long, shaped like those of Dunghil fowls; their claws black, and not so hooked as those of hawks.

Their food is carrion; in search after which they are always soaring in the air. They continue a long time on the wing, and with an easy, swimming motion mount and fall, without any visible moving of their wings. A dead carcass will attract together great numbers of them; and it is pleasant to observe their contentions in feeding. An eagle sometimes presides at the banquet, and makes them keep their distance while he satiates himself. This bird has a wonderful sagacity in smelling; no sooner there is a beast dead, but they are seen approaching from all quarters of the air, wheeling about, and gradually descending and drawing nigh their prey until at length they fall upon it. They are generally thought not to prey on anything living, though I have known them to kill lambs; and snakes are their usual food. Their custom is, to roost, many of them together, on tall dead pine or cypress trees, and in the morning continue several hours on their roost, with their wings spread open, I believe, that the air may have the greater influence to purify their filthy carcasses. They are little apprehensive of danger, and will suffer a near approach, especially when they are eating.

Editor's Note / Turkey Vulture (*Cathartes aura*)

The turkey vulture is so named because of the bare red skin of the head and neck and the dark body feathers that resemble a turkey. Called the turkey buzzard throughout the South, perhaps no bird is better known to the average person. Considered by most to be no more than ugly scavengers, turkey vultures are tremendously useful in cleaning up dead animals. These vultures eat almost any kind of carrion, fresh to putrid, ranging from dead alligators to pigs, skunks, opossums, raccoons, fish, and snakes, and have been known to kill newly born pigs and baby herons. They can be seen almost any day throughout the South soaring above with their widely outstretched pinions, often remaining on the wing for hours at a time. There has been considerable debate throughout the years as to how vultures locate their prey. Audubon was emphatic in his belief that they located prey by sight only and that if carrion or freshly killed animals were covered, vultures were unable to locate them. However, it has recently been shown that the turkey vulture has a well-developed olfactory food-locating mechanism. Unfortunately, vulture populations in the South have declined tremendously because of laws requiring the immediate disposal of dead farm animals.

The turkey vulture makes no nest to speak of, but simply deposits two eggs in a hollow log or a cave or on the ground. The young are white balls of fluffy down.

It is interesting to note here that Catesby followed John Lawson in recording only one species of vulture because both turkey and black vultures are quite common in the regions explored by the two men. Lawson stated: "The turkey-buzzard of Carolina is a small vulture which lives on any dead carcasses. They are about the bigness of the fishing-hawk, and have a nasty smell with them. They are of the kites color, and are reported to be an enemy to snakes by killing all they meet withal of that kind" (1709, 142). He made no mention of the cousin, the black vulture, which must have occurred alongside the turkey vulture wherever he went. Even Audubon noted: "They are daily seen in the streets of the southern cities, along with their relatives, and often roost with them on the same trees. . . . Charleston, Savannah, New Orleans, Natchez, and other cities, are amply provided with these birds [black vultures] which may be seen flying or walking about the streets the whole day in groups" (1840, 1:16–17). Another curious fact is that both Lawson and Catesby made a point of the supposed inclination of turkey vultures to kill snakes. In fact, while *dead* snakes are a favorite food of the vulture, it would be quite unusual for one actually to kill a snake. It seems quite possible that Catesby was simply following Lawson both in the omission of the black vulture and in the tale of the snakes.

PLATE 16

The Fishing Hawk (2)

This bird weighs three pounds and a quarter; from one end of the wing to the other extended, five foot five inches; the bill is black, with a blue cere; the iris of the eye yellow; the crown of the head brown, with a mixture of white feathers; from each eye, backwards, runs a brown stripe; all the upper part of the back, wing and tail dark brown; the throat, neck and belly white; the legs and feet are remarkably rough and scaly, and of a pale blue color; the talons black, and almost of an equal size; the feathers of the thighs are short, and adhere close to them, contrary to others of the hawk kind; which nature seems to have designed for their more easy penetrating the water.

Their manner of fishing is (after hovering awhile over the water) to precipitate into it with prodigious swiftness; where it remains for some minutes, and seldom rises without a fish; which the bald eagle (which is generally on the watch) no sooner spies, but at him

Accipiter Piscatorius.
The fishing Hawk.

T. 2

furiously he flies; the hawk mounts, screaming out, but the eagle always soars above him, and compels the hawk to let it fall; which the eagle seldom fails of catching, before it reaches the water. It is remarkable, that whenever the hawk catches a fish, he calls, as if were, for the eagle; who always obeys the call, if within hearing.

The lower parts of the rivers and creeks near the sea abound most with these eagles and hawks, where these diverting contests are frequently seen.

Editor's Note / Osprey (*Pandion haliaetus*)

The osprey, or fish-hawk, is the sole member of its family and is nearly cosmopolitan in the tropical and temperate regions of the world. Although it superficially resembles the bald eagle, the osprey has many distinctive features. It is smaller, and the underparts are white, as opposed to black in the eagle. In addition, the white head has a definite black line through the eye. The most distinctive feature of the osprey is its feet, which are well adapted for grasping slippery fish. They are large and strong and are equipped with scale-like structures, known as spicules, on the foot pads that are effective in holding fish. The claws are long, sharp, and powerful, and the outer toe is reversible. The food of ospreys consists entirely of fish taken alive.

Ospreys spend much of their time near the water, perched on a tall, often dead, tree, from which they fly out over fresh or salt water to search for fish. When it sights its prey, the osprey hovers for a moment, then plunges from thirty to one hundred feet above the surface straight into the water, often disappearing momentarily beneath the surface. Ospreys have been reported to carry fish weighing up to four pounds.

Like the bald eagle, the osprey builds its nest in a tall tree, often a pine or cypress; the nest, a bulky collection of sticks and other materials, may be added to year after year. Like eagles also, ospreys mate for life. Normally the female lays three eggs.

Ospreys were no doubt very abundant in colonial times, and both Lawson and Catesby have reasonable accounts of them. Both were quite intrigued with the piracy relationship between the bald eagle and the osprey. Lawson states, "The fishing-hawk is the eagle's jackal, which most commonly (though not always) takes his prey for him. . . . He is . . . the most dexterous fowl in nature at catching of fish, which he wholly lives on, never eating any flesh" (1709, 144).

PLATE 17

The Swallow-tail Hawk (4)

It weighs fourteen ounces; the beak black and hooked, without angles on the sides of the upper mandible, as in other hawks; the eyes very large, and black, with a red iris; the head, neck, breast and belly white; the upper part of the wing and back, dark purple; but more dusky towards the lower parts, with a tincture of green; the wings long, in proportion to the body; being four foot when extended; the tail dark purple, mixed with green, remarkably forked, the utmost and longest feather being eight inches longer than the middlemost, which is shortest.

Like swallows, they continue long on the wing, catching, as they fly, beetles, flies and other insects, from trees and bushes. They are said to prey upon lizards and other serpents; which has given them (by some) the name of snake-hawk. I believe they are birds of passage, not having seen any of them in winter.

Editor's Note / American Swallow-tailed Kite (*Elanoides forficatus*)

The swallow-tailed kite, truly one of the most beautiful of North American birds, was probably common during colonial times up the east coast from Florida to Virginia. Its numbers have been drastically reduced, however, and it is now common only in south Florida. Catesby probably encountered this bird frequently during his summers in the Charlestown region. Lawson had certain knowledge of this bird, which he called also the herring, and stated, quite accurately, that it never appeared except in the summer. He also stated: "His prey is chiefly on snakes" (1709, 145).

The flight of the swallow-tailed kite, a sight of remarkable beauty, was quite accurately and vividly described by Audubon: "Gliding along in easy flappings, it rises in wide circles to an immense height, inclining in various ways its deeply forked tail, to assist the direction of its course, dives with the rapidity of lightning, and, suddenly checking itself, reascends, soars away, and is soon out of sight. At other times a flock of these birds, amounting to fifteen or twenty individuals, is seen hovering around the trees. They dive in rapid succession amongst the branches, glancing along the trunks, and seizing in their course the insects and small lizards of which they are in quest" (1840, 1:78). Snakes of moderate size are among the most popular food items, and Audubon pictured his swallow-tailed kite holding a garter snake in its talons.

The courtship of the kite is a remarkable aerial show. Their nest is a stick structure placed near the top of a tall oak or pine tree near water; the female lays four to six eggs.

PLATE 18

The Bald Eagle (1)

This bird weighs nine pounds; the iris of the eye is white; over which is a prominence, covered with a yellow skin; the bill yellow, with the cere of the same color; the legs and feet are yellow; the talons black; the head, and part of the neck is white, as is the tail; all the rest of the body, and the wings, are brown.

Though it is an eagle of a small size, yet has great strength and spirit, preying on pigs, lambs, and fawns.

They always make their nests near the sea, or great rivers, and usually on old, dead pine or cypress trees, continuing to build annually on the same tree, till it falls. Though he is so formidable to all birds, yet suffers them to breed near his royal nest without molestation; particularly the fishing and other hawks, herons, etc. which all make their nests on high trees; and in some places are so near one another, that they appear like a rookery. This bird is called the bald eagle, both in Virginia and Carolina, though his head is as much feathered as the other parts of his body.

Both cock and hen have white heads, and their other parts differ very little from one another.

Editor's Note / Bald Eagle (*Haliaeetus leucocephalus*)

Although once widespread in North America, the bald eagle is abundant today only in Florida and Alaska. During colonial times the bald eagle was a relatively common bird, frequenting the shores of lakes and rivers as well as the coastline, where their preferred food, fish, is plentiful. The greatest part of the eagle's diet consists of dead fish gathered from the shores of lakes or rivers or from the surface of the water, but the eagle will also rob the osprey of its just captured fish or, as a last resort, will fish for itself. Eagles also eat carrion (often robbing vultures of their meals) and have been known to kill young lambs or pigs. Lawson tells us, "He is an excellent artist at stealing young pigs, which prey he carries alive to his nest, at which time the poor pig makes such a noise over head, that strangers that have heard them cry, and not seen the bird and his prey, have thought there were flying sows and pigs in that country" (1709, 142). Lawson also mentions a gray eagle, but only says that it is "the same sort of bird as the eagle in Europe." He may have been referring to the golden eagle (*Aquila chrysaetos*), but there is no more mention of it, and Catesby did not record the species. The golden eagle winters sparingly through the east and central United States to the Gulf states.

Both Lawson and Catesby described the nest of the eagle quite accurately; Lawson noted, "It is big enough to fill a handsome carts body, and commonly so full of nasty bones and carcasses that it stinks most offensively" (p. 142). Eagles mate for life and will build on to the same structure year after year; the overall accumulation can become a monstrous structure over the years. Normally the female lays two or three eggs, and the downy young are fed in the nest until fledged. The young attain the full white head and tail at approximately four years of age.

The powerful and stately bald eagle was adopted by the founders of our country as the national emblem

Aquila capite albo.
The White-headed Eagle.

The size of the Eagles head.

on 20 June 1782, and since that time it has appeared on virtually every official seal and document of the United States. There were those, however, such as Benjamin Franklin, who were quite aware of the daily habits of the bald eagle, especially its penchant for dead fish and other carrion. He argued for the adoption of the wild turkey as the national emblem. Franklin's comments were quoted by Sparks:

"Others object to the *bald eagle* as looking too much a *dindon*, or turkey. For my part, I wish the bald eagle had not been chosen as the representative of our country; he is a bird of bad moral character. . . . For in truth, the turkey is in comparison a much more respectable bird, and withal a true original native of America. Eagles have been found in all countries, but the turkey is peculiar to ours. . . . He is, besides (though a little vain and silly, it is true, but not a worse emblem for that), a bird of courage, and would not hesitate to attack a grenadier of the British guard, who should presume to invade his farmyard with a red coat on" (1840, 63–64).

Audubon also was greatly agitated over the selection of the bald eagle: "Suffer me, kind reader, to say how much I grieve that it should have been selected as the Emblem of my Country" (1840, 1:63).

Catesby, as Audubon would later, apparently also preferred the more appropriate name "white-headed eagle," as he inscribed his plate with it.

PLATE 19

The Little Hawk (5)

This bird weighs three ounces 16 penny-weight. The base of the upper mandible is covered with a yellow cere; the iris of the eye yellow; the head lead color with a large red spot on its crown; round the back of his head, are seven black spots regularly placed; the throat and cheeks are white, with a tincture of red; the back red, and marked with transverse black lines; the quill feathers of the wing dark brown; the rest of the wing blue, marked as on the back, with black; the tail red, except an inch of the end, which is black; the breast and belly of a bluish red; the legs and feet yellow.

The hen differs from the cock, as follows: her whole

is highly inaccurate and resembles the female more than the male.

wing and back is the same color as the back of the cock; the tail of the hen is marked as on the back, with the transverse black lines; her breast has not that stain of red as in the cock. They abide all the year in Virginia and Carolina, preying not only on small birds, but mice, lizards, beetles, etc.

Editor's Note / American Kestrel (*Falco sparverius*)

The handsome little sparrow hawk is the smallest and perhaps best known of the North American hawks. In the region of the Carolinas it is a breeding bird; in the winter the population greatly increases with the influx of migrants from the north. Sparrow hawks are commonly seen on telephone poles and wires in open country. From such vantage points it carefully scans the landscape beneath for the movement of a grasshopper or mouse. Or it might hover over a specific place that has aroused its interest and then suddenly drop to the ground, pouncing upon its victim and flying off with the prey in its talons. The sparrow hawk is considered one of the most beneficial of all the North American hawks; its food consists almost entirely of insects and small rodents, although small birds such as sparrows are included in the diet, especially in the cold winter months. Sparrow hawks nest usually in natural cavities of dead trees or in abandoned woodpecker nests where they deposit three to five eggs.

Lawson included the sparrow hawk in his list, stating, "He flies at the bush and sometimes kills a small bird, but his chiefest food is reptiles, as beetles, grasshoppers, and such small things" (1709, 143). Catesby's drawing of the sparrow hawk is marred by the presence of the seven black spots around the back of the head. The male has but two such spots. The overall drawing

PLATE 20

The Pigeon-hawk (3)

It weighs six ounces. The bill at the point black, at the base whitish; the iris of the eye yellow. The base of the upper mandible is covered with a yellow cere. All the upper part of the body, wings and tail is brown; the interior vanes of the quill feathers have large dusky red spots; the tail is transversely marked with four white lines; the throat, breast and belly white, intermixed with brown feathers; the small feathers that cover the thighs, reach within half an inch of the feet, and are white, with a tincture of red, beset with long spots of brown; the legs and feet yellow. It is a very swift and bold hawk, preying on pigeons and wild turkeys while they are young.

Editor's Note / Merlin (*Falco columbarius*)

It is somewhat curious that Catesby included this small falcon in his scanty list of birds of prey, for while Catesby gives only five types of hawks and eagles in his *Natural History*, he here included one of the least common, insofar as we can judge by historical documents. It is today only an unusual migrant and winter resident in the areas where Catesby worked. Lawson also recorded the "merlin," stating that "he very nimbly kills the smaller sorts of birds, and sometimes the partridge" (1709, 145). It seems more likely that Lawson probably included some of the larger falcons, such as the Cooper's hawk and the sharp-shinned hawk, with the merlin; all are bird eaters, but the little merlin seldom attacks anything larger than a jay.

The pigeon hawk is a small falcon, more or less the size of a bluejay; in many respects it is a miniature of the peregrine falcon, or duck hawk. It is primarily a bird of the open country in its wintering range, where it pursues small birds (the size of sparrows and thrushes) and insects.

PLATE 2 I

Urogallus Minor
(appendix, 1)

This bird was about a third part bigger than a common partridge. The bill was brown; the eyes black, with hazel-colored irises; the legs were covered with yellowish downy feathers to its toes; the tail was short, having the under part of a dusky black; except which, the plumage of the whole bird was of a reddish brown, marked transversely with black and white waved lines intermixed. The feathers of the crown of the head were long, and when erected, formed a little crest. But what is singular and extraordinary in this bird, and distinguishes it from all others yet known, are two tufts of feathers resembling little wings, three inches long, placed on the hind-part of the neck near the head, opposite to one another; each of these tufts were made up of five feathers lapping one over another, somewhat like those of a bird's wing, gradually decreasing in length.

These little wings (if so they may be called) were fixed to the neck in such a manner, that the bird has the power of contracting and dilating them; when disturbed, it would spread these little wings horizontally; at other times it would let them fall on each side of the neck. The hen had not these neck feathers; except which, there appeared very little difference between this and the cock. From the structure and resemblance of these neck feathers to real wings, they may possibly assist the bird in running or flying, or both; especially as the wings are short in proportion to its heavy body.

Some of these birds, in the year 1743, I saw at the right honorable the Earl of Wilmington's at Chiswick; who told me, they were natives of America, but from what particular part they came his Lordship knew not.

[Shooting Star]

The leaves of this plant are of a pale green, and resemble those of the common garden lettuce. From the middle of the leaves rises a single stalk about a foot high; on the summit of which are fixed together many reclining footstalks, on every one of which hang pendant a single flower; the whole forming a cluster of about twenty. The flower consists of a green calyx with five sections, and one reflexed petal divided almost to the bottom by five segments, in the manner of the autumn cyclamen. The apices are connected together in a point. Though the flowers hang down, the seed vessels afterwards turn up, and stand erect on their footstalks.

It flowered in Mr. Collinson's garden at Peckham, in September 1744, from seeds sent him by Mr. Bartram, who gathered them from beyond the Appalachian mountains, which lie parallel with Virginia. The seeds were contained in a long membranous capsule, which opens into four parts, and discharges its very small seeds.

To this new genus of plants, I have given the name of the learned Dr. Richard Mead, physician to His Majesty, and F.R.S. in gratitude for his zealous patronage of arts and sciences in general, and in particular for his generous assistance towards carrying the original design of this work into execution.

Editor's Note / Greater Prairie-Chicken (*Tympanuchus cupido*)

The now extinct population of the greater prairie-chicken, known as the heath hen or "pinnated grouse," is considered by some to have been a smaller, eastern race. Its scientific name comes from the Greek *tympanon*, meaning kettle drum, an allusion to the booming noise made by the males during courtship, and the Latin *cupido*, referring to the little wings on the neck which were likened to those of a cupid (which Catesby greatly exaggerated in his plate).

The heath hen was formerly a nonmigratory resident of the eastern seaboard, possibly from Massachusetts to Maryland and even Virginia, but the historical records are scanty. We do know that it was found in portions of the mid-Atlantic States, New England, New York (particularly Long Island), and Martha's Vineyard, where it is known to have preferred areas of sandy soil that were scrubby barrens with low pitch pines and scrub oaks and similar shrubbery. From this type of cover heath hens ventured out into farmlands to feed, although the birds did spend considerable time in the woods. Their diet is known to have included not only the tender shoots of grasses and other plants but also insects and, in the winter, berries, seeds, and especially acorns. The nest of the heath hen was a depression in the ground, lined with grasses, leaves, and so forth, and six to twelve eggs were the normal clutch.

Although the heath hen was quite numerous in certain localities, for example, in the Boston area and on Long Island, it was overhunted and fires devastated its rather limited habitat from time to time. Much of what Alexander Wilson (1829, 3:24–44) had to say concerning the "pinnated grous" came from a communication from a Dr. Samuel L. Mitchill of New York, who wrote an extensive account of this bird on "that peculiar tract generally known as the Brush plains of Long Island, having been, for time immemorial, the resort of the bird now before us." Mitchill stated: "The trees are mostly pitchpines of inferior size, and white oaks of a small growth. They are of a quality very fit for burning. Thousands of cords of both sorts of fire-wood are annually exported from these barrens. Vast quantities are occasionally destroyed by the fires which through carelessness or accident spread far and wide through the woods. The city of New York will probably for ages derive fuel from the grouse-grounds."

By 1869 it had been extirpated from the mainland and was thought to be restricted to Martha's Vineyard. Then in 1906 a fire swept through their breeding range and reduced the population to perhaps less than fifty. The population rebounded and established itself at from five hundred to one thousand birds, but it underwent similar declines and finally became extinct; the heath hen was last sighted on Martha's Vineyard on 11 March 1932. It is interesting to note that although Wilson wrote a long account of this species on Long Island, Audubon ignored the heath hen, believing it to be the same species as the prairie chicken he had encountered frequently in Kentucky.

Catesby's "Urogallus minor," for which he provided no common name, is illustrated with the shooting star (*Dodecatheon meadia*), a small, often cultivated perennial of open woods, fields, and prairies, particularly in the north and central United States.

PLATE 22

The American Partridge
(appendix, 12)

This is about half the size of the *Perdix cinerea*, or common partridge, which it somewhat resembles in color, though differently marked; particularly the head has three black lines; one above and two below the eyes, with two intermediate yellowish white lines. The bill is black; the iris of the eye red; the quill feathers of a dark brown, as is the tail; except which, the whole plumage of the body is of a reddish brown color, variously mixed, black and white: the legs and feet brown. They covey and roost on the branches of trees, frequenting woods and shady swamps more than open fields. Their flesh is remarkable white, and very delicate, but of a different taste from our common partridge: they lay as great a number of eggs.

The Attamusco Lily
(atamasco lily)

This plant sends forth from a bulbous root its narrow narciss-like leaves. The flowers grow singly on stalks about a foot in height, consisting of one leaf cut in six deep sections. From its center rises a style and six stamina, with yellow apices. The flower just before opening is stained with a rose color, which, as the flower declines, grows fainter. It is a native of Virginia and Carolina, where in particular places the pastures are as thick sprinkled with them and martagons, as cowslips and orchis's are with us in England.

Editor's Note / Northern Bobwhite
(*Colinus virginianus*)

Catesby's "American partridge" is our familiar bobwhite, or quail, which ranges over most of the eastern and central United States south to Guatemala; it also occurs in Cuba. These are short-tailed, chunky birds that have the appearance of miniature grouse; the male has a white throat and a white stripe above the eye. They occur as permanent residents throughout their range. Perhaps Wilson has described their habits as well as anyone: "They rarely frequent the forest, and are most numerous in the vicinity of well cultivated plantations, where grain is in plenty. They, however, occasionally seek shelter in the woods, perching on the branches, or secreting among the brush wood; but are found most usually in open fields, or along fences sheltered by thickets of briers. Where they are not too much persecuted by the sportsmen, they become almost half domesticated; approach the barn, particularly in winter, and sometimes in that severe season mix with the poultry, to glean up a subsistence" (1828, 3:39).

In the spring these birds are particularly evident by the male's clear whistle "bob-white," usually answered by a four-syllable whistle. They nest on the ground usually in places sheltered by small bushes or a clump of grass. A large clutch of twelve to eighteen eggs is normal. The bobwhite's varied diet comprises mostly weed seeds and grains, but also includes some insects.

Lawson commented of the "partridge," "They are a very beautiful bird, and great destroyers of the peas in plantations; wherefore, they set traps, and catch many of them" (1709, 144). Audubon, who called the bird the "common American partridge," stated, "In the States of Ohio and Kentucky, where they are very abundant, they are to be seen in the markets, both dead and alive, in large quantities" (1842, 5:59). He went on to describe how the partridges were caught in nets by roundups on horseback in the southern and western states and stated that hundreds were caught in a single day.

Catesby's "American partridge" is illustrated with the Atamasco lily (*Zephyranthes atamasco*), a member of the Amaryllis family that occurs from Virginia south to Florida and west to Mississippi.

PLATE 23

The Soree (70)

This bird, in size and form, resembles our water-rail. The whole body is covered with brown feathers; the under part of the body being lighter than the upper. The bill and legs are brown. These birds become so very fat in autumn, by feeding on wild oats, that they can't escape the Indians, who catch abundance by running them down. In Virginia (where only I have seen them) they are as much in request, for the delicacy of their flesh, as the rice-bird is in Carolina, or the ortolan in Europe.

[Soapwort Gentian]

This plant grows in ditches and shady moist places, rising usually sixteen inches high, with upright straight stems, having long sharp pointed leaves, set opposite to each other, spreading horizontally. From the joints of the leaves come forth four or five monopetalous blue flowers; which, before they open, are in form of a rolling-pin; but, when blown, are in shape of a cup, with the verge divided into five sections.

Editor's Note / Sora (*Porzana carolina*)

The sora is a small rail, somewhat reminiscent of a bantam chicken in general form. The adult has a chickenlike yellow bill with a black tip, and the throat and area at the base of the bill are black. Catesby's bird is clearly an immature specimen, beige brown all over and lacking these distinctive features. The sora is very common in the southern Atlantic states, especially during the fall and spring migrations when they may be encountered in great numbers in almost any kind of marshy situation, both freshwater and brackish, and wet meadows. Particularly during the fall migration, they carry a thick layer of fat, and in former years they were highly prized by hunters, who hunted them extensively when the tide was high and the birds were forced to take flight with the approach of a boat. T. G. Pearson stated, "They are highly esteemed for food and the bodies of great numbers of them formerly were dis-

played in the Wilmington [North Carolina] markets" (1959, 124). Their food consists largely of seeds, especially smartweed and wild rice, and small insects and aquatic animals.

Although Lawson (1709) mentioned marsh-hens in his list, it is impossible to ascertain to what species (and whether to one or more) he was referring. Catesby painted his soree (the name is thought to have been derived from the Indian name for the bird) next to the soapwort gentian (*Gentiana catesbaei*), a plant of the eastern United States that occurs in marshes, bogs, and similar wet areas. The name derives from their resemblance to the soapwort (*Saponaria*).

PLATE 24

The Hooping Crane (75)

It is about the size of the common crane. The bill is brown, and six inches long; the edges of both mandibles, towards the end, about an inch and half, are serrated. A deep and broad channel runs from the head more than halfway along its upper mandible. Its nostrils are very large. A broad white list runs from the eyes obliquely to the neck; except which, the head is brown. The crown of the head is callous, and very hard, thinly beset with stiff black hairs, which lie flat, and are so thin that the skin appears bare of a reddish flesh color. Behind the head is a peak of black feathers. The larger wing feathers are black. All the rest of the body is white. This description I took from the entire skin of

the bird, presented to me by an Indian, who made use of it for his tobacco pouch. He told me, that early in the spring, great multitudes of them frequent the lower parts of the rivers near the sea; and return to the mountains in the summer. This relation was afterwards confirmed to me by a white man; who added, that they made a remarkable hooping noise; and that he hath seen them at the mouths of the Savanna, Aratamaba, and other rivers nearer St. Augustine, but never saw any so far north as the settlement of Carolina.

The Bullet-bush

The largest part of the stem of this shrub is seldom bigger than the small of a man's leg. The height is usually five feet. The branches shoot forth near the ground and spread. The leaves are stiff like those of box, and about the same bigness, with notches at the ends. The berries hang to the smaller branches by footstalks not half an inch long, and are globular, somewhat larger than a black cherry, of a bluish black; and contain a single stone.

Editor's Note / Whooping Crane
(*Grus americana*)

Cranes are tall, long-legged wading birds that utter loud buglelike notes. Their numbers have been greatly reduced since the arrival of Europeans in the New World. They fly with their necks outstretched, unlike herons, with which they are often confused, which fly with their necks doubled back in an S shape. Further distinguishing them from herons, the face of the crane is nearly bare of feathers, and the young, instead of being born helpless, are born quite precocious with a dense covering of down feathers.

Of the two species of North American cranes, the whooping crane and the sandhill crane, the population of whoopers has been reduced to a dangerously low level. The remaining birds migrate from their northern nesting grounds to Texas each year, but the species has not been recorded in the Carolina region for well over a century. A specimen was taken on the Wacca-maw River in South Carolina in 1850, and the species probably visited the region with some frequency during colonial times. The account published by Audubon indicates that the whooper was still widespread in the early nineteenth century. "The Whooping crane reaches the Western Country about the middle of October, or the beginning of November, in flocks of twenty or thirty individuals, sometimes of twice or thrice that number; the young by themselves but closely followed by their parents. They spread from Illinois over Kentucky, and all of the intermediate States, until they reach the Carolinas on the southern coast" (1842, 5:189). The whooper's cousin the sand-hill crane is still a rare transient and winter visitor in coastal South Carolina and is occasionally found in North Carolina. Like the whoopers, these birds are fond of marshes and wet fields, where they search for frogs, insects, and small rodents.

Lawson recorded only the smaller sandhill crane. "Cranes use the savannas, low ground, and frogs; they are above five foot-high, when extended; are of a cream color, and have a crimson spot on the crown of their heads. Their quills are excellent for pens; their flesh makes the best broth, yet is very hard to digest. Among them often frequent storks, which are here seen, and nowhere besides in America, that I have yet heard of. The cranes are easily bred up tame, and are excellent in a garden to destroy frogs, worms, and other vermin" (1709, 149–50).

Catesby's "hooper" is illustrated with the Bahamian bullet-bush (*Reynosia septentrionalis*).

PLATE 25

The Chattering Plover (71)

This is about the size of the larger snipe. The eyes are large, with a scarlet circle. A black list runs from the bill under the eyes. The forehead is white; above which it is black. The rest of the head is brown. The throat, and round the neck, are white; under which there is a broad black list encompassing the neck. Another list of black crosses the breast, from the shoulder of one wing to that of the other. Except which, the breast and belly are white. The back and wings are brown; the larger quill feathers being of a darker brown. The small rump feathers, which cover three quarters of the tail, are of a yellowish red. The lower part of the tail is black. The legs and feet of a straw color. It hath no back toes. These birds are very frequent both in Virginia and Carolina; and are a great hindrance to fowlers, by alarming the game with their screaming noise. In Virginia they are called kill-deers, from some resemblance of their noise to the sound of that word. They abide in Carolina and Virginia all the year. The feathers of the cock and hen differ not much.

The Sorrel-tree

(or sourwood)

The trunk of this tree is usually five or six inches thick, and rises to the height of about twenty feet, with slender branches thick set with leaves, shaped like those of the pear tree. From the ends of the branches proceed little white monopetalous flowers, like those of the strawberry tree, which are thick set on short footstalks to one side of many slender stalks, which are pendant on one side of the main branch.

Editor's Note / Killdeer (*Charadrius vociferus*)

The name killdeer is a phonetic approximation for the loud cry of this bird, which is perhaps more of an insistent "kill-deeah," repeated along with a "dee-dee-dee." Usually seen in pairs or small flocks, the killdeer is the common, noisy resident plover of the Carolinas and Virginia. It frequents open country, such as pastures, large meadows, golf courses, and the like, and is the only plover that commonly occurs inland as well as at the coast. Its cry, which may be heard day or night, is familiar to all. Killdeers nest on the ground in a slight depression with some lining of small materials; four eggs are the normal clutch. They are versatile in their feeding, consuming great numbers of insects and grubs of all kinds. The killdeer is easily identified by the two large black stripes across the breast and the reddish rump, which appears when the bird flies.

Lawson's killdeer is clearly identifiable as such. "The Lap-wing or green-plover are here very common. They cry pretty much as the English plovers do, and differ not much in feather, but want a third of their bigness" (1709, 147).

Lawson also recorded another plover, which one can presume to be the black-bellied plover because of the reference to "whistling plover." "The gray or whistling plover are very scarce amongst us. I never saw any but three times that fell and settled on the ground. They differ very little from those in Europe, as far as I could discern. I have seen several great flocks of them fly overhead; therefore, believe they inhabit the valleys near the mountains."

Catesby's killdeer is a fairly accurate drawing of the species; it is depicted with a sorrel-tree or sourwood (*Oxydendrum arboreum*), so called because of the sour taste of the leaves. Sourwood honey is popular throughout its range.

PLATE 26

The Oyster Catcher (85)

Weighs one pound and two ounces. The bill is long, straight, and of a bright red color, contracted near the base, and towards the end compressed. The irises of their eyes are yellow, encompassed with a red circle. The whole head and neck are black, having a spot of white under the eyes; all the under part of the body is dusky white; the larger quill feathers are dusky black; the tail is short, black towards the end, and towards the rump is white. The upper part of the body and wings is brown, except a broad white line, which runs along the middle of each wing. The legs are long and thick, and of a reddish color. It has only three fore toes, wanting the back toe. Their feet are remarkably armed with a very rough scaly skin. In rivers, and creeks near the sea there are great quantities of oyster banks, which at low water are left bare; on these banks of oysters do these birds principally, if not altogether, subsist; nature having not only formed their bills suitable to the work, but armed the feet and legs for a defense against the sharp edges of the oysters. The hens differ from the cocks in not having the red circle around their eyes, and their bellies are of a more dirty white than in the cocks. In the maw of one was found nothing but undigested oysters.

This bird seems to be the *Haematopus* of Bellonius, Will. p. 297. notwithstanding there is some small dif-

ference in their description. I have seen them on the seacoasts both of Carolina and the Bahama Islands.

[Black or Honey Mangrove]

This grows to the size of a small tree; the leaves stand by pairs, on footstalks about an inch long; they are long, thick, and succulent. At the ends of the stalks grow in pairs, and sometimes singly, round flat seed vessels, about the breadth of a shilling; the fruit is of the substance of a bean, and, like that, divides in the middle; it is covered with a thin membrane of a pale green color. I had no opportunity of seeing the blossoms, though I was told they were very small and white. The bark of this tree is used for tanning of sole leather.

Editor's Note / American Oystercatcher (*Haematopus palliatus*)

This is the largest shorebird occurring along the southern Atlantic coast, where it frequents the beaches and tidal flats. And with its large red bill, black upper parts, and white underparts, it is also one of the most distinctive. These birds feed on a variety of bivalves, especially oysters, which they pry open by inserting their bill between the shells and then opening their bills. Oystercatchers are very noisy birds; particularly during the breeding season they constantly utter a loud "wheep, wheep, wheeop." The females deposit two or three eggs in a hollow in the sand. The young are very precocious and active almost immediately after hatching. Catesby's oystercatcher is pictured with the black or honey mangrove (*Avicennia germinans*), which is not a true mangrove (*Rhizophora*). The white spot under the oystercatcher's eye is apparently a mistake.

PLATE 27

The Turn-stone, or Sea-dottrel (72)

This bird has, in proportion to its body, a small head, with a straight taper black bill, an inch long. All the upper part of the body is brown, with a mixture of white and black. The quill feathers of the wings are

dark brown; the neck and breast are black; the legs and feet light red. In a voyage to America, in the year 1722, in 31 Deg. N. Lat. and 40 leagues from the coast of Florida, the bird, from which this was figured, flew on board us, and was taken. It was very active in turning up stones, which we put into its cage; but not finding under them the usual food, it died. In this action it moved only the upper mandible; yet would with great dexterity and quickness turn over stones of above three pounds weight. This property Nature seems to have given it for finding of its food, which is probably worms and insects on the seashore. By comparing this with the description of that in Will. *Ornithog.* which I had then on board, I found this to be the same kind with that he describes.

[Shanks]

This plant grows usually to the height of four or five feet, with many straight ligneous stems; to which are set, opposite to each other, at the distance of five or six inches, smaller single stems. The leaves grow opposite to one another on footstalks half an inch long, being narrow next the stalk, and broad at the end, where they are little pointed; in shape like a pear. The flowers grow in tufts, at the ends of the branches, on short footstalks; each flower being formed like a cup, with yellow apices.

Editor's Note / Ruddy Turnstone (*Arenaria interpres*)

The ruddy turnstone is easily distinguished from all of the other shorebirds by its pied appearance and reddish legs. Although these birds nest in the Arctic tundra, they migrate and winter along the coastal United States in some numbers where they stalk the beaches in search of small animal life, using their bills to turn over stones, shells, and other objects. Catesby's turnstone appears to be in typical winter plumage, although his description is more like that of one that was changing from nuptial to winter plumage. His statement that these birds can turn over stones weighing over three pounds is fanciful; the birds are probably not capable of turning over any stone greater than several inches in diameter. The turnstone is shown in association with the Bahamian plant shanks (*Salmea petrobioides*).

PLATE 28

The Laughing Gull (89)

This bird weighs eight ounces. The bill is red, hooked towards the point; the lower mandible having an angle towards the end; the head, of a dusky black; the eyes are edged above and below with white; half the quill feathers of the wing, towards the ends, are dusky black; all the rest of the body is white, as is the tail, the feathers of which are of an equal length, and not so long as the wings by two inches; the legs are black, as are also the feet, which are webbed.

These birds are numerous in most of the Bahama Islands. The noise they make has some resemblance to laughing, from which they seem to take their name. I know not whether the hen differs from this, which is a cock.

Editor's Note / Laughing Gull
(Larus atricilla)

The laughing gull, so named because of its laughing note, "ha, ha, ha, ha, haah, haah, haah . . . ," is common along the Atlantic and Gulf coasts during the summer. It is a distinctive bird with a dark gray mantle, a black head, and a red bill; the neck, tail, and underparts are white. Laughing gulls are often seen in the Atlantic states following after boats and ferries, seeking the spoils of fishing trips and bread from generous ferry passengers.

Laughing gulls build large, well-constructed nests in colonies along coastal islands or on tufts of grass in saltwater marshes; normally four eggs are laid.

Given the large number of species of gulls and terns that occur in the coastal regions of South Carolina, it is somewhat surprising that Catesby recorded only the laughing gull. Surely he would have recognized at least four or five other forms if he had ventured anywhere near the beaches. Lawson's gulls and terns are difficult to identify. He wrote: "The great gray gulls are good meat, and as large as a pullet. They lay large eggs, which are found in very great quantities on the islands in our sound, in the months of June and July. The young squabs are very good victuals, and often prove a relief to travelers by water, that have spent their provisions" (1709, 154). One might guess that Lawson was here referring to the large herring gull, although there are other possibilities. He also recorded another unidentifiable "little gray-gull" (p. 152) and a "sea-coch" that "crows at the break of day" (p. 151). Lawson was obviously referring to the laughing gull when he stated, "We have a great pied gull, black and white, which seems to have a black hood on his head; these lay very fair eggs which are good; as are the young ones in the season" (p. 154).

PLATE 29

The Noddy (88)

Weighs four ounces. The bill is black, long, and sharp. The eyes above and below are edged with white. The crown of the head is white, which grows gradually dusky towards the back part of the head. All the rest of these birds are brown, the tails and quill feathers being darkest. Their wings and tails are of an equal length.

They lay their eggs on bare rocks on many of the Bahama Islands, where they breed in company with boobies. It is pleasant to see them fishing, accompanied with variety of other sea birds in numerous flights, flying on the surface of the water, and continually dropping to snatch up the little fish, drove in shoals by larger ones to the surface of the water. This seems to be done with great pleasure and merriment, if we may judge from the various notes and great noise they make, which is heard some miles off. The shoals of fish they follow, cause a rippling and whiteness in the water, which is a plain direction for the birds to follow them, and may be seen from the hills several miles off. Where the rippling appears most, there the birds swarm thickest. This is done in breeding time, but that being past, these noddies roam the ocean over separately, and are seen several hundred leagues from any land, but are seldom met with without the tropics. They are stupid birds, and like the booby will suffer themselves to be laid hands on, and taken from off the yards or parts of ships on which they alight. The cocks and hens differ very little in color.

Editor's Note / Brown Noddy (*Anous stolidus*)

The terns are closely related to the gulls, but are in general smaller, more slender, and the bills are sharper, lacking the hook at the tip. Like the gulls, terns are birds of seacoasts and inland waters and feed primarily on fish and other aquatic life. Catesby encountered the beautiful little noddy in the Bahama Islands. Interestingly, seven species of terns are known there and four are commonly seen near the shoreline or even over land, but Catesby recorded only this rather unusual species. Unlike most terns, which are predominantly white, the brown noddy is, as the name implies, a dark sooty brown, with a distinctive white forehead and crown. Rather than the characteristic forked tail of terns, noddies have a wedge-shaped tail. The brown noddy breeds on the cays, away from the main islands.

PLATE 30

The Cut Water (90)

The bill, which is the characteristic note of this bird, is a wonderful work of nature. The base of the upper mandible is thick and compressed sideways gradually to the end, and terminates in a point, and is three inches long. The under mandible is more compressed than the upper, and very thin, both edges being as sharp as a knife, and is almost an inch longer than the upper mandible, which has a narrow groove or channel,

into which the upper edge of the lower mandible shuts. Half the bill, next the head, is red, the rest is black; the forepart of the head, neck, breast and belly white; the hindpart of the head, back and wings black, with a small mixture of white. The upper feather of the tail is black, the rest white. The legs are short and small, of a red color. The feet are webbed like those of a gull, with a small back toe. These birds frequent near the seacoasts of Carolina. They fly close to the surface of the water, from which they seem to receive somewhat of food. They also frequent oyster banks, on which, I believe, they feed. The structure of their bills seem adapted to that purpose. The cocks and hens are alike in color.

Editor's Note / Black Skimmer
(*Rynchops niger*)

It is unfortunate that Catesby's name "cut water" did not survive; it seems far more appropriate, as it vividly describes the manner in which the skimmer feeds, the longer lower mandible "cutting" the water in search of small fish as the bird flies along. Catesby listed the French name as *le coupeur d'eau*, a literal translation of his English name; in Louisiana today, however, the French name for this bird is *bec à ciseaux* (scissor beak).

Black skimmers are common breeding birds along the Atlantic coast to Florida and are familiar to almost all who go to the beaches. It is a large, long-winged bird that is distinctively black above and white beneath. The basal half of the bill is bright red tipped with black; the feet are also carmine. Skimmers lay four or five eggs, which are deposited on sand spits or islands littered with sea shells in a nest which it makes simply by turning its body around several times in the substrate.

Lawson apparently also recognized the skimmer, as he stated, "Old wives are a black and white pied gull, with extraordinary long wings, and a golden colored bill and feet. He makes a dismal noise as he flies, and ever and anon dips his bill in the salt-water. I never knew him eaten" (1709, 151).

PLATE 3 1

The Flamingo (73)

This bird is two years before it arrives at its perfect color; and then it is entirely red, except the quill feathers, which are black. A full-grown one is of equal weight with a wild duck; and, when it stands erect, is five feet high. The feet are webbed. The flesh is delicate and nearest resembles that of a partridge in taste. The tongue, above any other part, was in the highest esteem with the luxurious Romans for its exquisite flavor.

These birds make their nests on hillocks in shallow water; on which they sit with their legs extended down, like a man sitting on a stool. They breed on the coasts of Cuba and the Bahama Islands, and frequent salt water only. A man, by concealing himself from their sight, may kill great numbers of them for they will not rise at the report of a gun; nor is the sight of those killed close by them sufficient to terrify the rest, and warn them of the danger; but they stand gazing, and as

it were astonished, till they are most or all of them killed.

This bird resembles the heron in shape, excepting the bill, which being of a very singular form, I shall, in the next table, give the figure of it in its full size, with a particular description.

[Gorgonian Coral]

This plant ariseth from a short stem about two inches round, and about the same in height; where it divides into two larger branches, each of which divides again into two smaller; and so generally, at the distance of three or four inches, each branch divides in two smaller, till the whole plant is risen to about two feet, and the upper branches are become not thicker than a crow's quill; all pliant like horn or whalebone, and of a dark brown color. They are in great plenty at the bottom of the shallow seas and channels of the Bahama Islands, the water there being exceedingly clear. I have plainly seen them growing to the white rocks in above ten fathom water.

PLATE 3 2

The Bill of the Flamingo in Its Full Dimensions (74)

I need not attempt to describe the texture of the bill otherwise than Dr. Grew has done in his *Mus. R. Soc.* p. 67. His words are these: "The figure of each beak is truly hyperbolical. The upper is ridged behind; before, plain or flat, and pointed like a sword, and with the extremity bent a little down; within, it hath an angle or sharp ridge, which runs all along the middle. At the top of the hyperbole, not above a quarter of an inch high. The lower beak in the same place above one inch high, hollow, and the margins strangely expanded inward, for the breadth of above a quarter of an inch, and somewhat convexly. They are both furnished with black teeth, as I call them, from their use, of an unusual figure; *scil.* slender, numerous, and parallel, as in ivory-combs; but also very short, scarce the eighth part of an inch deep. An admirable invention of nature; by the help of which, and of the sharp ridge abovementioned, this bird holds his slippery prey the faster."

When they feed (which is always in shallow water) by bending their neck, they lay the upper part of their bill next the ground, their feet being in continual motion up and down in the mud; by which means they raise a small round sort of grain, resembling millet, which they receive into their bill. And as there is a necessity of admitting into their mouths some mud, nature has provided the edges of their bill with a sieve, or teeth, like those of a fine comb, with which they retain the food, and reject the mud that is taken in with it. This account I had from persons of credit; but I never saw them feeding myself, and therefore cannot absolutely refute the opinion of others, who say, they feed on fish, particularly eels, which seem to be the slippery prey Dr. Grew says the teeth are contrived to hold.

The accurate Dr. James Douglass hath obliged the world with a curious and ample description of this bird in *Phil. Trans.* No. 550.

[Gorgonian Coral]

This species differs from the former, in that it is black, and hath a large stem like the trunk of a tree, which rises up through the middle of the plant, and sends out several larger branches, from which arise the smaller twigs, which are more crooked and slender than those of the preceding. So that in the whole it resembles a tree without leaves.

This grows to rocks in the same places with the preceding.

Editor's Note / Greater Flamingo (*Phoenicopterus ruber*)

Flamingos are large, long-legged wading birds that are ancient derivatives of shorebirds. Like the ducks and geese, they possess webbed feet and lamellate bills, but the huge tongue is accommodated in the lower, instead of the upper, jaw. There it serves as a pump, and, with their heads inverted beneath the water, these master strainers sieve microscopic and tiny organisms from the water. Tiny toothlike projections located on both the tongue and the sides of the jaws catch any food material and strain out mud and water.

Although greatly reduced in numbers today, flamingos were no doubt extremely plentiful in the Bahamas when Catesby visited the islands. Catesby's flamingos are illustrated with the decorticated skeletons of gorgonian corals (*Plexaura*). That of Plate 31 is not identifiable; that of Plate 32 is *Plexaura flexuosa*.

PLATE 33

The Canada Goose (92)

This bird is described by Mr. Willoughby, p. 361. By comparing it with his description, and finding them agree, I conceive it sufficient to recite his account of it as follows:

"Its length, from the point of the bill to the end of the tail, or of the feet, is forty-two inches. The bill itself, from the angles of the mouth, is extended two inches, and is black of color. The nostrils are large. In shape of body it is like to a tame goose, save that it seems to be a little longer. The rump is black; but the feathers next above the tail, are white. The back is of a dark gray, like the common goose. The lower part of

the neck is white, else the neck is black. It hath a kind of white stay or muffler under the chin, continued on each side below the eyes to the back of the head. The belly is white; the tail black; as are also the greater quill feathers of the wings. The eyes are hazel colored. The edges of the eyelids are white; the feet are black, having the hind toe."

The white stay or muffler before mentioned is sufficient to distinguish it from all other of the goose kind.

In winter they come from the northern parts of America to Carolina, etc.

Editor's Note / Canada Goose
(*Branta canadensis*)

Considering the incredible numbers of geese and swans that must have spent the winters along the coastal plain of Virginia and "Carolina" during colonial times, it is indeed remarkable that Catesby painted only the Canada goose. Perhaps, though, many species appeared similar to those in Europe and were therefore of little interest. For a list of other species recorded by Catesby see his text (pp. 163–64). Lawson recorded numerous species of geese and swans:

Of the swans, we have two sorts; the one we call trumpeters, because of a sort of trumpeting noise they make.

These are the largest sort we have, which come in great flocks in the winter, and stay, commonly, in the fresh rivers till February, that the spring comes on, when they go to the lakes to breed. A cygnet, that is, a last year's swan, is accounted a delicate dish, as indeed it is. They are known by their head and feathers, which are not so white as old ones.

The sort of swans called hoopers, are the least. They abide more in the salt-water, and are equally valuable for food, with the former. It is observable that neither of these have a black piece of horny flesh down the head and bill, as they have in England.

Of geese, we have three sorts, differing from each other only in size. Ours are not the common geese that are in the fens in England, but the other sort, with black heads and necks.

The gray brant or barnacle, is here very plentiful, as all other water-fowl are, in the winter-season. They are the same which they call barnacles in Great Britain, and are a very good fowl, and eat well.

There is also a white brant, very plentiful in America. This bird is all over as white as snow, except the tips of the wings, and those are black. (1709, 150–51)

Lawson, then, recorded two species of swans and three species of geese—the first two are probably the Canada goose and the brant, and the last is clearly the snow goose.

The V-shaped bands of Canada geese migrating southward are a familiar sight during the autumn. They were, and still are, a common bird wintering along the Atlantic coastal plain, where they feed on grain or vegetation growing in marshy ponds and flats in salt or brackish water.

Catesby's Canada goose is illustrated with the rong bush (*Wedelia bahamensis*).

PLATE 34

The Summer Duck (97)

This is of a mean size, between the common wild duck and teal. The bill is red, with a black spot on the middle of it, and a black nail or horny substance on the end, the base of the bill is edged about with a yellow fleshy protuberance, pointing on each side towards the eyes, the irises of which are very large and red, encompassed with a red circle. The crown of the head is elegantly covered with a double plume of long feathers, composed of blue, green and purple colors, hanging down separately behind its head, and divided by a narrow white line, extending from the upper part of the base of the bill backward; the lower plume is likewise bordered with a white line, beginning at the eyes and running parallel with the other, dividing the plume

from the under part of the head, which is purple. The throat is white, from each side whereof proceed two white lines, one branching up towards the crown of the head, and the other below it, crossing the neck. The breast is of a muddy red, sprinkled thick over with white spots, like ermine. A little above the shoulder is a broad white line, extended transversely, below which, and joining to it, runs a broad black list. The back and upper parts of the wings are variously and changeably colored with brown, blue, and purple. The small feathers near the vent, are of a reddish purple, from amongst which spring two small yellow feathers. The tail is blue and purple. The lower part or verge of the wings are lapped over, and covered by the small downy side feathers, extending from the shoulders halfway the wings, displaying alternately and in a wonderful manner black and white pointed lines, varying in appearance according to the motion of the bird, and different position it puts its feathers into, which adds much to the beauty of it. The sides of the body below the wings are brown, with transverse waved lines, as in many of the duck kind; the legs and feet of a reddish brown. They breed in Virginia and Carolina, and make their nests in the holes of tall trees (made by woodpeckers) growing in water, particularly cypress trees. While they are young and unable to fly, the old ones carry them on their backs from their nests into the water; and at the approach of danger, they fix with their bills on the backs of the old ones, which fly away with them. The female is all over brown.

Editor's Note / Wood Duck (*Aix sponsa*)

The wood duck, or summer duck, is a permanent resident of the Carolinas and Virginia, where, more than any other duck species, it is a woodland bird. They are fairly common in the wooded swamps and rivers throughout the region, where they feed on nuts, especially acorns, and insects and other small animal life. Wood ducks nest in hollow trees from four to fifty feet off the ground, often in natural cavities or even abandoned woodpecker nests if the holes are sufficiently large. The birds take no nesting material to the nest; rather the female lines it with down from her breast. Although some still maintain that the adults carry the chicks to the ground when it is time for them to leave the nest, it is now generally believed that they jump. After the breeding season, wood ducks can be seen in small flocks over fresh water. The male is considered by many naturalists to be the most beautifully colored North American bird.

Lawson apparently recorded the wood duck as two separate species. He stated, "We have another duck that stays with us all summer. She has a great topping, is pied, and very beautiful. She builds her nest in a woodpeckers hole, very often sixty or seventy feet high" (1709, 152). He then went on to say, "Whistling duck.—Towards the mountains in the hilly country on the west-branch of Cape Fear Inlet, we saw great flocks of pretty pied ducks that whistled as they flew, or as they fed. I did not kill any of them."

While Catesby's failure to describe the incredible number of geese and swans along the coast of the Carolinas and illustrate some of the more spectacular species is enigmatic, his treatment of the ducks seems altogether adequate for the time. Nonetheless, Lawson had actually recorded more different species than Catesby. With some slight conjecture, Lawson's list is as follows:

Mallard	(*Anas platyrhynchos*)
American Black Duck	(*Anas rubripes*)
Wood Duck	(*Aix sponsa*)
Common Golden-eye	(*Bucephala clangula*)
Blue-winged Teal	(*Anas discors*)
American Wigeon	(*Anas americana*)
Green-winged Teal	(*Anas crecca*)
Northern Shoveller	(*Anas clypeata*)
Canvasback (bull-necks)	(*Aythya valisineria*)
Redhead	(*Aythya americana*)
Surf Scooter (black flusterers)*	(*Melanitta perspicillata*)
raft-fowl	includes all sorts . . . are of several sorts that we know no name for.
Red-breasted Merganser	(*Mergus serrator*)

*See McAtee, 1946.

Lawson recorded that "fishermen are like a duck, but have a narrow bill, with sets of teeth. They live on very small fish which they catch as they swim along. They taste fishy. The best way to order them is, upon occasion, to pull out the oil-box from the rump and then bury them five or six hours underground. Then they become tolerable" (1709, 157). Mergansers are winter residents along the coastal bays. They do not have teeth, but rather toothlike projections along the sides of the jaws. The oil-box is the oil gland of the tail or the uropygial gland.

PLATE 35

The Ilathera Duck (93)

This is somewhat less than the common tame duck. The bill is dusky blue, except on each side of the upper mandible; next the head is an orange-colored triangular spot: the throat and all the fore part of the neck to the eyes are white: the upper part of the head is of a mixed gray, inclining to yellow, as is the back and belly: the upper part of the wing and quill feathers are dark brown: in the middle of the wing is a row of green feathers, as in the common teal, bordered towards the quill ends with yellow, and their ends black, below which, and next to the quill feathers, is a row of yellow feathers: the feet are of a lead color.

These birds frequent the Bahama Islands, but are not numerous. I never having seen but one, which was a drake.

[Sea Ox-eye or Sea-bush]

This plant grows on rocks on the seashore to the height of four or five feet, with many pliant green stems arising from the root: the leaves are long, increasing in width gradually to the end, and in form resembling the leaves of the stock gillyflower; they are thick, succulent, and of a shining green, standing opposite to one another. The flowers grow singly at the ends of branches, on footstalks of four inches long.

Editor's Note / White-cheeked Pintail
(*Anas bahamensis*)

Catesby illustrated the white-cheeked pintail with the sea ox-eye or sea-bush (*Borrichia arborescens*). This duck, also known as the Bahama pintail, is common throughout the Bahamas; it has been recorded on all of the islands, where it is encountered on both freshwater and brackish lakes. It is easily identified by the white cheeks and throat on both the male and female.

PLATE 36

The Blue-wing Teal (99)

Is somewhat bigger than the common teal; the bill black, the head, and most part of the body of a mixed gray, like that of a wild duck, the back being darker than the under part of the body; the upper part of the wing is of a bright blue, below which ranges a narrow row of white feathers; next to them a row of green; the rest of the wing, being the quill feathers, is dark brown, the legs and feet, brown. The female is all brown, like a common wild duck.

In August these birds come in great plenty to Carolina, and continue till the middle of October, at which time the rice is gathered in, on which they feed. In Virginia, where no rice grows, they feed on a kind of wild oat growing in the marshes, and in both places they become extremely fat.

They are not only by the natives preferred to all other water fowl, but others, who have eat of them, give them the preference to all of the duck kind for delicacy of taste.

PLATE 37

The White-face Teal (100)

In bigness this exceeds a common teal; the bill black; the crown of the head is black, which extends along the base of the bill to the throat, between which and the eyes it is white; all the rest of the head is purple mixed with green; the breast and belly, in color, like that of a common teal; the upper part of the back, next the head is brown, curiously waved like the curdling of water; the lower part of the back is covered with long sharp-pointed feathers of a light brown color. The wings are colored as those of the blue-wing teal. The tail is brown, and somewhat longer than the wings; the vent feathers under the tail are black; the legs and feet yellow. The female is all over brown. They frequent ponds and fresh-water rivers in Carolina.

Editor's Note / Blue-winged Teal
(*Anas discors*)

The blue-winged teal is among the earliest of ducks to appear during the migration, in early fall. Many spend the winter along the Atlantic coast, and an occasional

pair may remain to breed. These teal are usually observed in small flocks of four or five birds on shallow ponds and flats along the coastal plain, where they feed on aquatic vegetation. They are among the swiftest of ducks in flight and are said to have attained speeds of up to 100 miles per hour. The female is rather nondescript, but the male is easily recognized by the white crescent in front of the eye. Catesby figured the female in Plate 36 as the blue-wing teal and the male in Plate 37 as the white-face teal. Lawson had also encountered this species, of which he stated, "The blue-wings are less than a duck, but fine meat. These are the first fowls that appear to us in the fall of the leaf, coming then in great flocks, as we suppose, from Canada, and the lakes that lie behind us" (1709, 152).

PLATE 38

The Blue-wing Shoveler (96)

This is somewhat less than a common duck. The eyes are yellow; the upper part of the wing is covered with pale blue feathers, below which is a row of white feathers, and below them a row of green; the rest of the lower part of the wing is brown; all the other part of the body is of a mixed brown, not unlike in color to the common wild duck. This bird does not altogether agree with that described by Mr. Willoughby, p. 370. But if, as he observes, they change their colors in winter, it is possible this may be the bird. However, as their bills are of the same form, and by which they may be distinguished from all others of the duck kind, I cannot describe it in better words than the above excellent author.

"Its bill is three inches long, coal black (though this is of a reddish brown, spotted with black) much broader toward the tip than at the base, excavated like a buckler, of a round circumference. At the end it hath

a small crooked hook or nail; each mandible is pectinated or toothed like a comb, with rays or thin plates inserted mutually one into another, when the bill is shut. The legs and feet are red." I am not certain whether this was a male or female.

Editor's Note / Northern Shoveler
(*Anas clypeata*)

The northern shoveler is a common winter resident throughout the coastal plain region of the Carolinas and Virginia. Also known to hunters as "spoonbill" because of the spoonlike shape of its bill, the male of the species is one of the most beautiful waterfowl of the region, sporting a green head, purplish bill, black back, and white breast with cinnamon breast and sides. Small flocks of shovelers are normally found on the shallower lakes and ponds, often accompanied by blue-winged teal and American wigeon. Their highly specialized bill permits them to feed from the surface of the water, but they also tip up in their pursuit of small aquatic plants and animals, which are strained through the spatulate bill. Lawson only noted, "Shovellers (a sort of duck) are gray, with a black head. They are a very good fowl" (1709, 152).

PLATE 39
The Buffel's Head Duck (95)

As to the size of this bird, it is between the common duck and teal. The bill lead color; on each side the head is a broad space of white; except which, the whole head is adorned with long loose feathers elegantly blended with blue, green and purple; the length and looseness of these feathers make the head appear bigger than it is, which seems to have given it the name of buffel's head, that animal's head appearing very big by its being covered with very thick long hair. The wings and upper part of the body have alternate lists of white and black, extending from the shoulders of the wings and back down to the rump, viz. The quill feathers are black; next to them extends a line of white, next to which is a line of black, then a line of white, and then black, which covers the middle of the back. The tail is gray; the legs are red.

The female is all over of a brown color; the head smooth, and without a ruff; the legs and feet brown. They frequent fresh waters, and appear in Carolina only in winter.

PLATE 40

The Little Brown Duck (98)

This duck has a large white spot on each side the head, and another on the lower part of the wing; except which, the head and all the upper part of the body and wings are dark brown. The breast and belly are light gray; the bill is black; the irises of the eyes are of a hazel color; this was a female. The male was pied black and white; but not being able to procure it, I am necessitated to be thus short in the description. They frequent the lower parts of rivers in Carolina, where the water is salt, or brackish.

Soap-wood
(joe-bush or ironwood)

This shrub or small tree rises to the height of about six or eight feet, and usually with one straight stem covered with a whitish bark. The leaves in size, shape and substance resemble those of box, and many of them grow concave and curling, with their edges inward. At the ends of the smaller twigs grow bunches of round pale green berries of the size of large peas, set on footstalks a quarter of an inch long with a small indented capsule. These berries contain an uncertain number of (four, five, and some six) small brown seeds covered with a mucilage. The bark and leaves of these seeds being beat in a mortar produces a lather; and is made use of to wash clothes and linen, to which last it gives a yellowness. The hunters, who frequent the

desolate islands of Bahama, (where this shrub grows on the seacoast) are frequently necessitated to use this sort of soap to wash their shirts, for want of better.

Editor's Note / Bufflehead (*Bucephala albeola*)

Plates 39 and 40 are both of the bufflehead, male and female, respectively. The bufflehead is a very small duck; the male of the species was one of the most beautiful of all the ducks of colonial America. They are commonly seen either as pairs or in small flocks in lakes and rivers, and especially in salt bays during the winter. Also known as "butterballs," they are excellent divers and feed on submerged vegetation as well as small aquatic crustacea and shellfish.

Catesby's female bufflehead (Plate 40) is illustrated with the joe-bush or ironwood (*Jacquinia keyensis*).

PLATE 41

The Round-crested Duck (94)

This bird is somewhat less than a common tame duck; the eyes are yellow; the bill is black and narrow; the upper mandible hooked at the end, and both mandibles serrated. This texture of the bill shows it to be of the kind of Mergi. *Vid.* Willoughby, p. 335, Tab. 64. The head is crowned with a very larger circular crest, or tuft of feathers; the middle of which, on each side, is white, and bordered round with black, which black extends to and covers the throat and neck. The breast and belly are white. The quill feathers of the wings are brown; just above which are some smaller feathers, whose exterior vanes are edged with white, with a little white intermixed in them, as in some of the other feathers likewise. The tail is brown, as is also the hindmost part of the belly near the vent, and under the wings. The rest of their wings and body is dusky black.

The females are all over of a brown color, having a smaller tuft of feathers of the same color. They frequent fresh waters, more especially mill-ponds in Virginia and Carolina.

Editor's Note / Hooded Merganser (*Lophodytes cucullatus*)

Catesby's description of the hooded merganser is quite accurate, and the painting is one of his better. He was

also correct in stating that the habitat was "mill-ponds," as hooded mergansers are inhabitants of wooded lakes, ponds, and rivers. Mergansers feed largely on fish and are therefore seldom short of food. The bill is highly adapted for catching fish; its edges bear a row of "teeth," or serrations, which permit them effectively to hold slippery fish. Mergansers swim around with a considerable portion of the body submerged and dive after prey and pursue fish underwater. The hooded merganser is a common winter resident in the area covered by Catesby.

PLATE 42

The White-crown'd Pigeon (25)

It is as big as the common tame pigeon. The base of the bill is purple; the end dusky white; the iris of the eye yellow, with a dusky white skin round it. The crown of the head is white; below which it is purple. The

hindpart of the neck is covered with changeable shining green feathers, edged with black. All the rest of the bird is of a dusky blue, the legs and feet are red. They breed in great numbers on all the Bahama Islands, and are of great advantage to the inhabitants, particularly while young. They are taken in great quantities from off the rocks on which they breed.

The Cocoa Plum
(coco-plum or pork-fat apple)

This is a shrub, which grows from five to ten feet high; not with a single trunk, but with several small stems rising from the ground, they grow many together in thickets. The flowers grow in bunches, are small and white, with many stamina. They produce a succession of fruit most part of the summer, which is of the size and shape of a large damson, most of them blue. Some trees produce pale yellow, and some red fruit. Each plum contains a stone shaped like a pear, chanulated

Columba capite albo
The White crown Pigeon.

with six ridges. They grow usually in low moist ground near the seaside. The leaves are as broad as a crown, thick, stiff, and shaped somewhat like a heart. The fruit is esteemed wholesome, and hath a sweet luscious taste. The Spaniards at Cuba make a conserve of them, by preserving them in sugar.

Editor's Note / White-crowned Pigeon (*Columba leucocephala*)

The white-crowned pigeon, also known in the Bahamas as "white head" is about the size of the common pigeon or rock dove, but has a conspicuous white crown. This species occurs throughout the West Indies and also in southern Florida and the Keys. As it is the principal game bird of the Bahamas and large numbers are killed each year, their numbers have been somewhat reduced. They are locally migratory, with large flocks leaving the Bahamas in October and November to spend the winter months in Cuba and Hispaniola.

Catesby's bird is shown with the coco-plum or pork-fat apple (*Chrysobalanus icaco*). The white-crowned pigeon is particularly fond of the fruit of the poisonwood

(*Metopium toxiferum*), illustrated by Catesby in Plate 97 with the Greater Antillean bullfinch. This plant is closely related to poison ivy, both belonging to the sumac family, and the plant produces a characteristic skin rash. The plant is common in the Bahamas, and many birds, but particularly the white-crowned pigeon, gorge on the fruit, and retrievers and hunters who clean the pigeons often break out in skin rashes (Campbell 1978, 51).

PLATE 43
The Turtle of Carolina (24)

This is somewhat less than a dove house pigeon; the eyes black, compassed with a blue skin; the bill black; the upper part of the head, neck, back, and upper part of the wings brown; the small feathers of the wing, next to the back, have large black spots; the lower part of the wing and quill feathers of a lead color, three or four of

the longest being almost black. The breast and belly of a pale carnation color. On each side of the neck, the breadth of a man's thumb, are two spots of the color of burnished gold, with a tincture of crimson and green; between which and its eye is a black spot. The wings are long, the tail much longer, reaching almost five inches beyond them, and hath fourteen feathers, the two middle longest, and of equal length, and all brown; the rest are gradually shorter, having their upper part lead color, the middle black, and the end white. The legs and feet are red. They breed in Carolina, and abide there always. They feed much on the berries of poke, i.e. *Blitum Virginianum*, which are poison. They likewise feed on the seeds of this plant; and they are accounted good meat.

The May Apple

This plant grows about a food and a half high; the flower consisting of several petala, with many yellow stamina surrounding the seed vessel, which is oval, unicapsular, and contains many roundish seeds. The leaves of the plant resemble the *Aconitum lycoctonum*

luteum C.B. Pin. The root is said to be an excellent emetic, and is used as such in Carolina which has given it there the name of Ipecacuana, the stringy roots of which it resembles. It flowers in March; the fruit is ripe in May; which has occasioned it in Virginia to be called may-apple.

Editor's Note / Mourning Dove (*Zenaida macroura*)

Catesby's beautiful "turtle of Carolina" is shown in association with the may-apple (*Podophyllum peltatum*), a flowering plant of twelve to eighteen inches that is normally found in rich, damp woods or woody clearings, a most unlikely spot for the mourning dove.

The mourning dove is in permanent residence over the entire eastern United States; during the winter months, the nesting population is complemented by migrants from the north. In the breeding season, mourning doves utter their mournful, cooing notes almost throughout the day. The nest, a flimsy structure, is placed in trees, usually at low heights, and two white eggs are the normal clutch. These birds have multiple broods, raising two and sometimes three broods per year, and the breeding season often extends from May to September. Mourning doves are birds of open fields with woodland margins, but they also occur in suburban areas. Their food consists almost entirely of seeds, especially weed seeds but including seeds from cultivated crops. Lawson noted: "Turtle doves are here very plentiful; they devour the peas; for which reason, people make traps and catch them" (1709, 146). The mourning dove population has no doubt drastically increased since colonial times with the destruction of forests and clearing of fields for agriculture.

PLATE 44

The Pigeon of Passage (23)

It is about the size of our English wood-pigeon; the bill black; the iris of the eye red; the head dusky blue; the breast and belly faint red. Above the shoulder of the wing is a patch of feathers that shines like gold; the wing colored like the head, having some few spots of black (except that the larger feathers of it are dark brown), with some white on their exterior vanes. The tail is very long, covered with a black feather; under which the rest are white; the legs and feet are red.

Of these there come in winter to Virginia and Carolina, from the North, incredible numbers; insomuch that in some places where they roost (which they do on one another's backs) they often break down the limbs of oaks with their weight, and leave their dung some inches thick under the trees they roost on. Where they light, they so effectually clear the woods of acorns and other mast, that the hogs that come after them, to the detriment of the planters, fare very poorly. In Virginia I have seen them fly in such continued trains three days successively, that there was not the least interval in losing sight of them, but that somewhere or other in the air they were to be seen continuing their flight south. In mild winters there are few or none to be seen. A hard winter drives them south for the greater plenty and variety of mast, berries, etc. which they are deprived of in the North by continual frost and snow.

In their passage the people of New York and Philadelphia shoot many of them as they fly, from their balconies and tops of houses; and in New England there are such numbers, that with long poles they knock them down from their roosts in the night in great numbers. The only information I have had from whence they come, and their places of breeding, was from a Canadian Indian, who told me he had seen them make their nests in rocks by the sides of rivers and lakes far north of the St. Lawrence River, where he said he shot them. It is remarkable that none are ever seen to return, at least this way, and what other route they may take is unknown.

The Red Oak
(turkey oak or scrub oak)

The leaves of this oak retain no certain form; but sport into various shapes more than other oaks do. The bark is dark colored, very thick and strong, and for tanning preferable to any other kind of oak; the grain is course, the wood spongy, and not durable. They grow on high land; the acorns vary in shape, as appears by the figures of them; they being from the same kind of oak.

Editor's Note / Passenger Pigeon
(*Ectopistes migratorius*)

The passenger pigeon was no doubt one of the best-known and most numerous birds of the colonial period in North America. It was very well known to Lawson; his account, the longest for any species, is given in its entirety following this note. Catesby was equally intrigued with the passenger pigeon; he depicted the bird with the turkey or scrub oak (*Quercus laevis*).

This magnificent species once ranged widely in eastern North America, from Canada south to the Gulf states and west to Montana and Texas. In fact, it inhabited nearly the entire forested portion of the eastern United States, breeding in the northern part of its range and migrating southward to the southern Atlantic and Gulf states and further south to spend the winter. It was a common transient through Virginia and North Carolina and a common winter resident in South Carolina. Like the mourning dove, the passenger pigeon built a small stick nest, but only deposited one egg. As many as fifty to a hundred nested in a single tree. The squabs being highly favored food, hunters attacked these breeding colonies and killed vast numbers. Often they cut down the trees to obtain the birds. But it was during the migration that the unbelievable numbers were slaughtered, and most of the early accounts of the passenger pigeon concern this massive killing.

The most definitive work on this species is that of A. W. Schorger (1955), in which he estimates that the population of the passenger pigeon at the time of the discovery of North America was three to five billion, and that it comprised approximately 25–40 percent of the entire bird population of what is now the United States.

Alexander Wilson wrote one of the best early accounts of the pigeon. He told of one nesting site in Kentucky that was several miles in breadth and over forty miles wide (1829, 3:1–11). "On some single trees upwards of one hundred nests were found, each containing one young only. . . . This is so extremely fat, that the Indians, and many of the whites, are accustomed to melt down the fat for domestic purposes as a substitute for butter and lard" (p. 3). Wilson also told of the massive destruction of these birds during their migration in the Atlantic States. "Wagon loads of them are poured into market, where they sell from fifty to twenty-five and even twelve cents per dozen; and pigeons become the order of the day at dinner, breakfast and supper, until the very name becomes sickening" (p. 9). Audubon likewise described this destruction in great detail, particularly in the areas in which they roosted. One such area was near Louisville where "for a week or more, the population fed on no other flesh than that of pigeons, and talked of nothing but pigeons" (1842, 5:27). The birds were still numerous in his time, however, and in 1830 Audubon bought 350 birds in a New York market which he carried alive to England and "distributed them amongst several nobleman, presenting some at the same time to the Zoological Society" (p. 32). In another example cited by Schorger, in 1874 at one nesting colony in Michigan, professional netters killed 25,000 birds daily for the market for twenty-eight days, or about 700,000 a month. By the turn of the century the species had been decimated; combined with the destruction of the forests, these mass killings resulted in the demise of the passenger pigeon. The last captive bird died in the Cincinnati Zoological Garden in 1914.

John Lawson's account of the passenger pigeon is given below in its entirety:

> Our wild pigeons, are like the wood-queese or stock-doves, only have a longer tail. They leave us in the summer. This sort of pigeon (as I said before) is the most like our stock-doves, or wood-pigeons that we have in England; only these differ in their tails, which are very long, much like a parrakeeto's? You must understand, that these birds do not breed amongst us, (who are settled at, and near the mouths of the rivers, as I have intimated to you before) but come down (especially in hard winters) amongst the inhabitants, in great flocks, as they were seen to do in the year 1707, which was the hardest winter that ever was known, since Carolina has been seated by the Christians. And if that country had such hard weather, what must be expected of the severe winters in Pennsylvania, New York, and New England, where winters are ten times (if possible) colder than with us. Although the flocks are, in such extremities, very numerous; yet they are not to be mentioned in comparison with the great and infinite numbers of these fowl, that are met withal about a hundred, or a hundred and fifty, miles to the westward of the places where we at present live; and where these pigeons come down, in quest of a small sort of acorns, which in those parts are plentifully found. They are the same we call turkey-acorns, because the wild turkies feed very much thereon; And for the same reason,

those trees that bear them, are called turkey-oaks. I saw such prodigious flocks of these pigeons, in January or February, 1701–2, (which were in the hilly country, between the great nation of the Esaw Indians, and the pleasant stream of Sapona, which is the west-branch of Clarendon, or Cape-Fear River) that they had broke down the limbs of a great many large trees all over those woods, whereon they chanced to sit and roost; especially the great pines, which are a more brittle wood, than our sorts of oak are. These pigeons, about sun-rise, when we were preparing to march on our journey, would fly by us in such vast flocks, that they would be near a quarter of an hour, before they were all passed by; and as soon as that flock was gone, another would come; and so successively one after another, for great part of the morning. It is observable, that wherever these fowl come in such numbers, as I saw them then, they clear all before them, scarce leaving one acorn upon the ground, which would, doubtless, be a great prejudice to the planters that should seat there, because their swine would be thereby deprived of their mast. When I saw such flocks of the pigeons I now speak of, none of our company had any other sort of shot, than that which is cast in molds, and was so very large, that we could not put above ten or a dozen of them into our largest pieces; wherefore, we made but an indifferent hand of shooting them; although we commonly killed a pigeon for every shot. They were very fat, and as good pigeons, as ever I eat. I inquired of the Indians that dwelled in those parts, where it was that those pigeons bred, and they pointed towards the vast ridge of mountains, and said, they bred there. Now, whether they made their nests in the holes in the rocks of those mountains, or build in trees, I could not learn; but they seem to me to be a wood-pigeon, that build in trees, because of their frequent sitting thereon, and their roosting on trees always at night, under which their dung commonly lies half a foot thick, and kills everything that grows where it falls. (1709, 145–46)

PLATE 45

The Ground Dove (26)

The weight of this dove was an ounce and a half. In size about the same as a lark. The bill is yellow, except the end, which is black. The iris of the eye red; the breast and whole front of the birds is of a changeable purple color, with dark purple spots. The large quill feathers and tail are of a muddy purple. The legs and feet dirty yellow. In short, the whole bird has such a composition of colors, so blended together, that no perfect description by words can be given of it. And I have observed some of them to differ in color from others. From which causes probably may be the reason why Nieremberg, Margravius, and others who have described it, have varied in their descriptions of it. They fly many of them together, and make short flights from place to place, lighting generally on the ground. They are natives of most countries in America lying between the tropics. They sometimes approach so far north as Carolina, and visit the lower parts of the country near the sea, where these trees grow, and feed on the berries, which gives their flesh an aromatic flavor.

The Pellitory, or Tooth-ache Tree
(Hercules-club)

This tree seldom grows above a foot in thickness, and about sixteen feet high. The bark is white, and very rough. The trunk and large limbs are in a singular manner thick set, with pyramidal-shaped protuberances, pointing from the tree; at the end of every one of which is a sharp thorn. These protuberances are of the same consistence with the bark of the tree, of various sizes, the largest being as big as walnuts. The smaller branches are beset with prickles only. The leaves are pinnated, standing on a rib six inches long, to which the lobes are set one against another, with footstalks half an inch long. The lobes are awry, their greatest vein not running in the middle, but on one side, being bigger than the other. From the ends of the branches shoot forth long stalks of small pentapetalous white flowers with reddish stamina. Every flower is succeeded by four shining black seeds, contained in a round green capsule. The leaves smell like those of orange; which with the seeds and bark, is aromatic, very hot and astringent, and is used by the people inhabiting the seacoasts of Virginia and Carolina for the tooth-ache, which has given it its name.

Editor's Note / Common Ground-Dove
(*Columbina passerina*)

Smallest of the American doves, the common ground-dove is found in only the southeastern coastal region of North Carolina but is a fairly common resident in South Carolina, which is no doubt where Catesby encountered it. Appropriately named, this species spends most of its time on the ground, walking along and frequently jerking the tail; the bird will allow a person to approach within a few yards before taking flight a short distance to land on the ground once again. In the Carolina region it primarily inhabits shrubs and grasses in sandy areas, although it may also be seen in towns. The ground dove builds a nest similar to that of its cousin the mourning dove, either on the ground or in low shrubs, and two eggs are normal. Its voice is a mournful cooing, also somewhat similar to that of the mourning dove.

Its food consists of seeds and berries of various types. Catesby's comment that the flesh has an aromatic flavor because of the berries they eat cannot be confirmed; Audubon simply noted, "Their flesh is excellent" (1842, 3:22). Supporting his view, however, Catesby illustrated his ground dove with the Hercules-club, or toothache-tree (*Zanthoxylum clava-herculis*), a tree with spreading branches that grows in moist, sandy soils near the coast and is highly aromatic. The aromatic bark is a local home remedy for toothache, as chewing the bark numbs the pain. Alexander Wilson stated that these doves "feed on rice, various seeds and berries, particularly those of the tooth-ache tree, under or near which, . . . they are almost sure to be found" (1829, 3:15).

PLATE 46

The Parrot of Carolina (11)

This bird is of the bigness, or rather less than a blackbird, weighing three ounces and a half; the fore part of the head orange color; the hind part of the head and neck yellow. All the rest of the bird appears green; but upon nearer scrutiny the interior vanes of most of the wing feathers are dark brown; the upper parts of the exterior vanes of the larger wing or quill feathers, are yellow, proceeding gradually deeper colored to the end, from yellow to green, and from green to blue; the edge of the shoulder of the wing, for about three inches down, is bright orange color. The wings are very long, as is the tail; having the two middle feathers longer than the others by an inch and half, and end in a point; the rest are gradually shorter. The legs and feet are white; the small feathers covering the thighs, are green, ending at the knees with a verge of orange color. They feed on seeds and kernels of fruit; particularly those of cypress and apples. The orchards in autumn are visited by numerous flights of them; where they make great destruction for their kernels only; for the same purpose they frequent Virginia; which is the furthest north I ever heard they have been seen. Their guts are certain and speedy poison to cats. This is the only one of the parrot kind in Carolina; some of them breed in the country; but most of them retire more South.

The Cypress of America
(baldcypress)

The cypress (except the tulip-tree) is the tallest and largest in these parts of the world. Near the ground some of them measure 30 feet in circumference, rising pyramidally six feet, where it is about two thirds less;

Psittacus Carolinensis
The Parrot of Carolina

from which to the limbs, which is usually 60 or 70 feet, it grows in like proportion of other trees. Four or five feet around this tree (in a singular manner) rise many stumps, some a little above ground, and others from one to four feet high, of various shape and size, their tops round, covered with a smooth red bark. These stumps shoot from the roots of the tree, yet they produce neither leaf nor branch, the tree increasing only by seed, which in form are like the common cypress, and contain a balsamic consistence of a fragrant smell. The timber this tree affords, is excellent, and particularly for covering houses with, it being light, of a free grain, and resisting the injuries of the weather better than any other here. It is an aquatic, and usually grows from one, five and six feet deep in water; which secure situation seems to invite a great number of different birds to breed in its lofty branches; amongst which this parrot delights to make its nest, and in October, (at which time the seed is ripe) to feed on their kernels.

Editor's Note / Carolina Parakeet (*Conuropsis carolinensis*)

Now completely extinct, the Carolina parakeet was the only endemic parrot of North America; it was common along the Atlantic coastal plain from Florida to southern Virginia (and occasionally northward to New York), and west to Texas, Oklahoma, and Colorado and northward to Iowa and Wisconsin. The last sure report of this species was in Florida in 1920, although in the 1930s there were some reported sightings (now thought to have been invalid) in the Santee Swamp in South Carolina. The Carolina parakeet was bred successfully in captivity, and the last captive bird died in the Cincinnati Zoological Gardens in September 1914. What a shame to have lost our only native parrot.

These birds were well known to early travelers in the New World. In his notes on the flora and fauna of "Virginia" which he compiled on the 1585 expedition to the Carolina coast under the sponsorship of Sir Walter Raleigh, Thomas Hariot recorded the parrot on Roanoke Island. "There are also Parats, Faulcons & Marlin haukes" (1588, reprinted in Quinn 1955, 359).

Another early record is that of William Hilton, who came from Barbados in the fall of 1663 to explore parts of "Carolina." He wrote that in the woods there were great flocks of "parrakeeto's," and in enumerating the game taken stated, "We killed of wild fowl, four swans, ten geese, twenty-nine cranes, ten turkies, forty duck and mallard, three dozen of parrakeeto's, and six or seven dozen of other small fowls, as curlues and plovers, etc." (Salley 1911, 46, 53). John Lawson also was quite familiar with these birds:

> The parrakeetos are of a green color, and orange-colored half way their head. Of these and the alligators, there is none found to the northward of this province. They visit us first, when mulberries are ripe, which fruit they love extremely. They peck the apples, to eat the kernels, so that the fruit rots and perishes. They are mischievous to orchards. They are often taken alive, and will become familiar and tame in two days. They have their nests in hollow trees, in low, swampy ground. They devour the birch-buds in April, and lie hidden when the weather is frosty and hard. (1709, 146–47)

Alexander Wilson gave perhaps the first extensive account of this species, stating that along the east coast the parrots were seldom seen north of Maryland. He correctly stated that the favorite food of the Carolina parrot was the cockle-burr and the "seeds of the cypress-tree and hackberry, as well as beech-nuts." "I have known a flock of these birds alight on an apple-tree, and have myself seen them twist off the fruit, one by one, strewing it in every direction around the tree." Wilson also witnessed the manner by which the Indians had been able to destroy vast numbers of the birds. He stated, "Having shot down a number, some of which were only wounded, the whole flock swept repeatedly around their prostrate companions, and again settled on a low tree, within twenty yards of the spot where I stood. At each successive discharge, though showers of them fell, yet the affection of the survivors seemed rather to increase; for after a few circuits around the place, they again alighted near me." Wilson also described their roosting. "They are particularly attached to the large sycamores, in the hollow of the trunks, and branches of which, they generally roost, thirty or forty, and sometimes more, entering the same hole." What seemed to intrigue him the most about the parakeets, however, was Catesby's statement, which in his time he considered to be "a very general opinion," that "the brains and intestines of the Carolina Paroquet are a sure and fatal poison to cats." Wilson's cats survived some considerable experimentation on this point, but

Wilson himself reserved judgment, pointing out that the parrots from which he had extracted the intestines had not recently fed on the cockle-burr (1828, 1:153–63).

During Audubon's time the Carolina parrot was abundant. He described their depredations on stacks of grain put up in fields. They were so numerous that "they present[ed] to the eye the same effect as if a brilliantly colored carpet had been thrown over them. . . . The gun is kept at work; eight or ten, or even twenty, are killed at every discharge" (1841, 4:307). Although most were probably killed by persons trying to protect crops, great numbers were killed to satisfy the demands of the millinery trade. By the latter part of the nineteenth century the Carolina parrot had been nearly extirpated even in the center of its range, and after that period there were only occasional sightings up into the 1920s when the last survivors had apparently faded away.

Catesby's "parrot of Carolina" is pictured feeding on one of its favorite trees, the baldcypress (*Taxodium distichum.*)

PLATE 47

The Parrot of Paradise of Cuba (10)

It is somewhat less than the common African gray parrot; the bill white, the eyes red; the upper part of the head, neck, back and wings, of a bright yellow, except the quill feathers of the wing, which are white; the neck and breast scarlet; below which is a wide space of yellow; the remainder of the under part of the body scarlet; halfway of the under part of the tail next the rump red, the rest yellow. All the yellow, particularly the back and rump, have the ends of the feathers tinged with red; the feet and claws white. The figure of this bird has the disadvantage of all the rest, it being painted only from the case; for as every different bird have gestures peculiar to them, it is requisite they should be drawn from the living birds, otherwise it is impracticable to give them their natural air; which method, except in a few birds, has been practiced through the whole collection. It was shot by an Indian, on the island of Cuba; and being only disabled from flying, he carried it to the Governor of Havana, who presented it to a gentlewoman of Carolina, with whom it lived some years, much admired for its uncommonness and beauty.

Red-wood
(smooth snake-bark)

This tree usually grows from sixteen to twenty feet high, with a small trunk, and slender branches; the leaves shaped not unlike those of the bay-tree; three black seeds are contained in every capsule; the bark of a russet color, and smooth; the grain of a fine red; but being exposed a little time to the air, fades, and loses much of its luster. They grow plentifully on the rocks in most of the Bahama Islands.

Editor's Note / Cuban Parrot
(*Amazona leucocephala*)

Although the description given by Catesby and his painting of this bird are less than definitive for a positive identification, there can be little doubt that he intended to illustrate and describe the Cuban parrot (*Amazona leucocephala*). However, the species is predominantly green, not yellow, as he showed it, and has a white forehead. The Cuban parrot occurs today in remote lowland and mountain woodlands in Cuba, where it feeds on fruits, berries, and seeds, especially the seeds of palms. It is also found on the Isle of Pines, the Cayman Islands, and the Bahama Islands. Catesby illustrated his parrot with the smooth snake-bark (*Colubrina elliptica*).

PLATE 48

The Cuckow of Carolina (9)

It is about the size of a black-bird; the bill a little hooked and sharp; the upper mandible black, the under yellow; the large wing feathers reddish; the rest of the wing, and all the upper part of the body, head and neck, ash color; all the under part of the body, from the bill to the tail, white; the tail long and narrow, composed of six long and four shorter feathers; the two middlemost ash color, the rest black, with their ends white; their legs short and strong, having two back toes, and two before. Their note is very different from ours, and not so remarkable to be taken notice of. It is a solitary bird, frequenting the darkest recesses of woods and shady thickets. They retire at the approach of winter.

The Chinkapin
(chinkapin or chinquapin)

It is a shrub which seldom grows higher than sixteen feet, and usually not above eight or ten; the body commonly eight or ten inches thick, and irregular; the bark rough and scaly; the leaves are serrated, and grow alternately of a dark green, their back-sides being of a greenish white; and the joints of the leaves shoot forth long spikes of whitish flowers, like those of the common chestnut, which are succeeded by nuts of a conical shape, and the size of a hazel-nut; the shell which encloses the kernel, is of the color and consistence of that of a chestnut, enclosed in a prickly burr, usually five or six hanging in a cluster. They are ripe in September.

Cuculus Carolinensis
The Cuckow of Carolina.

Castanea pumila Virginiana.
The Chinkapin.

These nuts are sweet, and more pleasant than the chestnut; of great use to the Indians, who for their winter's provision lay them up in store.

Editor's Note / Yellow-billed Cuckoo (*Coccyzus americanus*)

Of the nearly 130 species of cuckoos worldwide, only a handful inhabit the New World, and, except for the strange tropical anis (see Plate 49), the yellow-billed and black-billed cuckoos are the only representatives in North America. Of these last 2, only the yellow-billed commonly occurs in the region covered by Catesby. It is a common summer resident throughout most of eastern North America and then migrates to South America for the winter. Cuckoos differ from typical songbirds, or passerines, in that they are yoke-toed, or zygodactyl, which means that they have two toes directed forward and two backward.

The yellow-billed cuckoo, commonly known to farmers as the "rain crow," is thought to foretell the coming of rain by its resonant call, a "keow-keow-keow," which one often hears without sighting the secretive bird. It is one of our most beneficial birds: one of the few avian species which eats the tent caterpillar, it consumes them in enormous numbers. The nest is a simple structure which it places in a dense bush or tree, and two to four pale blue eggs are the normal clutch. Lawson listed a cuckoo as one of his species, but his description noted that cuckoos sucked the eggs of small birds, a habit never observed for this cuckoo but common for the blue jay. Catesby's cuckoo of Carolina is pictured in the chinkapin (*Castanea pumila*), a tree that was greatly esteemed by the Indians, who called its nuts *checkinquamins*.

PLATE 49

The Razor-billed Black-bird of Jamaica
(appendix, 3)

This bird is somewhat less than our jackdaw. It appears at a distance all over black, but at a nearer view some of the feathers were blended with shining purple and green. The singular make of the bill resembles that of the razor-bill, Willoug, p. 323, tab. 65, the upper mandible being remarkably prominent, rising arch-wise, with a high and very thin edge.

Sir Hans Sloane informs us that it subsists on beetles and grasshoppers. It also feeds on fruit and grain. They appear in flocks and are querulous and very noisy. They are numerous in Jamaica, Hispaniola, etc.

[Pink Lady's Slipper or Pink Mocassin-flower]

This plant produces the most elegant flower of all the Helleborine tribe, and is in great esteem with the North American Indians for decking their hair, etc. They call it the moccasin flower, which also signifies, in their language, a shoe, or slipper.

Editor's Note / Smooth-billed Ani (*Crotophaga ani*)

Catesby's "razor-billed blackbird of Jamaica" is the smooth-billed ani, a moderate-sized cuckoo ranging from south Florida through the West Indies and many of the Caribbean islands, down to Argentina. These are grackle-sized all-black birds with long tails. They appear to be very clumsy, and their flight is a slow alternation of flaps and glides. Anis are very communal, and groups of ten to fifteen can be seen sitting very close together on the same wire or branch. They are birds of bush-covered fields and scrub, where they nest communally; several females may deposit eggs in the same nest, which is a large structure of sticks and other similar materials. As many as twenty-nine eggs have been found in a single nest. The several pairs that deposit the eggs share the responsibilities of incubating the eggs and feeding the young. Anis are characterized by their huge bills with high curved ridges. They feed mainly on insects, which they often obtain around grazing livestock, but will also eat fruits and berries.

Catesby's bird is illustrated with the pink lady's slipper or pink mocassin-flower (*Cypripedium acaule*), one of our largest native orchids, which is found in pine words and dry forests of the eastern and central United States.

PLATE 50

The Little Owl (7)

Is about the size of, or rather less than a jackdaw; has large pointed ears; the bill small, the iris of the eye of a deep yellow or saffron color; the feathers of its face white, with a mixture of reddish brown; the head and upper part of the body a fulvous or reddish brown color; the wings are of the same color, except they are verged about with white, have some white spots on the

search for insects, small mice, and so forth, which constitute their main food. In the cold winter months they may take an occasional small bird.

Because the screech owl is nocturnal, it is more commonly known by its call, or "screech," which is a mournful "whinny," normally descending in pitch. The screech owl places its nest in a natural cavity of a tree or takes an abandoned flicker's nest; four eggs are the normal clutch. It is thought that the male and female mate for life.

Although Catesby recorded but a single owl, which he called the little owl, Lawson noted that there were several types (1709, 149). He listed the "Scritch" owls as being "much the same as in Europe." But, he also said that of "Owls, . . . we have two sorts: the smaller sort are like ours in England; the other sort is as big as a middling Goose, and has a prodigious head. They make a fearful hollowing in the nighttime, like a man, whereby they often make strangers lose their way in the woods." Why Catesby recorded only a single species of owl is a mystery.

PLATE 5 I

The Goat-sucker of Carolina (8)

This bird agrees with the description of that in Mr. Willoughby, p. 107, of the same name, except that this is somewhat less. They are very numerous in Virginia and Carolina, and are called there East India bats. In the evening, they appear most, and especially in cloudy weather; before rain, the air is full of them, pursuing and dodging after flies and beetles. Their note is only a screep; but by their precipitating and swiftly mounting again to recover themselves from the ground, they make a hollow and surprising noise; which to strangers is very observable, especially at dusk of the evening, when the cause is not to be seen. This noise is like that made by the wind blowing into a hollow vessel; wherefore I conceive it is occasioned by their wide mouth forcibly opposing the air, when they swiftly pursue and catch their prey, which are flies, beetles, etc.

They usually lay two eggs, like in shape, size and color to those of lapwings, and on the bare ground.

Its stomach was filled up with half-digested scarabei, and other insects; and amongst the remains there seemed to be the feet of the grillotalpa, but so much consumed, that I could not be certain; they being both nocturnal animals, makes the probability the greater. They disappear in winter.

quill feathers, and five larger white spots on the upper part of each wing; the breast and belly is dusky white, intermixed with reddish brown feathers; the tail dark brown, a little longer than the wings; the legs and feet light brown, feathered and hairy down to the toes, armed with four semicircular black talons.

The hen is of a deeper brown, without any tincture of red.

Editor's Note / Eastern Screech-Owl
(Otus asio)

These little owls come in two phases, red and gray; the sexes are alike in each phase. A given brood may produce individuals of both gray and red phases, and males and females from the different phases may mate. Obviously Catesby painted the red phase, but apparently thought that the gray phase, which is actually a brownish-gray color, was the female. Generally found around farmhouses, gardens, and orchards, these little owls are strictly nocturnal in their habits; during the day they remain hidden in thick vegetation and are seldom seen. In late evening they begin their nightly

The grillotalpa is found both in Virginia and Carolina, in the like marshy grounds as in England, and seems not to differ from ours.

PLATE 52

The Whip-poor-will
(appendix, 16)

This nocturnal bird is about a third part less than the caprimulgus, or goat-sucker of Europe. The length of it, from the bill, is eight inches; and from the shoulder of the wing to the end of it, is seven inches. The length of the bill, from the base of the upper mandible to the end of it, is half an inch long; two-thirds of which being covered with feathers, there is visible so small a part of it, that, in proportion to the bigness of the bird, it seems to have the smallest bill of any other. From the base of the bill shot forth some stiff bristly hairs. The throat has a white list half round its neck. The breast is white, faintly stained with red and transverse dark lines. The quill feathers of the wings are of a dark brown color, except a broad white list crossing five of them on the middle of each wing. The tail feathers, except the three uppermost, have also two white spots near their ends. The plumage of all the rest of the body is brown, irregularly mixed, or powdered with an obscure reddish color. The legs are very short, being but half an inch in length, and formed like those of the goat-sucker; having also the inside of the middle toe serrated.

This bird I have mentioned in the addenda to the volume; but having since received two of them from Virginia, it has enabled me to exhibit the figure of it, and also to add to the description of it some remarks sent me by Mr. Clayton concerning it, as follows:

"The whip-poor-will is not so large as the bird called here the East-India bat, i.e. caprimulgus; but in shape, and color of the feathers, it very much resembles it; having also at each side of its mouth three or four stiff black hairs like those of a horse's mane, two or three inches long. These birds visit us about the middle of April, from which time, till the end of June, they are heard every night, beginning about dusk, and continuing till break of day; but it is chiefly in the upper or western parts that they are so very frequent. I never heard but one in the maritime parts, although my abode has been always there; but near the mountains, within a few minutes after sunset, they begin, and make so very loud and shrill a noise all night, which the echoes from the rocks and sides of mountains increase to such a degree, that the first time I lodged there I could hardly get any sleep. The shooting them in the night is very difficult, they never appearing in the day-time. Their cry is pretty much like the sound of the pronunciation of the words whip-poor-will, with a kind of chucking noise between every other or every two or three cries, and they lay the accent very strong upon the last word will, and least of all upon the middle one.

"The Indians say these birds were never known till a great massacre was made of their countryfolks by the English, and that they are the souls or departed spirits

of the massacred Indians. Abundance of people here look upon them as birds of ill omen, and are very melancholy if one of them happens to light upon their house, or near their door, and set up his cry (as they will sometimes upon the very threshold) for they verily believe one of the family will die very soon after. These birds, as I have been credibly informed, breed exactly as the goat-sucker before mentioned, which is thus: they lay only two eggs of a dark greenish color, spotted and scrawled about with black, in the plain beaten paths, without the least sign of any nest, upon which they sit very close, and will suffer a very near approach before they fly off."

The Ginseng
or Ninsin of the Chinese.

Ginseng is the root of a medicinal plant of the highest esteem with the Chinese. Their principal physicians have wrote many volumes of its virtues. Most of the writers of China take notice of the Ginseng; yet it was very little known till Father Jartoux, a Jesuit and missionary in China, who being employed, by order of the Emperor, in making a map of Tartary, in the year 1709, had an opportunity of seeing it growing in a village, about four leagues from the kingdom of Corea. That father took the opportunity to make a draught of the plant, and give an accurate description thereof, which, being published in the *Memoirs of the Academy of Sciences at Paris*, gave light to the discovery of the same plant in Canada and Pennsylvania; from which last place it was sent to Mr. Collinson, in whose curious garden at Peckham it has, the preceding two or three years, and also this year 1746, produced its blossoms and berries as it appears in the figure here exhibited, and agrees so exactly to the father's description of the Chinese ginseng, that no doubt can be made of its being the very species he describes. But as the Jesuit's account is too long to be inserted here, I shall recite only what is most remarkable, adding to my figure the blossoms, which the father owns he never saw. The father's account is as follows:

"The place of its growth is between the 39th and 46th degree of latitude, upon the declivities of mountains, in thick forests, and upon the banks of torrents. That part of the country in which this precious root grows, is on every side secured by a barrier of wooden stakes, and about which guards continually patrol, to hinder the Chinese from going out and looking after this root. Yet how vigilant soever they are, greediness after gain incites the Chinese to lurk about privately in these deserts, sometimes to the number of two or three thousand, at the hazard of losing their liberty, and all the fruit of their labor, if they are taken either as they go out of, or come into, the province it grows in.

"The Emperor, having a mind that the Tartars should reap all the advantage that is to be made of this plant, rather than the Chinese, gave orders, in 1709, to 10,000 Tartars, to go and gather all that they could of the ginseng, upon condition that each person should give him two ounces, and that the rest should be paid for, weight for weight, in pure silver. It was computed that, by this means, the Emperor would get this year about 20,000 Chinese pounds of it, which would not cost him above one fourth part of its real value.

"The ginseng (says Father Jartoux) we have observed, is an ingredient in most of the medicines which the Chinese physicians prescribe to the better sort of patients. They affirm that it is a sovereign remedy for all weaknesses, occasioned by excessive fatigues, either of body or mind; that it attenuates and carries off pituitous humors, cures weakness of the lungs and the pleurisy, stops vomiting, strengthens the stomach, and helps the appetite, disperses fumes or vapors, fortifies the breast, and is a remedy for short and weak breathing, strengthens the vital spirits, and is good against dizziness of the head and dimness of sight, and that it prolongs life to extreme old age.

"Nobody can imagine (adds the Father) that the Chinese and Tartars would set so high a value upon this root, if it did not constantly produce a good effect. Those that are in health often made use of it to make themselves more vigorous and strong; and I am persuaded (adds the Father) it would prove an excellent medicine in the hands of any European who understands pharmacy, if he had but a sufficient quantity of it to make such trials as are necessary, to examine the nature of it chemically, and to apply it in a proper quantity, according to the nature of the disease for which it may be beneficial." It is certain that it subtilizes and increases the motion of, and warms, the blood; that it helps digestion, and invigorates in a very sensible manner.

"After I had designed the root (he goes on) I observed the state of my pulse, and then took half of the root, raw as it was, and unprepared; in an hour after I found my pulse much fuller and quicker; I had an appetite, and perceived myself much more vigorous, and could bear labor better and easier than before. Four days after, finding myself so fatigued and weary that I could scarce fit on horseback, a Mandarin, who was in company with us perceiving it, gave me one of these roots; I took half of it immediately, and in an hour after I was not the least sensible of any weariness. I have often made use of it since, and always with the same success." Thus far Father Jartoux.

This plant had a straight round stem, and arose to about the height of ten inches; from the tip of which shoot forth three smaller stalks of three or four inches long; each of which had at their ends five serrated leaves on short footstalks. From the summit of the stem arose perpendicularly another shorter stalk, on the tip of which was placed a globular bunch of red berries; the pedicles of which spreading circularly, formed the radii of a sphere. These berries were double, containing each two flattish rough seeds covered with a thin skin. The flowers were very small, composed of five round white petals, with five stamina and a stilus, rising from a calyx with five sections.

The root is white, three or four times the size of the stem, and grows tapering to the end, and is usually about three inches in length, more or less; and it often parts in two or three branches.

Editor's Note / Catesby's Goatsucker

The strange "ghosts of the night" called goatsuckers acquired this unlovely and absurd ordinal name in very ancient times in rural Europe. There, as elsewhere, these large-mouthed, elusive, batlike birds feed at dusk on the wing, flying low over fields and pastures. It was thought that they pilfered milk while they darted around the legs of grazing goats in their endless search for insects.

The names of goatsuckers usually allude to the birds' loud, distinctive night cries. Some of the cries are extraordinarily weird, and local folk often have a superstitious dread of these "ghosts" or "wandering voices." Other goatsuckers, however, are diurnal and go by more conventional names, such as the nighthawk, a common bird in the eastern United States. All of these birds have long wings and tails and small feet and are somberly dressed in browns and grays, which blend with their surroundings in what biologists call cryptic coloration.

The most striking part of their architecture is the huge mouth, armed with a tiny, almost useless beak. The sides of this immense gape are usually lined with a series of specialized, hairlike feathers called rictal bristles. These long, stiff feathers prevent the escape of insect prey by fencing in the edges of the mouth. All of the goatsuckers have exceptionally large eyes, well adapted for their world of twilight and night. Most of their feeding activity is in flight, and they are capable of only a short shuffle on the ground.

The people of colonial America and, to a not much lesser degree, colonial naturalists, including Mark Catesby, were totally confused as to the number of species of goatsuckers and their characteristics. The common nighthawk (*Chordeiles minor*) was commonly seen, and its characteristic voice noted, during the daytime, but at nighttime the woods resounded with the different but somewhat similar calls of the elusive whip-poor-will (*Caprimulgus vociferus*) and chuck-will's-widow (*Caprimulgus carolinensis*). European settlers, familiar with their own single "nightjar," simply combined these three species of goatsuckers and their various features.

Editor's Note / Common Nighthawk (*Chordeiles minor*)

Catesby's goatsucker of Carolina (Plate 51) is a strange combination of the common nighthawk and the chuck-will's-widow, and probably also the whip-poor-will, although this last is uncertain. The white wing patch is that of a nighthawk, but the tail and rictal bristles are characteristic of a "chuck" or "whip." If he had intended it as a nighthawk, he should have given it a large white patch on the throat, horizontal streaking on the breast, and no rictal bristles. Regardless, Linnaeus was later to designate Catesby's bird simply as the common European nightjar (*Caprimulgus europeaus*), with which he was familiar. In 1789, however, the industrious German professor of natural history Johann Friedrich Gmelin used Catesby's goatsucker for his description and designation of the chuck-will's-widow (*Caprimulgus carolinensis*). Gmelin, with no practical experience, spent most of his life compiling inadequate natural history information on beasts he had never seen.

The common nighthawk (*Chordeiles minor*) is not a hawk at all, although it does "hawk" insects on the wing, primarily at noon or near dusk. It is a very common summer breeding bird over much of North America and the Bahamas; in the fall it makes a lengthy migration to spend the winter months in South America, from Venezuela down to central Argentina. In the Carolinas and Virginia, the nighthawk is present in numbers from April to October, and in the fall migrating flocks numbering in the thousands may be encountered. In the spring the vanguard of nighthawks has reached the eastern states by the middle of April, and, as in the fall, large flocks have been reported.

The scientific name *Chordeiles* is derived from two Greek words, *Chorde*, meaning a stringed instrument, and *deile*, meaning evening; this is in reference to the hollow, booming noise made by the nighthawk in his courting ritual. While this noise is most frequently heard in the evening hours, nighthawks are active throughout the day, particularly in the early hours and then again in the hours preceding dusk. They are birds of open country, unlike their nocturnal cousins, and fly in erratic patterns, often in small groups, over pastures and other clearings in their incessant pursuit of all sorts of insects, ranging from dragonflies, large moths, and beetles to the tiniest flies and mosquitoes. Catesby's statement that "in the evening they appear most, and especially in cloudy weather; before rain, the air is full of them, pursuing and dodging after flies and beetles" obviously refers to this commonly observed behavior of the nighthawk, and not in any way to the chuck.

A very adaptable bird, the nighthawk has taken to life in our cities, coursing high over tall buildings and alighting on graveled rooftops. In their normal rural setting, they are silent when not in flight and remain perched lengthwise on fence rails, branches, or the tops of houses and barns. When in flight they are a delight to watch as they course buoyantly through the air in erratic zigzag patterns high and low, circling upwards or suddenly passing capriciously to the right or the left to catch an insect, always emitting an incessant nasal, buzzing noise, usually characterized as a "peent."

Like the other goatsuckers, the nighthawk can consume insects in astonishing quantities. The name mosquito hawk was used by Lawson, who noted, "East-India bats or mosquito hawks, are the bigness of a cuckoo, and much of the same color. They are so called, because the same sort is found in the East-Indies. They appear only in the summer, and live on flies, which they catch in the air, as gnats, mosquitos, etc." (1709, 148–49). Lawson was no doubt referring to the breeding West Indian race of the nighthawk, which is a common breeding summer resident throughout the Bahamas, Jamaica, and Puerto Rico and is present from early April to October, but the North American race also passes through the Bahamas during migration both in the spring and autumn.

The courtship ritual is the hallmark of the nighthawk, for unlike his cousins, the whip and chuck, the nighthawk performs most of his courtship on the wing in a spectacular aerial display. At somewhat regular intervals he rises to a great height, some three hundred feet or more, and then suddenly dives down with wings and tail half closed toward his mate on the ground. As he approaches her, and appears to be on the verge of crashing into the ground, he brakes, stretching-out the wings and expanding the tail, and makes an abrupt turn upward; the wind rushing through the flight feathers produces the well-known loud hollow "boom" sound of the courtship display. The male continues his aerial displays throughout the breeding season. The female places her two pale creamy eggs, spotted with grays and pale purple, in gravelly places in open fields or on large rocks or, perhaps most commonly nowadays, on the graveled roofs of city buildings.

With its prominent daytime courting display the nighthawk was no doubt well known to the Indians. Many Indian names for this bird were onomatopes of its various calls, examples being the Hudson Bay Indians' name "peesk" or the Chippewas' "besh-que" for the nighthawk. The Chippewas, in fact, were able to distinguish the nighthawk from the whip-poor-will, calling the whip "Gwen-og-wi-a. As mentioned above, early settlers—and naturalists—totally confused the goatsuckers, and it was not until some fifty years after Catesby that American ornithologist Alexander Wilson made the same distinction.

Along with the other goatsuckers the nighthawk played a prominent role in the myths and legends of early Americans. In Louisiana, for example, the species was called *crapaud volant* (flying toad) by the Creoles; in Virginia the name was simply "bat." In fact, today perhaps the most common name for the nighthawk in the South is "bullbat," and in many southern states the species was seriously depleted by extensive shooting of "bullbat" for sport.

Editor's Note / Chuck-will's-widow (*Caprimulgus carolinensis*)

The chuck-will's-widow is the largest and most handsome of the eastern goatsuckers. It is commonly found in a variety of habitats, ranging from thickly wooded regions or swampy ravines to extensive pine woodlands. In the Carolinas and Virginia the "chuck" is a common summer bird mainly along the coastal plain regions and less frequent or even transient in the piedmont.

The chuck returns to its breeding grounds in mid-March to early April. On calm nights as the sun disappears and the nocturnal insects emerge from their burrows, the woods literally resound with the cry "chuck-will's-widow," which is usually repeated six or eight times at intervals of about 2½ seconds. Chucks raise and lower the head with each successive note. The many claims of record counts of consecutive calls include one astonishing record of over eight hundred by a single bird. The call has been variously interpreted as "chip-fell-out-a-white-oak" or "twixt-hell-and-white-oak." It is only at rather close hand that the first note, the low-toned "chuck," is audible; the "will's-widow," however, can be heard at great distance. Throughout the South the songs of the chuck and whip-poor-will are confused, but the chuck's call is distinctively four syllabled, the emphasis being on the "will's" and the first syllable of the "widow."

The female deposits two eggs on the dead leaves of the forest floor. The eggs are cream colored, mottled with pale buff and browns as protective coloration. If disturbed, the birds pick up the eggs in their prodigious mouths and carry them to new locations. If they are disturbed after the fluffy young have emerged, they transport them to a new location, carrying them between the legs just as the woodcock does her young. The chuck has an uncanny ability to return to place its eggs in the same nesting site year after year; in one documented case a bird nested only ten feet from the site it had used twelve years earlier.

The chuck-will's-widow, with its enormous mouth of two-inch breadth, has a voracious appetite for insects, Its food consists primarily of large night-flying beetles and moths, but it might also eat an occasional small bird, such as a wood warbler, wren, sparrow, or hum-mingbird, and there is at least one case of a chuck actively pursuing warblers.

Catesby, somewhat misleadingly, illustrated his goatsucker of Carolina with a mole cricket, very likely the common eastern species *Gryllotalpa hexadactyla* (from the Latin *gryllus*, cricket, and *talpa*, mole). While Catesby may indeed have identified the "feet of the *Grillotalpa*" from the stomach of the "Carolina goatsucker," the mole cricket is without a doubt a very uncommon food item for either the common nighthawk or the chuck-will's-widow. These insects are about an inch or more long. Their rather large scoop-like front legs are used in digging their burrows, where they feed on small roots and insects. Adult mole crickets rarely emerge from their burrows and are therefore only rarely seen; they can sometimes be encountered stridulating at the entrances to their burrows, especially following a rain. They do have wings, however; they can occasionally be seen flying around night lights, and there have been numerous observations of chucks alighting at dusk or night along a road or path to pick up insects. On these excursions mole crickets could occasionally become food for the chuck.

Editor's Note / Whip-poor-will (*Caprimulgus vociferus*)

With only minor modifications, a great deal of what has been said of the habits of the chuck-will's-widow applies to the whip-poor-will, the northern "night" goatsucker in America. In Virginia and the Carolinas the whip is a fairly common summer resident in the mountains, piedmont, and inner coastal plain. Some whips may be present in the winter in eastern South Carolina and coastal North Carolina, but remain silent and are not easily encountered. Most spend the winter further south, from South Carolina to Central America. I have a favorite spot in the North Carolina piedmont near the Virginia border where I can encounter both the chuck and the whip side by side during the breeding season. On calm spring nights one may hear a "whip-poor-will" and, after a brief pause, a more distant "chuck-will's-widow." Here, where the two occur together, within easy "hearing" distance to one another, they seem to have ecologically divided the area rather precisely: the whip restricts itself to more upland woodland areas near or surrounding pastures and cultivated fields, while the chuck remains in the low, primarily deciduous woods located along the banks of a deep ravine with a creek.

Lawson's brief account of the "Whippoo Will" probably applies primarily to the whip, but no doubt applies also to the chuck, as there is no mention of the latter. "Whippoo-Will, so named, because it makes those words exactly. They are the bigness of a thrush, and call their note under a bush, on the ground, hard to be seen, though you hear them never so plain. They are more plentiful in Virginia, than with us in Carolina; for I never heard but one that was near the settlement, and that was hard-by an Indian Town" (1709, 150).

The whip-poor-will arrives in the Carolinas and Virginia from mid to late March or early April (in the Boston area in late April or early May), and the woods immediately begin to resound with their calls. Apparently, whips migrate in groups by night; one can hear the first arrivals begin to sing singly, and then suddenly during the same night dozens can be heard singing in the same vicinity. Shortly after their arrival, courtship begins, and, like the chuck, the female whip places two white eggs on the forest floor on bare ground or dry leaves in the open or under a small bush.

Whip-poor-wills feed in open fields, near the ground; the chuck feeds in much the same manner, but prefers to remain closer to the edges of woodlands or even small openings in woodlots. Whips are frequently encountered as two shining ruby red, phosphorescent eyes reflected in the headlights of cars as the birds sit in the middle of country roads, no doubt catching insects either on the ground or by flying up. The whip is entirely insectivorous; his diet includes a large number of moths, as well as crickets, grasshoppers, and even mosquitoes.

Catesby's whip-poor-will (Plate 52) is somewhat of an enigma, for while Lawson mentions and describes the bird in 1709, there is little evidence that Catesby came into contact with the whip in America except through its voice or perhaps hearsay from the locals and Indians. At least at the beginning, Catesby lumped the goatsucker of Carolina and the whip into one bird; but then he described the goatsucker as a nighthawk. The whip was included only as an afterthought in the appendix to the second volume, in 1743, so it was only then that Catesby had a night-calling goatsucker in America. Given that the chuck and whip must have been extremely common birds, such an oversight is hard to understand.

It seems, though, that Catesby became aware of his oversight because around 1741 he wrote to John Bartram: "There is a bird in Virginia and Carolina, and I suppose in Pennsylvania, that at night calls Whipper Will, and, sometimes, Whip Will's widow, by which names it is called (as the bird clinketh, the fool thinketh). I have neglected to describe it, and therefore should be glad of it. I believe it is a kind of cuckoo" (in Darlington 1849, 321–22). This letter indicates that

Catesby was still confused by the whip and chuck. A year later Catesby's friend Peter Collinson wrote to Bartram: "Friend John: Mr. Catesby Deposes that thou wilt look after a night bird called Whipper-Will—if this can be shot & sent in its Feathers being first, boweled, and Dried in a oven, and then tied up in tobacco leaves or packed up in tobacco dust—Pray observe if it is cock or hen—this may be seen in taking out its guts, if it has testicles or no" (Darlington 1849, 154). We know that specimens were later sent from Virginia, probably by John Clayton, whose description of the habits of the whip Catesby quotes in the appendix to volume 2. The real enigma is that while the description is that of a whip, the figure is more like that of a nighthawk; it is a small, brown bird with large feet for a goatsucker. The horizontal streaks on the breast, alternating tail bars, and white wing patches belong to the nighthawk, but the bird is shown with hairlike rictal bristles on the mouth, and these are found not in the nighthawk but in the chuck and whip.

Regardless of the hybrid nature of Catesby's plate, it later became the basis for the first accepted designation of the common nighthawk (*Chordeiles minor*) by Johann Reinhold Forster in 1771. Catesby's nighthawk-whip is standing (which goatsuckers almost never do) under a recognizable ginseng plant (*Panax quinquefolius*). The name is derived from the Latin *Panax*, a plant with cure-all properties, and *quinquefolius*, referring to the five-leaved arrangement of the three compound leaves from which the small flowers arise; the fruit is a cluster of red berries. The plant grows to a height of eight to twenty-four inches. The common name is a corruption of the Chinese *Jin-chen*, meaning manlike, in reference to the forked, fleshy root, which is highly prized by the Chinese, who consider it an aphrodisiac and heart stimulant. In this country it has been in great demand for some time as an ingredient in tonic, and now, with the increase in interest in the occult, it is valued for its superstitious powers. Because of overcollection to satisfy all these markets, the plant is now considered rare.

It is unlikely that Catesby thought that there was any real association between the whip and the ginseng plant, as he himself admitted to having almost no firsthand experience with the bird. Rather, the plant and bird were no doubt placed together because of the mystical and superstitious connotations attached to both.

PLATE 5 3

The American Swallow
(appendix, 8)

This is a little less than the English house-swallow, but very like it in shape. It is all over of a brown color, except that the under part of the body and tail is of a lighter brown; particularly the throat is almost white. The cock has some feathers faintly stained with purple, except which he differs not in color from the hen. The singularity of this bird is, that the shafts of the tail feathers are very stiff, sharp-pointed and bare of feathers at their ends, which seem designed by nature for the support of their bodies, while they are in an erect posture building their nests, which they do in chimneys, with little sticks interwoven and cemented together with a kind of glue or gum. Their periodical retiring from, and returning to Virginia and Carolina, is at the same seasons as our swallows do in England: therefore the place they retire to from Carolina is, I think, most probably Brazil, some part of which is in the same latitude in the Southern Hemisphere, as

Carolina is in the northern; where, the seasons reverting, they may, by this alternate change, enjoy the year round an agreeable equality of climate: and what strengthens the probability of it is, that the description of the Brazilian andorinha of Margravius agrees well with that of this bird, except the he takes no notice of the spines in the tail, which he might probably overlook.

N.B. If it were ascertained that this Virginia swallow was the same of Margravius's andorinha, it would, I think, confirm that most probable hypothesis, That birds of passage (particularly swallows) pass to the same latitude in the Southern Hemisphere, as the northern latitude from whence they came.

[Wood Lily]

This lily rises from the ground with one, two, or three straight stalks; each of them bearing a single flower at the height of about sixteen inches. The leaves are narrow, and stained at their ends with purple. The flower consists of a pointal and six stamina, rising from the center of six deep scarlet petals spotted with very dark red or purple, and their backsides covered with a hairy roughness, as is also the upper part of the stalk. It is a native of Pennsylvania, and blossomed in Mr. Peter Collinson's garden at Peckham, *Anno* 1743.

Editor's Note / Chimney Swift (*Chaetura pelagica*)

Catesby's "American swallow" is the common chimney swift, which is common over much of southern Canada and the United States as a breeding bird. Swifts belong to the bird family Apodidae, from the Greek meaning "without feet," so named because their feet are very small and weak. They do, though, have very sharp, curved claws for clinging on vertical surfaces. Equally well adapted for this purpose is the tail; each tail feather terminates in a spine which aids the bird in propping itself on vertical surfaces. In this it is similar to the woodpeckers. The chimney swift has often been described as a flying cigar; the small, blackish, swallow-like birds with stiff pointed wings are most often seen in groups in flight, uttering their chippering notes. They feed entirely on insects caught on the wing during the day; at dusk they fly into a hollow tree or chimney where they roost and where they have their nests.

Considered swallows practically until Audubon's time, chimney swifts were known even in colonial times as chimney nesters; remarkably, these birds must have made the transition from nesting in tree cavities to nesting in chimneys almost immediately upon the arrival of the first settlers, and it may be that its population has steadily increased since that time with the availability of more and more nesting sites. Alexander Wilson, who called this bird the chimney swallow, stated that they arrived in April or May and then dispersed themselves "over the entire country wherever there are vacant chimneys in summer sufficiently high and convenient for their accommodation. In no other situation with us are they observed at present to build. . . . Where did these birds construct their nests before the arrival of Europeans in this country, when there were no such places for their accommodation? . . . One of the first settlers in the state of Kentucky informed me that he cut down a large hollow beech tree which contained forty or fifty nests of the Chimney Swallow" (1828, 2:426). Wilson also described the nest accurately: "The nest of this bird is of singular construction, being formed of very small twigs, fastened to-

gether with a strong adhesive glue or gum, which is secreted by two glands, one on each side of the hind head, and mixes with the saliva. With this glue, which becomes hard as the twigs themselves, the whole nest is thickly besmeared. The nest itself is small and shallow, and attached by one side or edge to the wall. . . . The eggs are generally four and white. They generally have two broods in the season" (p. 427). Later Audubon investigated several of these, and stated, "I had a tree of this kind cut down, which contained about thirty of their nests in its trunk, and one in each of the hollow branches" (1840, 1:164). On another occasion in Louisville, Audubon was led to a massive hollow sycamore that in July accommodated a huge roosting colony of postbreeding swallows. He calculated that "the number of Swallows, therefore, that roosted in this single tree was 9000" (1840, 1:168).

By October the chimney swift begins its migration to South America, where it spends the winter primarily in Peru, roosting in large hollow trees or in chimneys where they are available.

Catesby's "American swallow" is illustrated with the wood lily (*Lilium philadelphicum*). Obviously, bird and plant are associated in the wild only accidentally.

PLATE 54

The Humming-bird (65)

There is but one kind of this bird in Carolina, which in the summer frequents the northern continent as far as New England. The body is about the size of a bumble bee. The bill is straight, black, and three-quarters of an inch long. The eyes are black; the upper part of the body and head of a shining green; the whole throat adorned with feathers placed like the scales of fish, of a crimson metallic resplendency; the belly dusky white; the wings of a singular shape, not unlike the blade of a Turkish cymiter; the tail is copper color, except the uppermost feather, which is green. The legs are very short and black. It receives its food from flowers, after the manner of bees; its tongue being a tube, through which it sucks the honey from them. It so poises itself by the quick hovering of its wings, that it seems without motion in the air. They rove from flower to flower, on which they wholly subsist. I never observed nor heard, that they feed on any insect, or other thing than flowers. They breed in Carolina, and retire at the approach of winter.

What Lerius and Thevet say of their singing, is just as true as what is said of the harmony of swans; for they have no other note than screep, screep, as Margravius truly observes.

Hernandes bespeaks the credit of his readers by saying, 'tis no idle tale, when he affirms the manner of their lying torpid, or sleeping, all winter, in Hispaniola, and many other places between the tropics. I have seen these birds all the year round, there being a perpetual succession of flowers for them to subsist on.

The Trumpet-flower
(trumpet creeper)

These plants climb upon trees; on which they run a great height; and are frequently seen to cover the dead trunks of tall trees. The leaves are winged, consisting of many serrated lobes, standing by couples, opposite to each other on one rib. In May, June, July and August, it produces bunches of red flowers, somewhat like the common foxglove. Each flower shoots from a long reddish-colored calyx; is monopetalous, swelling in the middle, and opens a-top into five lips, with one pointal arising from the calyx, through the middle of the flower. In August, the cods or seed vessels appear.

They are, when full grown, eight inches long, narrow at both ends, and divide into two equal parts, from top to bottom, displaying many flat winged seeds.

The hummingbirds delight to feed on these flowers; and, by thrusting themselves too far into the flower, are sometimes caught.

Editor's Note / Ruby-throated Hummingbird (*Archilochus colubris*)

The more than three hundred species of hummingbirds are predominantly birds of the tropical regions and are entirely restricted to the New World. Several species get up into North America, but only one, the ruby-throated, occurs as a breeding bird in eastern North America, where it is common during the summer months. These birds first arrive in the early part of April and remain through the summer, the males leaving by mid-September and the young and females remaining for another month. There are some records of hummingbirds spending the winter in South Carolina.

These fascinating birds are familiar to almost everyone in this country, both because of their small size and because of their aerial antics, being able to fly forwards and backwards and at very rapid speeds. They are perhaps most commonly seen along woodland edges and in gardens, where they feed by hovering at flowers to obtain the nectar with their long, extrusible tongues. They prefer tubular flowers, and Catesby has characteristically illustrated his hummingbird feeding on the trumpet creeper (*Campsis radicans*), a favorite of the hummer and the flower that Audubon later chose to illustrate with his birds. The popular conception is that hummers live entirely on nectar obtained from flowers, but their diet also consists of large numbers of small insects, and often when they are hovering, they are actually in search of their tiny prey. The indigestible hard parts of the insects are later ejected in small pellets. Hummingbirds build a remarkable nest, a walnut-sized structure of plant material and lichens, bound with spider webs, which it places from four to fifty feet off the ground. Two eggs are the normal brood.

Lawson's account of the hummingbird is worth repeating.

> The humming-bird is the miracle of all our winged animals; he is feathered as a bird, and gets his living as the bees, by sucking the honey from each flower. In some of the larger sort of flowers, he will bury himself, by diving to suck the bottom of it, so that he is quite covered, and oftentimes children catch them in those flowers,

and keep them alive for five or six days. They are of different colors, the cock differing from the hen. The cock is of a green, red, aurora, and other colors mixed. He is much less than a wren, and very nimble. His nest is one of the greatest pieces of workmanship the whole tribe of winged animals can shew, it commonly hanging on a single brier, most artificially woven, a small hole being left to go in and out at. The eggs are the bigness of peas. (1709, 149)

PLATE 55

The King-fisher (69)

This kind of king-fisher is somewhat larger than a blackbird. The bill is two inches and a half long, and black. The eyes are large. His head is covered with long bluish feathers. Under the eye there is a white spot, and another at the base of the upper mandible of the bill. All the upper part of the body is of a dusky blue. The neck is white, with a broad list of dusky blue cross it; under which the breast is muddy red. The belly is white. The quill feathers of the wing are black,

having some white on their interior vanes, edged with blue and black, with transverse white spots, not appearing but when the wing is spread open. The tail is dusky blue, with the end white, as are most of the quill feathers. It has four toes, one only being behind. Its cry, its solitary abode about rivers, and its manner of feeding, are much the same as those in England. It preys not only on fish but likewise on lizards.

The Narrow-leaved Candleberry Myrtle
(waxmyrtle or candleberry)

These are usually but small trees or shrubs, about twelve feet high, with crooked stems, branching forth near the ground irregularly. The leaves are long, narrow, and sharp-pointed. Some trees have most of their leaves serrated; others not. In May, the small branches are alternately and thick set with oblong tufts of very small flowers resembling, in form and size, the catkins of the hazel-tree, colored with red and green. These are succeeded by small clusters of blue berries, close connected, like bunches of grapes. The kernel is enclosed in an oblong hard stone, incrustated over with an unctuous mealy consistence; which is what yields the wax; of which candles are made in the following manner.

In November and December, at which time the berries are mature, a man with his family will remove from his home to some island or sandbanks near the sea, where these trees most abound, taking with him kettles to boil the berries in. He builds a hut with palmetto leaves, for the shelter of himself and family while they stay, which is commonly three or four weeks.

The man cuts down the trees, while the children strip off the berries into a porridge pot; and having put water to them, they boil them until the oil floats, which is skimmed off into another vessel. This is repeated until there remains no more oil. This, when cold, hardens to the consistence of wax, and is of a dirty green color. Then they boil it again, and clarify it in grass kettles; which gives it a transparent greenness.

These candles burn a long time, and yield a grateful smell. They usually add a fourth part of tallow; which makes them burn clearer.

Editor's Note / Belted Kingfisher
(*Ceryle alcyon*)

Kingfishers are primarily birds of the Old World, there being only six species in the New World. The ancient Greeks called kingfishers *halkyons* (*halcyon* in Latin), referring to the belief that they nested in the open sea. They were so favored by the gods that the sea was calmed at their nesting time; since then days of calm have been known as "halcyon days."

The belted kingfisher is a common bird throughout most of the United States and Canada, up to Alaska. It is usually seen perched on limbs overhanging water of all sorts, from small ponds to fast-flowing rivers; along the coast it stays primarily in the sounds, often perching on piers. In feeding, the kingfisher usually flies below the level of tree limbs along the course of the banks of streams. Its food consists primarily of small fishes, although it may take tadpoles, insects, lizards, snakes, young birds, and even mice. It utters its rattling call both in flight and on its perch. Kingfishers nest in a three-to-seven-foot burrow which they excavate in a bank overlooking water; five to eight eggs is the normal clutch.

Lawson mentioned the "little fisher or dipper," saying that "we have the little dipper or fisher that catches fish so dexterously, the same as you have in the islands of Scilly" (1709, 152). Catesby's kingfisher is clearly a male; the female has a rusty breastband that extends down along the sides. It is illustrated with the waxmyrtle or candleberry (*Myrica cerifera*), an aromatic and resinous coastal evergreen shrub of the southern Atlantic and Gulf states widely used today as an ornamental shrub. Colonists boiled the fruit to separate its waxy covering, which they used to make fragrant-burning candles.

PLATE 5 6

The Red-headed Wood-pecker
(20)

This bird weighs two ounces; the bill sharp, somewhat compressed sideways, of a lead color; the whole head and neck, deep red; all the under part of the body and rump white; as are the smaller wing feathers; which, when the wings are closed, joins to the white on the rump, and makes a broad white patch cross the lower part of the back; the upper part of which is black, as are the quill feathers and tail, which is short and stiff. In

Virginia very few of these birds are to be seen in winter; in Carolina there are more, but not so numerous as in the summer; wherefore I conceive they retire southward, to avoid the cold. This is the only one of the wood-peckers that may be termed domestic, frequenting villages and plantations, and takes a peculiar delight in rattling with their bill on the boarded houses; they are great devourers of fruit and grain.

The hen in color differs little or nothing from the cock.

The Water-Oak

These grow nowhere but in low waterish lands; the timber not durable, therefore of little use, except for fencing in fields. In mild winters they retain most of their leaves. Their acorns are small and bitter, and are rejected by the hogs, while others are to be found.

[Twin-berry]

This plant grows in moist places, usually under trees, on which it sometimes creeps a little way up, but most commonly trails on the ground, many stems rising close together near the ground, about six inches long, which have some side branches. The leaves are small, in the form of a heart, and grow opposite to each other on very small footstalks. Its flowers are tetrapetalous, very small, and in form and color like those of the white lilac, and are succeeded by red berries of an oval form and of the size of large peas, having two small holes, and contain many small seeds. It retains the leaves all year.

Editor's Note / Red-headed Woodpecker (*Melanerpes erythrocephalus*)

The woodpeckers are tree-trunk foraging birds that nest in holes in trees, usually excavated by the birds themselves. Unlike typical songbirds, which have three toes in front and one hind toe, woodpeckers are yoke-toed, or zygodactyl; that is, they have two front and two hind toes. They also have very stiff tail feathers with spiny shafts that aid them in hitching up tree trunks. Their very long, extensible tongues are equipped with sharp barbs that aid in capturing insects of various sorts. Woodpeckers are easily recognized at a distance by their characteristic undulating flight.

Catesby's eight woodpeckers included all of the common woodpeckers in the area he explored. His plates of these birds are striking, not only because these are among his best bird drawings but also because he pictured a different oak tree with each. There is no particular association between woodpeckers and oak trees; he apparently placed them together simply as a means of exhibiting each. Lawson also was cognizant of woodpeckers in the New World; his list of birds mentioned five types. Only four different species, however, were described later in the text. These are recognizable as the ivory-billed, northern flicker, red-bellied, and either hairy or downy.

The red-headed woodpecker is a year-round resident throughout most of its range in the Atlantic states, although in certain areas there may be some movement with changing seasons. This is a very distinctive species, with a beautiful red head, black back with white wing patches, and white belly. Red-heads have a decided preference for residential areas and parks. Catesby noted this preference as well as their habit of rattling with their bills on the sides of houses during the courting season. He found this species uncommon in Virginia, but it is possible that the red-head population actually increased over the years with the arrival of Europeans in the New World. Like other woodpeckers, it feeds on insects, grubs, and a variety of nuts and berries; like other woodpeckers also, it excavates a hole in a tree for its nest. Since the introduction of the European starling into America in the last part of the nineteenth century and its subsequent spread over the country, the red-headed woodpecker has declined in numbers because the starling usurps the nest cavity the woodpecker has so laboriously excavated. Catesby's red-headed woodpecker appears on the water oak (*Quercus nigra*) with the twin-berry (*Mitchella repens*) below.

PLATE 5 7

The Red-bellied Wood-pecker (19)

Weighs two ounces, six penny-weight. The bill black; the eyes of a hazel color; all the upper part of the head and neck, bright red; below which, it is ash color; as is the under part of the body, except the belly near the vent, which is stained with red; the upper part of the body, including the wings, is marked regularly with transverse black and white lines; the tail black and white; the feet black.

The hen is of the same color with the cock, with this only difference, that the forehead of the hen is brown.

The Hairy Wood-pecker (19)

Weighs two ounces; the crown of the head black; a red spot covers the back part of the head; between which and the eye it is white; the rest of the head and neck black, with a white line in the middle; the back is black, with a broad white stripe of hairy feathers, extending down the middle to the rump; the wings are black, with both vanes of the feathers, spotted with large white spots; the tail black; all the under part of the body white.

The hen differs from the cock, only in not having the red spot at the back of the head.

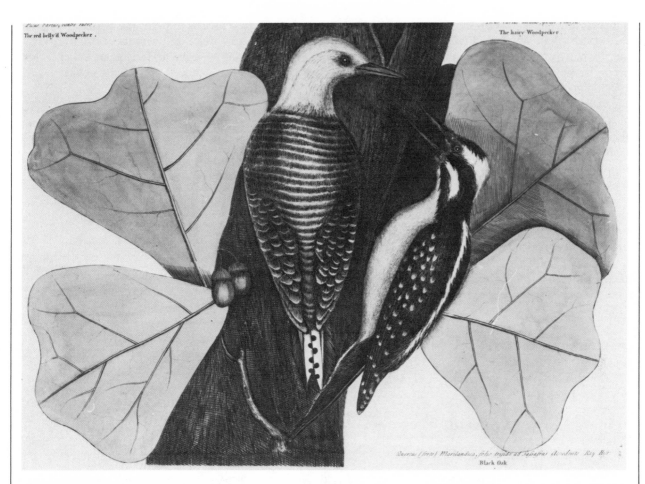

The red belly'd Woodpecker.

The hairy Woodpecker

Quercus (Iris) Marilandica, folio trifido ad Sassafras accedente Ray Hist.

Black Oak

The Black Oak
(blackjack oak)

Usually grows on the poorest land, and is small; the color of the bark black, the grain course, and the wood of little use but to burn; some of these oaks produce leaves ten inches wide.

Editor's Note / Red-bellied Woodpecker (*Melanerpes carolinus*)

The "red-bellied" would at first glance appear to be misnamed, but upon careful inspection one finds that there is indeed a red wash to the lower underparts. This red is not normally seen in field conditions, however, and the bird is much more easily recognized by the back, which is transversely barred with black and white, and the head, which is red in the male and the back of the head red in the female. This species, one of the commonest and most conspicuous woodpeckers in Virginia and the Carolinas, is a resident bird of deciduous woodlands, residential areas, farms, and orchards.

Red-bellies eat a great variety of insects and berries, as well as fruit and some corn. Like the other woodpeckers, they nest in holes excavated in trees, where they deposit four or five white eggs. Lawson told of a woodpecker that was "pied with black and white, has a crimson head, without a topping, and is a plague to the corn and fruit; especially the apples. He opens the covering of the young corn, so that the rain gets in, and rots it" (1709, 147). Catesby drew the red-bellied and hairy woodpecker on the same plate with the blackjack oak (*Quercus marilandica*).

Editor's Note / Downy Woodpecker (*Piocoides pubescens*) and Hairy Woodpecker (*Piocoides villosus*)

Although not depicted on the same plate, the hairy and downy woodpeckers are appropriately discussed together because they are sister species, having evolved directly from the same ancestor. The hairy (Plate 57) is the larger form (9 inches); the downy (Plate 58), the smaller (6 inches). Both are very similar in appearance, and unless they are side by side are often difficult to distinguish. Both downy and hairy woodpeckers have large white patches extending down their otherwise black backs; the black wings have white spots all over them. Both species are common residents along the Atlantic states, where they occur in a variety of woodland situations, the hairy being more common in densely wooded areas than the downy, which is very common in residential areas. Both excavate nest holes in dead limbs or in stumps, where they deposit four to six white eggs. Lawson described a hairy-downy type of woodpecker as "a black and white speckled, or mottled; the finest I ever saw. The cock has a red crown; he is not near so big as the others; his food is grubs, corn, and other creeping insects. He is not very wild, but will let one come up to him, then shifts on the other side of the tree, from your sight; and so dodges you for a long time together. He is about the size of an English lark" (1709, 147).

PLATE 58

The Smallest Spotted Wood-pecker (21)

Weighs fourteen penny-weight. It so nearly resembles the hairy wood-pecker, Tab 19, in its mark and color, that were it not for disparity of size, they might be thought to be the same. The breast and belly of this are light gray. The four uppermost feathers of the tail are black; the rest are gradually shorter, and transversly marked with black and white. The legs and feet are black. Thus far this differs from the description of the above mentioned.

The hen differs from the cock in nothing but wanting the red spot on its head.

The White Oak

This nearest resembles our common English oak in the shape of its leaves, acorns, and manner of growing. The bark is white, the grain of the wood fine, for which and its durableness it is esteemed the best oak in Virginia and Carolina. It grows on all kinds of land; but most on high barren ground amongst pine trees.

There is another kind of white oak, which in Virginia is called the scaly white oak, with leaves like this. The bark is white and scaly, the wood of great use in building. They grow on rich land both high and low.

The White Oak with Pointed Notches
(northern red oak or red oak)

The leaves of this oak are notched, and have sharp points. The bark and wood are white, but has not so close a grain as the precedent. Dr. Pluknet has figured a leaf shaped like this by the name of *Quercus virginiana rubris venis muricata*. This has no red veins. *Vid.* Pluk. *Phytograph.* Tab. LIV. fig. 5.

The Yellow Belly'd Wood-pecker (21)

Weighs one ounce thirteen penny-weight. Its bill is of a lead color; all the upper part of the head is red, bordered below with a list of black, under which runs a list of white, parallel with which runs a black list from the eyes to the back of the head, under which it is pale yellow. The throat is red, and bordered round with black. On the neck and back the feathers are black and white, with a tincture of greenish yellow. The breast and belly are of a light yellow, with some black feathers intermixed. The wings are black, except towards the shoulders, where there are some white feathers; and both edges of the quill feathers are spotted with white; the tail is black and white.

The hen is distinguishable by not having any red about her.

Editor's Note / Downy Woodpecker
(*Piocoides pubescens*)

Discussed above (see Plate 57).

Editor's Note / Yellow-bellied Sapsucker
(*Sphyrapicus varius*)

The yellow-bellied sapsucker is a common winter resident in the Atlantic states from about September to
May. This species receives its name from its feeding
habits, which include drilling parallel rows of small
holes in trees, causing the sap to exude; the sapsucker
then returns to feed on the sap and the small insects
that are attracted to the sap. Sapsuckers may return to
the same tree or trees day after day in their pursuit of
food and may cause some damage to the trees, although surely the beneficial aspects of their insect eating outweigh the injury to trees, which is slight. Plate
58 illustrates the leaf of a white oak (*Quercus alba*), left,
and that of a northern red oak or red oak (*Quercus
rubra*), right.

PLATE 59

The Gold-winged Wood-pecker
(18)

This bird weighs five ounces. The bill is black, an inch
and a half long, and a little bending. From the angles of
the mouth, on each side, runs down a broad black list,
about an inch long. The upper part of the head and
neck is of a lead color. On the hind part of the head, is
a large scarlet spot. The hind part of the neck, throat,
and about the eyes, is of a bay color. The back and part
of the wing next to it, are intermixed with black spots,
in the form of half moons. The larger wing feathers are
brown. What adds the elegancy of this bird, and what
alone is sufficient to distinguish it, is, that the beams of
all the wing feathers are of a bright gold color. The
breast has in the middle of it a large black spot, in form
of a crescent; from which to its vent it is of a dusky
white, and spotted with round and some heart-shaped
black spots. The rump is white; the tail black; which
with the feet, are formed as others of this kind. It
differs from other wood-peckers in the hookedness of
its bill, and manner of feeding, which is usually on the

ground, out of which it draws worms and other insects. Neither do they alight on the bodies of trees in an erect posture as wood-peckers usually do, but like other birds.

The hen wants the black list, which is at the throat of the cock; except which, she differs not from him in color.

The Chestnut-oak

This oak grows only in low and very good land, and is the tallest and largest of the oaks in these parts of the world; the bark white and scaly; the grain of the wood not fine, though the timber is of great use; the leaves are large, indented round the edges, like those of the chestnut. None of the other oaks produce so large acorns.

Editor's Note / Northern Flicker (*Colaptes auratus*)

Catesby's name for this bird, golden-winged woodpecker, and the more recently used yellowhammer and yellow-shafted flicker are far more appropriate and descriptive names than northern flicker, the common name in current use. Flickers are known as ground woodpeckers, for they are equally at home on the ground or in trees, where they may appear either clinging to the sides of tree trunks in typical woodpecker fashion, hitching up, or perched on a limb in typical "perching" bird fashion. Flickers are common permanent residents throughout the Carolinas and Virginia, where the population is greatly augmented during the winter by migrants from the more northern parts of the range. They are common in open woodlands as well as in suburbs. Flickers feed primarily on the ground, hopping around in quest of ants, which make up a large percentage of their diet; in fact, it is said that flickers eat more ants than any other North American bird. They also eat various other sorts of insects as well as some fruits, particularly berries. Flickers nest either in cavities in trees or on the ground; they lay five to ten eggs.

Catesby's description of the flicker's feeding habits is quite accurate, but he apparently mistook the long extensible tongue of the flicker for a worm, stating that it "draws worms and other insects." The flicker is shown with the chestnut oak (*Quercus prinus*).

PLATE 60

The Larger Red-crested Wood-pecker (17)

Weighs nine ounces; the bill angular, two inches long, of a lead color; the neck is small; the iris of the eye gold color, encompassed with a lead-colored skin; the whole crown of the head is adorned with a large scarlet crest; under which, and from the eyes back, runs a narrow white line, and under that a broad black list; a patch of red covers some of the lower mandible of the bill and neck; the rest of the neck (except the hind part, which is black) of a pale yellow, with a small stripe of black dividing it; the upper part of the exterior vanes of the quill feathers is white; above which on the edge of the wing, is a white spot or two; on the middle of the back is a broad white spot; all the rest of the upper part of

the body and tail black; the under part of the body of a dusky black.

That which distinguishes the cock from the hen, is the red which covers some part of his under jaw; which in the hen is black. And whereas the whole crown of the cock is red, in the hen the forehead is brown. These birds (besides insects, which they get from rotten trees, their usual food) are destructive to maize, by pecking holes through the husks that enclose the grain; and letting in wet.

The Live-oak

The usual height of the live oak is about 40 feet; the grain of the wood course, harder and tougher than any other oak. Upon the edges of salt-marshes (where they usually grow) they arrive to a large size. Their bodies are irregular, and generally lying along, occasioned by the looseness and moisture of the soil, and tides washing their roots bare.

On higher lands they grown erect, with a regular

pyramidal-shaped head, retaining their leaves all the year. The acorns are the sweetest of all others; of which the Indians usually lay up store, to thicken their venison soup, and prepare them other ways. They likewise draw an oil very pleasant and wholesome, little inferior to that of almonds.

Editor's Note / Pileated Woodpecker (*Dryocopus pileatus*)

Also known as the "Indian hen" and "log-god," the pileated woodpecker is the second largest North American woodpecker, after the ivory-bill. Although a bird of heavily wooded regions of both hardwood or pine, the pileated's diet is not so restricted as that of its larger cousin. Pileated woodpeckers feed on all types of insects and ants, acorns, beechnuts, wild grapes, cherries, sumac berries, and so forth. The pileated woodpecker appears to have maintained a healthy population level despite the devastation of the North American forests. Audubon noted this: "Even now, when several species of our birds are becoming rare, destroyed as they are, either to gratify the palate of the epicure, or to adorn the cabinet of the naturalist, the pileated woodpecker is every where to be found in the wild woods, although scarce and shy in the peopled districts" (1842, 4:226).

Although, according to reports, pileated woodpeckers do not today feed on corn, Catesby noted that they were "destructive to maize." Audubon noted this, stating that "the maize it attacks while yet in its milky state, laying it bare, like the redheads or squirrels. For this reason, it often draws upon itself the vengeance of the farmer, who, however, is always disposed, without provocation, to kill the 'woodcock,' or 'logcock' as it is commonly named by our country people" (p. 229).

The pileated nests in a cavity excavated by the birds in a dead tree usually forty or so feet high; three to six eggs are normal.

Catesby's pileated woodpecker is shown with the live oak (*Quercus virginiana*).

PLATE 61

The Largest White-bill Wood-pecker (16)

Weighs twenty ounces. It is about the size of, or somewhat larger than a crow. The bill, white as ivory, three inches long, and channeled from the base to the point; the iris of the eye, yellow; the hind part of the head adorned with a large peaked crest of scarlet feathers; a crooked white stripe runs from the eye on each side of the neck, towards the wing; the lower part of the back and wings (except the large quill feathers) are white. All the rest of the bird is black.

The bills of these birds are much valued by the Canada Indians, who make coronets of them for their princes and great warriors, by fixing them around a wreath, with their points outwards. The northern Indians having none of these birds in their cold country, purchase them of the southern people at the price of two, and sometimes three buck-skins a bill.

These birds subsist chiefly on ants, wood-worms, and other insects, which they hew out of rotten trees; nature having so formed their bills, that in an hour or two of time they will raise a bushel of chips; for which the Spaniards call them *carpenteros*.

The Willow Oak

This oak is never found but in low moist land. The leaves are long, narrow and smooth-edged; in shape like the willow; the wood is soft, and course-grained; and of less use than most of the other kinds of oak. In mild winters they retain their leaves in Carolina; but in Virginia they drop.

Editor's Note / Ivory-billed Woodpecker (*Campephilus principalis*)

The ivory-billed woodpecker, largest of the North American woodpeckers, was once a permanent resident of the primeval forests of South Carolina and southeastern North Carolina. Today it is essentially extinct, and only a small number, if any, survive in some remote regions of Louisiana and the South Atlantic states. The ivory-bill is a beautiful bird, approximately twenty-one inches long, solid black with large white patches on the wings and two white stripes running down either side of the back. The bills are a beautiful ivory white, and the males have a large red crest. Lawson surely knew of these birds, as he told of a bird "with a white cross on his back, his eyes circled with white, and on his head stands a tuft of beautiful scarlet feathers. His cry is heard a long way; and he flies from one rotten tree to another, to get grubs, which is the food he lives on" (1709, 147).

A resident of heavily wooded lowlands, the ivory-bill covers vast expanses of territory in a single day in its quest for food, which consists almost entirely of wood-boring insects and grubs found beneath the bark of dying mature trees in virgin woodland. The destruction of large expanses of virgin woodland and the restricted diet are no doubt responsible for the near demise of this great bird in North America.

Apparently, ivory-bills were not uncommon throughout parts of South Carolina (especially the Santee River swamp) and are known to have occurred as far north as Wilmington, North Carolina, as Alexander Wilson took a specimen at some point near Wilmington and described it in 1811 in his *American Orni-*

thology. Wilson commented that the people had a "vulgar prejudice" against the bird (2:11), but there is no further evidence to indicate that the bird was specifically singled out for persecution by hunters. The bills, however, were prized by Indians as ornamental jewelry (see account in Catesby). Catesby's ivory-bill is pictured with a willow oak (*Quercus phellos*), but there is no particular biological association of bird and tree.

Wilson's account of the ivory-bill in Wilmington is given below in its entirety.

The first place I observed this bird at, when on my way to the south, was about twelve miles north of Wilmington, in North Carolina. There I found the bird from which the figure in the plate was taken. This bird was only wounded slightly in the wing, and on being caught, uttered a loudly-reiterated, and most piteous note, exactly resembling the violent crying of a young child; which terrified my horse so, as nearly to have cost me my life. It was distressing to hear it. I carried it with me in the chair, under cover, to Wilmington. In passing through the streets, its affecting cries surprised every one within hearing, particularly the females, who hurried to the doors and windows, with looks of alarm and anxiety. I drove on, and on arriving at the piazza of the hotel, where I intended to put up, the landlord came forward, and a number of other persons who happened to be there, all equally alarmed at what they heard; this was greatly increased by my asking whether he could furnish me with accommodations for myself and my baby. The man looked blank, and foolish, while the others stared with still greater astonishment. After diverting myself for a minute or two at their expense, I drew my Woodpecker from under the cover, and a general laugh took place. I took him up stairs, and locked him up in my room, while I went to see my horse taken care of. In less than an hour I returned, and on opening the door he set up the same distressing shout, which now appeared to proceed from grief that he had been discovered in his attempts at escape. He had mounted along the side of the window, nearly as high as the ceiling, a little below which he had begun to break through. The bed was covered with large pieces of plaster; the lath was exposed for at least fifteen inches square, and a hole, large enough to admit the fist, opened to the weather-boards; so that in less than another hour he would certainly have succeeded in making his way through. I now tied a string round his leg, and fastening it to the table, again left him. I wished to preserve his life, and had gone off in

search of suitable food for him. As I reascended the stairs, I heard him again hard at work, and on entering had the mortification to perceive that he had almost entirely ruined the mahogany table to which he was fastened, and on which he had wreaked his whole vengeance. While engaged in taking the drawing, he cut me severely in several places, and on the whole, displayed such a noble and unconquerable spirit, that I was frequently tempted to restore him to his native woods. He lived with me nearly three days, but refused all sustenance, and I witnessed his death with regret. (1828, 2:11–12)

PLATE 62

The Little Brown Fly-catcher (54)

Weighs nine penny-weight. The bill is very broad and flat; the upper mandible black; the lower yellow. All the upper part of the body of a dark ash color. The wings are brown, with some of the smaller feathers edged with white; all the under part of the body dusky white, with a tincture of yellow; the legs and feet are black.

The Red-ey'd Fly-catcher (54)

Weighs ten penny-weight and a half. The bill is lead color; the iris of the eyes are red. From the bill, over the eyes, runs a dusky white line, bordered above with a black line. The crown of the head is gray. The rest of the upper part of the body is green. The neck, breast and belly are white; the legs and feet red. Both these breed in Carolina, and retire southward in winter.

[Horse-sugar]

This shrub has a slender stem, and grows usually about eight or ten feet high. Its leaves are in shape like those of a pear, growing alternately on footstalks of an inch long; from between which proceeds small whitish flowers, consisting of five petals; in the middle of which shoot forth many tall stamina, headed with yellow apices. The roots of this plant are made use of in decoctions, and are esteemed a good stomachic and cleanser of the blood. The fruit I have not seen. This plant grows in moist and shady woods, in the lower parts of Carolina.

Editor's Note / Eastern Wood-Pewee
(*Contopus virens*)

This little nondescript flycatcher is a common summer resident in the Atlantic states, arriving from its wintering grounds in Central and South America by mid-April and remaining until October. It is most commonly encountered in wooded groves, orchards, or similar situations, where it often perches at medium heights in trees. From there it flies out on frequent sorties to catch insects on the wing, making an audible snap of its bill each time it takes an insect. Less often seen than heard, the sparrow-sized wood-pewee is well known by its voice, a plaintive whistle, "pee-a-wee, pee-wee," that can be heard throughout the long days of summer. It places its cup-shaped nest, composed of grasses, mosses, and lichens, on a horizontal limb about twenty to forty feet up, and four eggs are the

normal clutch. Catesby's "little brown fly-catcher" is shown in the horse-sugar (*Symplocos tinctoria*), a deciduous shrub or small tree of shady thickets, in association with the red-eyed vireo.

Editor's Note / Red-eyed Vireo
(*Vireo olivaceus*)

Found only in the New World, vireos are small, drab birds usually of olive green coloration; they closely resemble the wood warblers, but have a hooked bill. The red-eyed vireo is certainly the most common bird of this group throughout the eastern United States, arriving from its winter home in the Amazon Basin in mid-April and departing around mid-October. This fairly nondescript bird is olive green above and white below, with a bluish gray head marked by a white line extending over the deep red eyes. Common arboreal birds, vireos constantly glean insects from the surrounding branches; they may also eat berries of various kinds. They build a cup-shaped nest of plant material in a tree or shrubs, and four eggs are the normal clutch.

PLATE 63

The Blackcap Fly-catcher (53)

The bill is broad and black; the upper part of the head, of a dusky black; the back, wings and tail are brown; the breast and belly white, with a tincture of yellowish green. The legs and feet are black. The head of the cock is of a deeper black than that of the hen, which is all the difference between them. I don't remember to have seen any of them in winter. They feed on flies and other insects. They breed in Carolina.

[Yellow Jessamine]

This plant grows usually in moist places, its branches being supported by other trees and shrubs on which it climbs. The leaves grow opposite to each other from the joints of the stalks; from whence likewise shoot forth yellow tubulous flowers; the verges of which are notched or divided into five sections. The seeds are flat

cup-shaped nest of all sorts of grasses and other materials cemented together with mud and placed in a sheltered place, such as an overhanging cliff or a window or door frame. Four or five eggs are the normal number, and two broods are not uncommon. Catesby's eastern phoebe is pictured with the yellow jessamine (*Gelsemium sempervirens*), a high-climbing vine common throughout parts of the South. This plant is poisonous and can be lethal to livestock.

and half winged, contained in an oblong pointed capsule, which, when the seeds are ripe, splits to the stalk and discharges them. The smell of the flowers is like that of the wall-flowers. These plants are scarce in Virginia, but are everywhere in Carolina. They are likewise at Mr. Bacon's at Hoxton; where, by their thriving state, they seem to like our soil and climate. Though Mr. Parkinson calls it *semper virens*, I have always found it loses its leaves in winter.

Editor's Note / Eastern Phoebe
(*Sayornis phoebe*)

In the southern Atlantic states the eastern phoebe is a fairly common permanent resident in the mountains and in the piedmont and parts of the upper coastal plain, but is absent in most of the coastal regions during the breeding season, appearing from September to March as a winter resident. Like the eastern wood-pewee, phoebes often perch in trees at moderate heights, from which they sally out to catch flying insects on the wing. From these perches they are frequently heard to utter a hoarse "fee-be." They are most frequently seen in open woodlands or around the wooded margins of fields. The phoebe builds a bulky,

PLATE 64

The Crested Fly-catcher (52)

Weighs one ounce. The bill is black and broad; the upper part of the body of a muddy green; the neck and breast of a lead color; the belly is yellow; the wings brown, having most of the vanes of the quill feathers edged with red. The two middle feathers of the tail are all brown; the interior vanes of the rest are red. The legs and feet are black. It breeds in Carolina and Virginia, but retires in winter. This bird, by its ungrateful brawling noise, seems at variance and displeased with all others.

[China-root, Hellfetter or Bamboo Greenbrier]

This plant shoots forth with many pliant thorny stems, which, when at full bigness, are as big as a walking cane, and jointed; and rises to the height usually of twenty feet, climbing upon and spreading over the adjacent trees and shrubs, by the assistance of its tendrils. In autumn it produces clusters of black round berries, hanging pendant to a footstalk, above three inches long, each berry containing a very hard roundish seed. The roots of this plant are tuberous, divided into many knots and joints; and, when first dug out of the ground, are soft and juicy, but harden in the air to the consistency of wood. Of these roots the inhabitants of Carolina make a diet drink, attributing great virtues to it in cleansing the blood, etc. They likewise in the spring boil the tender shoots and eat them prepared like asparagus. This is called there China root.

Editor's Note / Great Crested Flycatcher (*Myiarchus crinitus*)

The crested flycatcher is a common summer resident throughout the entire eastern United States, where it arrives from its winter home in central and northern South America in late March and April and departs again in September. The crested flycatcher nests in either a natural cavity in a tree or stump or a manmade cavity; there it builds a small cup nest that is invariably lined with a cast snake skin. Four eggs are the normal clutch.

As the name implies, these birds are principally insect eaters, but they supplement their diet with berries of various sorts as the summer progresses. Unlike the kingbird, the crested flycatcher is a bird of open woodlands and is not uncommon in wooded residential areas. Catesby figured his crested flycatcher with crest erected in China-root, hellfetter, or bamboo greenbrier (*Smilax tamnoides*), a southern species of catbrier with triangular leaves and stout thorns. These plants are closely related to the sarsaparilla-vine (illustrated with the bluebird, Plate 72) and are placed in the same genus.

PLATE 65

The Tyrant (55)

The bill is broad, flat and tapering. The crown of the head has a bright red spot, environed with black feathers; which, by contracting, conceals the red; but, when they are spread, it appears with much luster after the manner of the *Regulus cristatus*. The back, wings and tail are brown; the neck, breast and belly white; the legs and feet black. There appears little or no difference between the cock and hen. They appear in Virginia and Carolina about April, where they breed, and retire at the approach of winter. The courage of this little bird is singular. He pursues and puts to flight all kinds of birds that come near his station, from the smallest to the largest, none escaping his fury; nor did I ever see any that dared to oppose him while flying; for he does not offer to attack them when sitting. I have seen one of them fix on the back of an eagle, and persecute him so, that he has turned on his back into various postures in the air, in order to get rid of him, and at last was forced to alight on top of the next tree, from whence he dared not move, till the little tyrant was tired, or thought fit to leave him. This is the constant practice of the cock while the hen is brooding. He sits on top of a bush, or small tree, not far from her nest; near which if any small birds approach, he drives them away; but the great ones, as crows, hawks, and eagles, he won't suffer to come within a quarter of a mile of him without attacking them. They have only a chattering note, which they utter with great vehemence all the time they are fighting.

When their young are flown, they are as peaceable as other birds. It has a tender bill, and feeds on insects only. They are tame and harmless birds. They build their nest in an open manner on low trees and shrubs, and usually on the sassafras tree.

[Sassafras Tree]

This is generally a small tree; the trunk usually not a foot thick. The leaves are divided into three lobes by very deep incisures. In March comes forth bunches of small yellow flowers with five petals each; which are succeeded by berries, in size and shape not unlike those of the bay-tree, hanging on red footstalks, with a calyx like that of an acorn; which calyx is also red. The berries are at first green, and, when ripe, blue. These trees grow in most parts of the northern continent of America, and generally on very good land. The virtue of this tree is well known, as a great sweetener of the blood; I shall therefore only add, that in Virginia a strong decoction of the root has been sometimes given with good success for an intermitting fever. This tree will bear our climate, as appears by several now at Mr. Collinson's at Peckham, and at Mr. Gray's in Fulham; where they have withstood the cold of several winters.

Editor's Note / Eastern Kingbird
(*Tyrannus tyrannus*)

Also known as the "field martin," this large flycatcher is a conspicuous part of the summer avifauna of the entire eastern United States, arriving from its wintering grounds in South America in March and April and departing normally by the middle of September. Kingbirds are black above and white below, with a white tip on the tail and a red patch on the crown which is not frequently seen but is shown in Catesby's painting. These birds are most frequently seen perched on fences bordering pastures or on telephone lines along rural roads. They are truly birds of open groves and fields, where they dart out periodically to catch passing insects on the wing. According to an old country tale kingbirds use the bright red crown patch to lure insects in for the kill. Also known as "bee martins," these birds have often drawn the wrath of beekeepers, as they consume large quantities of those insects; the good that they perform, though, far outweighs any harm they might have caused to bee populations.

The name "kingbird" or "tyrant" derives from the fact that these birds are absolutely fearless in defense of their nesting territories against the likes of hawks, crows, and even eagles. Audubon told of this behavior: "Should he spy a crow, a vulture, a martin, or an eagle, in the neighborhood or at a distance, he spreads his wings to the air, and pressing towards the dangerous foe, approaches him, and commences his attack with fury. He mounts above the enemy, sounds the charge, and repeatedly plunging upon the very back of his more powerful antagonist, essays to secure a hold. In this manner, harassing his less active foe with continued blows of his bill, he follows him probably for a mile" (1840, 1:205). Kingbirds are apparently effective in territorial encounters with all but the purple martin, who is far more agile but equally aggressive. Audubon recounted a story of a martin actually killing a male kingbird that nested nearby.

The kingbird nests in low-lying bushes frequently in orchards or similar situations, where its nest, a fairly bulky structure of sticks and weeds, accommodates usually four eggs.

Catesby's tyrant is pictured in a sassafras tree (*Sassafras albidum*), a tree that, because of its aromatic root bark, early colonists thought to be a panacea; it was not only used in America but also shipped to Europe. The roots and bark of the roots produce an oil that was used to perfume soap and to flavor drinks such as tea.

PLATE 66

The Lark (32)

In size and shape this resembles our sky-lark. The crown of the head is mixed with black and yellow feathers. Through the eyes runs a stripe of yellow. From the angle of the mouth runs a black stripe, inclining downward; except which, the throat and neck are yellow. The upper part of the breast is covered with a patch of black feathers, in form of a crescent. The remaining part of the breast and belly of a brown straw color. It has a long heel. It has a single note, like that of our sky-lark in winter; at which time and in cold

Editor's Note / Horned Lark
(*Eremophila alpestris*)

The horned lark was illustrated by Catesby with sea oats (*Uniola paniculata*), a well-known member of the grass family that grows on sand dunes from Virginia south to Florida on the Atlantic coast. The horned lark is the only true North American lark (family Alaudidae), having the characteristic elongated hind claw. During the breeding season it has a musical, high display flight characteristic of larks. Although the horned lark nests in parts of the Atlantic piedmont, along the coastal regions where it was encountered by Catesby this species is a migrant and winter resident, being found in open fields or near the shore. These larks feed primarily on seeds of grasses and weeds in addition to a variety of insects and small animal matter. Horned larks are usually seen traveling in small, scattered flocks that alight and walk along the ground. Lawson's "lark" referred to Catesby's "large lark," the meadowlark (Plate 103).

weather only, they appear in Virginia and Carolina. They come from the North in great flights, and return early in the spring. From their near resemblance to our sky-lark, I conceive they mount up and sing as ours do; but they appearing here only in winter, I cannot determine it. They frequent the sandhills upon the seashore of Carolina, and there feed on these oats, which they find scattered on the sands.

The Sea-side Oat
(sea oats)

This plant I observed growing nowhere but on sandhills; so near the sea, that at high tides the water flows to it. Its height is usually four and five feet.

PLATE 67
The Purple Martin (51)

Is larger than our common martin. The whole bird is of a dark shining purple; the wings and tail being more dusky and inclining to brown. They breed like pigeons in lockers prepared for them against the houses, and gourds hung on poles for them to build in; they being of great use about houses and yards, for pursuing and chasing away crows, hawks, and other vermin, from the poultry. They retire at the approach of winter, and return in the spring to Virginia and Carolina.

[Coral Beads or Moon Seed]

The stalks of this plant are slender, running up the walls of old houses, and twining about posts and trees. They resemble our common ivy. I never saw it in flower; bears red berries, about the bigness of small peas, which are in clusters.

Editor's Note / Purple Martin (*Progne subis*)

Purple martins are well-known summer residents throughout Virginia and the Carolinas, arriving in numbers by March and April and then departing for their South American wintering grounds by October. They are extremely useful birds, consuming large quantities of insects on the wing, including dragonflies, wasps, and other day-flying varieties. Long before the arrival of the first settlers men made efforts to attract these popular birds into their midst. The Indians hung clusters of gourds to serve as nesting houses, and the settlers made pottery "bird bottles." Farmers also value them for their ability to ward off hawks with their pugnacious attacks and therefore keep the chicken yard free from those predators. Lawson stated of the purple martin, "The planters put gourds on standing poles, on purpose for these fowl to build in, because they are a very warlike bird, and beat the crows from the plantations" (1709, 149). In ancient times martins nested in tree cavities of various kinds, no doubt including abandoned woodpecker holes. The small nest of grasses and twigs accommodates four or five eggs, which are deposited in April or May.

Catesby's purple martin is illustrated with coral beads or moon seed (*Cocculus carolinus*), a climbing vine; in September, when they ripen, the fruits resemble whitish-powdered grapes.

PLATE 68

The Blew Jay (15)

It is full as big, or bigger, than a starling; the bill black. Above the base of the upper mandible are black feathers, which run in a narrow stripe cross the eyes, meeting a broad black stripe, which encompasses the head and throat; its crown feathers are long, which it erects at pleasure; the back is of a dusky purple; the interior vanes of the larger quill feathers, black; the exterior, blue; with transverse black lines cross every feather, and their ends tipped with white; the tail blue, marked with the like crosslines as on the wings. They have the like jetting motion of our jay; but their cry is more tuneful.

The hen is not so bright in color; except which, there appears no difference.

The Bay-leaved Smilax
(greenbrier or bamboovine)

This plant is usually found in moist places; it sends forth from its root many green stems, whose branches overspread whatsoever stands near it, to a very considerable distance; and it frequently climbs above sixteen feet in height, growing so very thick, that in summer it makes an impenetrable shade, and in winter a warm shelter for cattle. The leaves are of the color and consistence of laurel, but in shape more like the bay, without any visible veins, the middle rib only excepted.

The flowers are small and whitish. The fruit grows in round clusters, and is a black berry, containing one single hard seed, which is ripe in October, and is food for some sorts of birds, particularly this jay.

Editor's Note / Blue Jay (*Cyanocitta cristata*)

Catesby's blue jay, which is drawn in the greenbrier or bamboovine (*Smilax laurifolia*), is truly one of his more animated drawings and captures the real personality of this well-known bird. The "jay" was also well known to Lawson, who commented, "Jays are here common and very mischievous in devouring our fruit and spoiling more than they eat. They are abundantly more beautiful and finer feathered than those in Europe" (1709, 145). Jays are placed in the same family as the crows and ravens, and it is interesting to note that while

Lawson clearly recorded the latter two forms, Catesby made no mention of either, probably because they were not new types for Europeans.

The blue jay is an abundant permanent resident throughout the Atlantic states, and the population is augmented during the winter months with the arrival of migrants from the more northern parts of the range. Common in almost any woodland situation, these birds are particularly fond of areas inhabited by man. They place their three to five eggs in a bulky nest of sticks and other materials up to fifty feet high in trees. Perhaps no account of the habits of the blue jay could match that of Audubon, who depicted three blue jays eating the eggs of another bird. "Reader, Look at the plate in which are represented three individuals of this beautiful species—rogues though they may be, and thieves, as I would call them, were it fit for me to pass judgment on their actions. See how each is enjoying the fruits of his knavery, sucking on the egg which he has pilfered from the nest of some innocent Dove or harmless Partridge! Who could imagine that a form so graceful, arrayed by Nature in a garb so resplendent,

should harbor so much mischief;—that selfishness, duplicity, and malice should form the moral accomplishments of so much physical perfection!" (1842, 4:110).

PLATE 69

The Crested Titmouse (57)

It weighs thirteen penny-weight. The bill is black, having a spot a little above it of the same color; except which, all the upper part of the body is gray. The neck and all the under part of the body is white, with a faint tincture of red, which just below the wings is deepest. The legs and feet are of a lead color. It erects its crown feathers into a pointed crest. No difference appears between the cock and hen. They breed in and inhabit Virginia and Carolina all the year. They do not frequent near houses, their abode being only amongst the

Editor's Note / Tufted Titmouse
(*Parus bicolor*)

The tufted titmouse is, as the name implies, a small, gray bird with a tufted crest. These familiar birds are permanent residents throughout the entire eastern United States; they are well known not only by their appearance but also by their constant clear whistle, "peter, peter, peter." Also known as "tomtits," these birds frequent deciduous woodlands and wooded residential areas; there they busily pursue insects throughout the day, sometimes hanging upside down in their arboreal acrobatics in search of prey. Titmice nest in cavities, often an abandoned woodpecker nest or a natural cavity in a tree, where the female deposits four to eight eggs. Catesby's "crested titmouse" is shown on the swamp honeysuckle (*Rhododendron viscosum*), a large shrub that grows along the borders of streams and bogs.

forest trees from which they get their food; which is insects.

The Upright Honeysuckle
(swamp honeysuckle)

This plant rises usually with two or three stiff straight stems, which are small except where the soil is very moist and rich; where they grow to the size of a walking cane, twelve or sixteen feet high, branching into many smaller stalks, with leaves alternately placed. At the ends of the stalks are produced bunches of flowers, resembling our common honeysuckle; not all of a color, some plants producing white, some red, and others purplish, of a very pleasant scent, though different from ours. The flowers are succeeded by long pointed capsules, containing innumerable very small seeds. This is a native of Virginia and Carolina, but will endure our climate in the open air, having for some years past produced its beautiful and fragrant blossoms at Mr. Bacon's at Hoxton, at Mr. Collinson's at Peckham; and at Mr. Christopher Gray's, at Fulham.

PLATE 70

The Nuthatch (22)

Weighs thirteen penny-weight, 5 grains. The bill and upper part of the head and neck black, the back gray. The wings of a dark brown, edged with light gray; the uppermost two feathers of the tail are gray; the rest black and white. At the vent is a reddish spot, the legs and feet are brown. The back claw is remarkably bigger and longer than the rest, which seems necessary to support their body in creeping down as well as up trees, in which action they are usually seen pecking their food (which are insects) from the chinks or crevices of the bark.

The hen differs but little from the cock in the color of her feathers. They breed and continue the whole year in Carolina.

The Small Nuthatch (22)

This weighs six penny-weight; the bill black; the upper part of the head brown; behind which is a dusky white spot; the back is gray; as are the two uppermost tail feathers; the rest being black; the wings are dark brown; the throat and all the under part of the body

dusky white; the tail is short; the back toe is largest. They abide all year in Carolina. Their food, and manner of taking it, is the same as that of the larger nuthatch.

The Highland Willow Oak
(bluejack oak or upland willow oak)

This is usually a small tree, having a dark-colored bark with leaves of a pale green, and shaped like those of a willow. It grows on dry poor land, producing but few acorns, and those small. Most of these oaks are growing at Mr. Fairchild's.

Editor's Note / White-breasted Nuthatch (*Sitta carolinensis*) and Brown-headed Nuthatch (*Sitta pusilla*)

Both white-breasted and brown-headed nuthatches are permanent residents in Virginia and the Carolinas.

These small birds are masters at gleaning limbs and tree trunks. They creep along the trunk with head up, or as frequently with head down, and probe and peck into the bark to find small insects and grubs. The name "nuthatch" refers to their habit of placing a nut seed in a crack of bark and then "hatching" it until it is broken. Nuthatches lack the stiff tail feathers of woodpeckers and must depend on their well-adapted legs and sharp claws for climbing. The white-breasted nuthatch frequents deciduous forests throughout its range, while the smaller (tiny) brown-headed nuthatch prefers pine woods. However, the two frequently occur together in mixed pine and deciduous forests, and both are frequent visitors to bird feeders. These two species are also easily recognized by their calls: the white-breasted utters an incessant "yank-yank-yank," while the brown-headed's note may be described as a metallic "dee-dee-dee." White-breasted nuthatches either excavate their own nest holes or use old abandoned woodpecker nests; the brown-headed always excavates its own nest hole. Five or more eggs are the normal brood. Catesby's nuthatches are drawn on the bluejack or upland willow oak (*Quercus incana*).

PLATE 7 1

Regulus Cristatus
(appendix, 13)

As this is an English as well as an American bird, I shall only observe, that, by comparing this American one with the description of Mr. Willughby's European one, they agreed in every particular; and therefore I refer to his *Ornithology*, p. 227. of the English edition.

This bird, which is the least of all European birds, is likewise an inhabitant in the parallel latitudes of the Old and New World.

In winter sunshine days, they are wont to associate with other creepers, particularly the certhia, the sitta, the parus-ater, the parus caudata, and other tit-mice; ranging the woods together, from tree to tree, as if they were all of one brood; running up and down the bark of lofty oaks, from the crevices of which they collect their food, which are insects lodged in their winter dormitories, in a torpid state. In like manner, the same little birds feed in America, frequenting juniper, fir, and pine-trees; this repeating zilzilperle, as Gesner relates his parus sylvaticus to do.

Steuartia
(silky-camellia or Virginia Stewartia)

This shrub rises from the ground, with several stiff inflexible stems, to an ordinary height. The leaves are serrated, and grow alternately, resembling those of the syringa. The flower resembles that of a single rose, consisting of five white concave petals, with a pointel rising from a pale green ovarium, surrounded by many purple stamina, with bluish apices. It is remarkable, that one particular petal in every flower is stained with a faint greenish yellow. The calyx is divided into five segments. The capsule has a hairy roughness on the outside, is of a conic form, and when ripe splits open and discloses five membranous cells, every one of which contains a single oblong brown shining seed. For this elegant plant I am obliged to my good friend Mr. Clayton, who sent it me from Virginia, and three months after its arrival it blossomed in my garden at Fulham, in May, 1742.

Sir,

"The plant which you shewed me by the name of *Steuartia*, I take to be a new genus of plants, the same that I called *Malachodendron*. But I humbly conceive, that the generical character of it, which you shewed me in the *Acta Suecica*, is so faulty, that it will not even determine the proper class of this plant in any system of botany, instead of establishing the true genus. It is there referred to the class of *Polyandria Monogynia, Linnaei*, whereas it properly belongs to the class of *Monadelphia Polyandria*, in which it makes a new tribe or order of *Pentagynia*, which alone distinguishes it from all the tribe of malvaceous plants, under which it is properly included in all systems of botany: for the petals are connected at the base, and drop off united together, which (according to Ray and Tournefort) makes the flower monopetalous. The stamina are connected in a ring at their base, and are inserted to the base of the petal. There are five styles, as I shewed you in a specimen I have. The fruit is a dry capsule with five sharp angles, five cells, and five valves, which open at top, and are not crowned with the calyx, which remains on their base. The seeds are single in each cell, of an oblong, oval, triangular shape."

John Mitchell.

The right honorable and ingenious Earl of Bute will, I hope, excuse my calling this new genus of plants after his name.

Editor's Note / Golden-crowned Kinglet
(*Regulus satrapa*)

Kinglets are tiny arboreal "birdlets" that belong to the family of Old World warblers (Sylviidae), only a handful of species of which occur in the New World. The golden-crowned kinglet is a nesting species of conifer forests; in the eastern United States it breeds in the mountains down through Virginia and North Carolina, but otherwise it is a winter bird only in the Carolinas. During the winter kinglets are most frequently encountered in stands of various evergreen trees and bushes, where they glean small insects and spiders from the leaves and twigs. They are very active while feeding, constantly flicking their tiny tails.

These tiny olive-green birds can be recognized by their white wing bars and yellow crown patch, which has a central orange streak in the male. The crown is edged with black. Catesby recognized his *Regulus cristatus* as being "an English as well as an American bird," thinking that it was the same as the goldcrest (*Regulus regulus*), a "very common kinglet" of Great Britain and quite similar in appearance to the golden-crowned kinglet. It is illustrated with an unidentifiable ichneumon fly and is perched in the silky-camellia or Virginia Stewartia (*Stewartia malacodendron*), a shrub or small tree that has large white or yellow flowers with a purple center. It occurs from eastern Virginia south to northern Florida and west.

These birds are common in most parts of North America, I having seen them in Carolina, Virginia, Maryland, and the Bermuda Islands.

PLATE 7 2

The Blew Bird (47)

This bird weighs nineteen penny-weight, and is about the bigness of a sparrow. The eyes are large. The head and upper part of the body, tail and wings are a bright blue, except that the ends of the wing feathers are brown. The throat and breast, of a dirty red; the belly white. This is a bird of a very swift flight, its wings being very long; so that the hawk generally pursues it in vain. They make their nests in holes of trees, are harmless birds, and resemble our robin-red-breast. They feed on insects only.

[Sarsaparilla-vine]

This plant sometimes trails on the ground, the leaves resembling those of the birth-wort, set alternately on its slender stalks; from which hang clusters of small red berries of an oval form but pointed, each containing a very hard round seed.

Editor's Note / Eastern Bluebird (*Sialia sialis*)

The eastern bluebird is a fairly common resident species over much of the eastern United States, where it is

normally encountered in somewhat open country with scattered trees. It is, however, migratory in the northern part of its range. Bluebirds are well known for their nesting habits: they build a simple nest of small sticks or grasses in a natural cavity in a tree, where the female deposits four or five pale blue eggs. Today, persons all over the country put up nesting boxes for this spectacular species, and the birds have been known to usurp rural mail boxes. Bluebirds are predominantly insect eaters during the summer months; when winter arrives they feed to a large extent on berries of various kinds and are particularly fond of pyracantha berries.

Placed with the kinglets and Old World warblers until the time of Audubon, the bluebird is now properly placed with the robin among the true thrushes. Catesby drew his bluebird in such an absurd pose that one must wonder if he had seen much of this bird in the wild. It is shown with a most unlikely partner, the sarsaparilla-vine (*Smilax pumila*), a low-lying perennial of swamp forests and wooded coves of the piedmont and mountains. These plants have vinelike tendrils that climb over other vegetation. The round clusters of flowers produce a strong carrionlike odor, and are thus pollinated by flies.

PLATE 73

The Little Thrush (31)

In shape and color it agrees with the description of the European mavis, or song-thrush, differing only in bigness; this weighing no more than one ounce and a quarter. In never sings, having only a single note, like the winter note of our mavis. It abides all the year in Carolina. They are seldom seen, being but few, and those abiding only in dark recesses of the thickest woods and swamps. Their food is the berries of holly, haws, etc.

The Dahoon Holly
(Christmas berry)

This holly usually grows erect, sixteen feet high; the branches shooting straighter, and being of quicker growth than the common kind. The leaves are longer, of a brighter green, and more pliant; not prickly, but serrated only. The berries are red, growing in large clusters. This is a very uncommon plant in Carolina, I having never seen it but at Col. Bull's plantation on Ashley River, where it grows in a bog.

Editor's Note / Little Thrush
(*Hylocichla or Catharus sp.?*)

Although conceivably a wood thrush (*Hylocichla mustelina*) from the description and certain of its characteristics, Catesby's little thrush is simply not identifiable. The bird figured by Catesby was analyzed in detail by Alexander Wilson, who stated, "It is difficult to discover, either from the figure or description, what particular species is meant" (1828, 2:115–16). It is drawn in the Christmas-berry or dahoon holly (*Ilex cassine*), a small evergreen tree with bright red berries that grows along streams and swamps from southeastern North Carolina to Florida.

PLATE 74

The Fieldfare of Carolina (29)

Weighs two ounces three quarters; about the size and shape of the European fieldfare. That part of the bill, next to the head, is yellow. Over and under the eye are two white streaks. The upper part of the head is black, with a mixture of brown. The wings and upper part of the body brown; the tail dark brown; the throat black and white; the breast and belly red; the legs and feet brown. In winter they arrive from the north in Virginia and Carolina, in numerous flights, and return in the spring as ours in England. They are canorous, having a loud cry like our miffel-bird, which the following accident gave me an opportunity of knowing. Having some trees of alaternus full of berries (which were the first that had been introduced in Virginia) a single fieldfare seemed so delighted with the berries, that he tarried all the summer feeding on them. In Maryland, I am told, they breed and abide the whole year.

The Snake-root of Virginia
(snake-root)

This plant rises out of the ground in one, two, and sometimes three pliant stalks, which at every little distance are crooked, or undulated. The leaves stand alternately, and are about three inches long, in form somewhat like the *Smilax aspera*. The flowers grow close to the ground on footstalks an inch long, of a singular shape, though somewhat resembling those of the birthworts, of a dark purple color. A round chanulated capsule succeeds the flower, containing many small seeds, which are ripe in May. The usual price of this excellent root, both in Virginia and Carolina, is about six pence a pound when dried, which is money hardly earned. Yet the Negro slaves (who only dig it) employ much of the little time allowed them by their masters in search of it; which is the cause of there being seldom found any but very small plants. By planting them in a garden they increased so in two years time, that one's hand could not grasp the stalks of one plant. It delights in shady woods, and is usually found at the roots of great trees.

Editor's Note / American Robin
(*Turdus migratorius*)

The migratory arrival of the American robin is considered one of the best signs of the onset of spring, but in fact the robin is a common winter bird throughout the Atlantic states. In early spring most wintering birds migrate back to their breeding grounds to the north and robins from further south move in to become breeding birds in the summer. However, many birds that breed in a given area may spend the winter there if the supply of berries and fruit is sufficient. Robins are noted for taking earthworms and insects, but they are also fond of berries and other wild fruits. They often nest is residential areas, placing their nests of twigs and grasses cemented with mud in the crotches of trees; three or four blue eggs are the normal clutch. Robins may raise two or even three broods in one season.

The American robin no doubt got its name from colonial settlers who were reminded of the European robin, or "robin redbreast" (*Erithacus rubecula*), a common bird of Europe not closely allied or related to our robin. The European blackbird (*Turdus merula*), the bird of "four and twenty blackbirds baked in a pie," is in fact their "robin." Catesby's robin, a dead bird figured on a stump of the snake-root (*Aristolochia serpentaria*), is today one of his least desired plates. Snake-root was prized during colonial days as an antidote for snake bite.

PLATE 75

The Red Leg'd Thrush (30)

Weighs two ounces and a half; has a dusky black bill; the inside of the mouth is more red than usual; the iris of the eye red, with a circle of the same color encompassing it. The throat is black; all the rest of the body of a dusky blue, except that the interior vanes of the large wing feathers are black, as is the tail when closed; but when spread, the outermost feathers appear to have their ends white, and are gradually shorter than the two middlemost. The legs and feet are red.

The hen differs from the cock no otherwise than in being about a third part less. In the gizzard of one were the berries of the tree described below. In its singing, gestures, etc. this bird much resembles other thrushes. I saw many of them on the islands of Andros and Ilathera.

The Gum-elimy Tree
(gum-elemi tree)

This is a large tree; the bark remarkably red and smooth. The leaves are pinnate; the middle rib five or six inches long, with the pinnae set opposite to one another, on footstalks half an inch long. The blossoms (which I did not see) are succeeded by purple-colored berries bigger than large peas, hanging in clusters on a stalk of about five inches long, to which each berry is joined by a footstalk of an inch long. The seed is hard, white, and of a triangular figure, enclosed within a thin capsule, which divides in three parts, and discharges the seed. This tree produces a large quantity of gum, of a brown color, and of the consistence of turpentine. It is esteemed a good vulnerary, and is much used for horses. Most of the Bahama Islands abound with these trees.

Editor's Note / Red-legged Thrush
(*Turdus plumbeus*)

Although five species of thrushes visit the Bahama Islands as migrants or winter visitors, only the red-legged thrush is a resident species. This bird has striking colors for a thrush, being predominantly gray, with a bright orange bill, red eye ring, and red feet. Normally found in wooded areas, but also in gardens and similar situations, it feeds on insects and fruits, as well as small reptiles. This characteristic Bahamian bird is illustrated with the common gum-elemi tree (*Bursera simaruba*).

PLATE 76

The Cat-bird (66)

This bird is about the size of, or somewhat bigger than a lark. The crown of the head is black; the upper part of the body, wings and tail, dark brown; particularly the tail approaches nearest to black. The neck, breast, belly, are of a lighter brown. From the vent, under the tail, shoot forth some feathers of a dirty red. This bird is not seen on lofty trees; but frequents bushes and thickets; and feeds on insects. It has but one note, which resembles the mewing of a cat; and which has given it its name. It lays a blue egg, and retires from Virginia in winter.

[Sweet Pepperbush]

This shrub grows in moist places, and sometimes in water, from which it rises, with many slender stems, to the height of ten or fourteen feet. The leaves are some-

what rough, placed alternately, serrated, and in shape not unlike those of the white thorn. In July there shoots from the ends of the branches, spikes of white flowers, four or five inches long. Each flower consists of five petals, and a tuft of small stamina. These flowers are thick set on footstalks a quarter of an inch long; and are succeeded by small oval pointed capsules, containing many chaffy seeds. This plant endures our climate in the open air, and flourishes at Mr. Bacon's at Hoxton.

Editor's Note / Gray Catbird
(*Dumetella carolinensis*)

Closely allied with the mockingbird and brown thrasher, the catbird is the third member the family of "mimic thrushes" to occur in the eastern United States. It is a common breeding bird from southern Canada south through the eastern and central United States to the Gulf states and also commonly winters in the southern parts of its range in the United States. Like the brown thrasher, the catbird is primarily a bird of low bushes and shrubs. Its characteristic call resembles the mewing of a cat. The nest, a deep structure of sticks and twigs and dead leaves, is normally placed at moderate heights. Several broods per season are common, and four or five blue eggs are the normal clutch. The food of the catbird consists of berries and fruits, as well as insects. Catesby's catbird is illustrated on sweet pepperbush (*Clethra alnifolia*).

PLATE 77

The Mock-bird (27)

This bird is about as big or rather less than a blackbird, and of a slenderer make. The bill is black; the iris of the eye of a brownish yellow; the back and tail dark brown; the breast and belly light gray; the wings brown, except that the upper part of the quill feathers have their exterior vanes white; and some of the small feathers, near the shoulder of the wing, are verged with white. The cocks and hens are so alike, that they are not easily distinguished by the color of their feathers.

Hernandez justly calls it the queen of all singing birds. The Indians, by way of eminence or admiration, call it *cencontlatolly*, or four hundred tongues; and we call it (though not by so elevated a name, yet very properly) the mock-bird, from its wonderful mocking and imitating the notes of all birds, from the humming-bird to the eagle. From March till August it sings incessantly day and night with the greatest variety of notes; and, to complete his compositions, borrows from the whole choir, and repeats to them their own tunes with such artful melody, that it is equally pleasing and surprising. They may be said not only to sing but dance, by gradually raising themselves from the place where they stand, with their wings extended, and falling with their head down to the same place; then turning round, with their wings continuing spread, have many pretty antic gesticulations with their melody.

They are familiar and sociable birds, usually perching on the tops of chimneys or trees, amongst the inhabitants, who are diverted with their tuneful airs most part of the summer. Their food is haws, berries and insects. In winter, when there is least variety and plenty, they will eat the berries of dogwood.

Cornus mas &c.   *Turdus minor &c.*
                                                        The Mock-bird.

The Dogwood Tree
(flowering dogwood)

This is a small tree, the trunk being seldom above eight
or ten inches thick. The leaves resemble our common
dogwood, but are fairer and larger, standing opposite to
each other on footstalks of about an inch long, from
among which branch forth many flowers in the following manner. In the beginning of March the blossoms
break forth; and though perfectly formed and wide
open, are not so wide as a six-pence; increasing gradually to the breadth of a man's hand, being not at their
full bigness till about six weeks after they begin to
open. Each flower consists of four greenish white
leaves, every leaf having a deep indenture at the end.
From the bottom of the flower rises a tuft of yellow
stamina; every one of which opens a-top into four small
leaves or petals. The wood is white, has a close grain,
and very hard like that of box. The flowers are succeeded by clusters of berries having from two to six in a
cluster, closely joined, and set on footstalks an inch
long. These berries are red, of an oval form, and of the
size of large haws, containing a hard stone. As the
flowers are a great ornament to the woods in summer,
so are the berries in winter, they remaining full on the
trees usually till the approach of spring; and being very
bitter are little coveted by birds, except in time of
dearth. I have observed mockbirds and other kinds
of thrushes to feed on them. In Virginia I found one of
these dogwood trees with flowers of a rose color, which
was luckily blown down, and many of its branches had
taken root, which I transplanted into a garden. That
with the white flower Mr. Fairchild has in his garden.

Editor's Note / Northern Mockingbird
(*Mimus polyglottos*)

The mockingbird was in colonial times, as it is now,
one of the best-known North American birds. Lawson
was very familiar with the "mocking-bird." "They sing
with the greatest diversity of notes, that it is possible for
a bird to change to. They may be bred up, and will sing

with us tame in cages.... They often sit upon our chimneys in summer, ... and sing the whole evening and most part of the night" (1709, 147). Perhaps one tradition from colonial times that has not carried over is the hobby of caging these birds. Alexander Wilson told of the domesticated mockingbird: "In his domesticated state, when he commences his career of song, it is impossible to stand by uninterested. He whistles for the dog; Caesar starts up, wags his tail, and runs to meet his master. He squeaks out like a hurt chicken, and the hen hurries about with hanging wings.... The barking of the dog, the mewing of the cat, the creaking of a passing wheelbarrow, follow, with great truth and rapidity" (1828, 2:99). In the wild these birds can imitate twenty or thirty species of birds. Mockingbirds are also known for their fierce territoriality; they will chase all other birds from their territory both during the summer and winter months. They build a nest in trees about five to twelve feet above the ground and place three to five eggs in it. Their diet includes a large variety of insects as well as berries, especially during the winter months.

Catesby's "mockbird" is pictured with the flowering dogwood (*Cornus florida*). Catesby painted the pink form of the dogwood (forma *rubra*), of which he was quite fond.

PLATE 78

The Fox Coloured Thrush (28)

This is somewhat larger than the mockbird, and of a more clumsy shape. Its bill somewhat long, and a little hooked. The eyes yellow. All the upper part of its body of a muddy red, or fox color, except the interior vanes of the quill feathers which are dark brown, and the ends of the covert wing feathers which are edged with dusky white. Its tail is very long, and of the same color of the back and wings. The neck, breast, and all the under part of the body, of a dusky white, spotted with dark brown. The legs and feet are brown. This bird is called in Virginia the French mockbird. It remains all the year in Carolina and Virginia. It sings with some variety of notes, though not comparable to the mockbird.

The Clustered Black Cherry
(wild cherry)

This tree, in the manner of its growing, resembles much our common black cherry, in the thick woods of Carolina, where these trees most abound. They seldom grow bigger than a man's leg; but by being removed to more open places, they become large, some of them being two feet in diameter. In March it produces pendulous bunches of white flowers, which are succeeded by small black cherries of a greenish cast, hanging in clusters of five inches long, in the manner of currants. The fruit of some of these trees is sweet and pleasant; others are bitter. They are esteemed for making the best cherry brandy of any other, and also for stocks to graft other cherries upon. They are much coveted by birds, particularly those of the thrush kind.

Editor's Note / Brown Thrasher
(*Toxostoma rufum*)

Placed in the same family as the mockingbird, the brown thrasher is found throughout most of the Carolinas and Virginia, where it is a bird of thickets and brush and is also common in residential areas. Lawson stated, "There is another sort [of mockingbird] called the ground-mocking-bird. She is the same bigness, and of a cinnamon color. This bird sings excellently well, but is not so common amongst us as the former" (1709, 147–48). Lawson's name is quite appropriate, as this species is mainly seen either in thorny bushes low to the ground or walking rapidly on the ground itself. The thrasher's nest, which is usually placed in brambles or bushes near the ground, is an attractive target for the black snake, and the pugnacious adults must often repel such attacks. In fact, Audubon painted the brown thrasher at its nest under attack by a large black snake. Brown thrashers may produce several broods of three to six each year. Their diet consists of fruit and berries and a variety of insects.

During and after colonial times, brown thrashers, like mockingbirds, were kept in cages, for they had a great reputation as songsters. Catesby's "fox coloured thrush" is pictured with the wild cherry (*Prunus virginiana*).

PLATE 79

The Chatterer (46)

It weighs an ounce; and is rather less than a sparrow. The bill black; the mouth and throat large. From the nostrils runs a black list to the back of its head, like velvet, with a line of white on the lower edge, in which stand the eyes. The rest of its head and neck, brown. On its crown is a pyramidal crest of the same color. The breast is brown; the back and covert feathers of the wing somewhat darker; the belly pale yellow. What distinguishes this bird from others, are eight small red patches at the extremities of eight of the smaller wing feathers, of the color and consistence of red sealing wax. When the wing is closed these patches unite, and form a large red spot. The tail is black, except the end which is yellow.

[Sweet Shrub or Sweet Betsy]

This shrub usually grows about eight or ten feet high. The leaves are set opposite to each other. The flowers resemble, in form, those of the star-anemone, composed of many stiff copper-colored petals, enclosing a tuft of short yellow stamina. The flowers are succeeded by a roundish fruit flat at top. The bark is very aromatic, and as odoriferous as cinnamon. These trees grow in the remote and hilly parts of Carolina, but nowhere amongst the inhabitants.

Editor's Note / Cedar Waxwing (*Bombycilla cedrorum*)

Although a nesting species in the northern section of the northern piedmont, the cedar waxwing is a nomadic wanderer throughout most of Virginia and the Carolinas, and it was certainly in this context that Catesby discovered it. These distinctive, sleek, crested, olive brown birds have red, waxlike droplets on the secondaries of the wings, the function of which remains unknown. From September to May flocks of waxwings wander all over their range in search of their food, which consists of a great variety of fruits and berries. Catesby's waxwing is pictured on the sweet shrub or sweet betsy (*Calycanthus floridus*), a plant of the southeastern United States that is normally found on stream banks and hillsides in the piedmont. The association of the waxwing and this plant is most unlikely.

Editor's Note / Red-Eyed Vireo (*Vireo olivaceus*), see p. 90.

PLATE 80

The Finch-creeper (64)

It weighs five penny-weight. The upper mandible of the bill is brown. The under, yellow. The head blue. It hath a white spot over, and another under each eye. The upper part of the back is of a yellowish green. The rest of the upper part of the body, wings, and tail, of a dusky blue, the scapular feathers having some white spots. The throat is yellow. The breast, of a deeper yellow, divided by a dark blue lift. The belly white. Near the breast some feathers are stained with red. The feet are dusky yellow. The feathers of the hen are black and brown. These birds creep about the trunks of large trees; and feed on insects, which they gather from the crevices of the bark. They remain the winter in Carolina.

[Carolina Silverbell or Opossum-wood]

The trunk of this shrub is slender. Sometimes two or three stems rise from the same root to the height usually of ten feet. The leaves are in shape like those of a pear. In February and March, come white flowers, in form of a bell, hanging usually two and three together, on inch-long footstalks, from the sides of the branches. From the middle of the flower shoot forth four stamina, with a stylus extending half an inch beyond them, of a reddish color. These flowers are succeeded by oblong quadrangular seed vessels, pointed at the ends.

Editor's Note / Northern Parula (*Parula americana*)

This warbler is a breeding bird throughout much of southeastern Canada and the eastern United States. In the Carolinas this species arrives by March and is fairly common along the coast, especially in woodlands where Spanish moss is found. Catesby no doubt encountered this species near Charleston, where it is particularly abundant, being the most common summer warbler along the South Carolina coast. Like the yellow-throated warbler, this bird prefers to build its nest in clumps of Spanish moss; five eggs are the normal clutch and several broods are common per year. Catesby's "finch creeper" is illustrated with the Carolina silverbell or opossum-wood (*Halesia tetraptera*). His comment that "they remain in winter" is somewhat questionable, as only a few individuals are known to spend the winter in southeastern South Carolina.

PLATE 81

The Yellow Titmouse (63)

It is less than a wren. It appears all yellow; but, on a near view, is as follows. The bill is slender. The head, breast, and belly are bright yellow. The back is of a greenish yellow. The tail brown, with a mixture of yellow. The hen is not of so bright a yellow as the cock. It breeds in Carolina, but retires at the approach of winter.

Carolinas it is primarily a bird of the higher interior regions; birds arrive along the coast during the migration period (April to May) and then retire to the inland regions. The nest of the yellow warbler is a typical warbler cup nest placed in a bush or small tree; four or five eggs is the normal clutch. Catesby's yellow titmouse is illustrated with the red bay (*Persea borbonia*).

The Red Bay

The leaves of this tree are in shape like those of the common bay, and of an aromatic scent. The berries, when ripe, are blue, growing two, and sometimes three together, on footstalks of two or three inches long, of a red color, as is the calyx or cup of the fruit, and indented about the edges. These trees are not common in Virginia, except in some places near the sea. In Carolina they are everywhere seen, particularly in low swampy lands. In general, they arrive to the size of but small trees and shrubs; though in some islands, and particular places near the sea, they grow to large and straight-bodied trees. The wood is fine-grained, and of excellent use for cabinets, etc. I have seen some of the best of this wood selected, that has resembled watered satin; and has exceeded in beauty any other kind of wood I ever saw.

Editor's Note / Yellow Warbler (*Dendroica petechia*)

This species has the most yellow color of all the warblers. The yellow warbler breeds over much of the United States, but is generally absent in the lower southeastern states as a breeder. In Virginia and the

PLATE 82

The Yellow-rump (58)

This is a creeper, and seems to be of the tit-kind. The most distinguished part of this bird is its rump, which is yellow. All the rest of the feathers are brown, having a faint tincture of green. It runs about the bodies of trees, and feeds on insects, which it pecks from the crevice of the bark. The hen differs little from the cock in the color of its feathers. They are found in Virginia.

The Lilly-leaf'd Hellebore
(rosebud orchid)

This plant has a bulbous root, from which arises a single stem of about a foot high, encompassed by the bottom part of one leaf as by a sheath. At the top grows the flower, composed of six petals; three of them long, and of a dark purple color; the other three shorter, of a pale rose color, and commonly turning back, with a pistillum in the middle. It grows in wet places.

Dogs-bane
(devil's potato-root or rubber vine)

This plant climbs upon and is supported by shrubs and trees near it. Its leaves grow opposite to each other, on footstalks less than an inch long. The flowers grow usually four or five in a cluster, are white, and consist of five petals, succeeded by long cylindrical pods, growing by pairs, containing many flat seeds not unlike the rest of the Apocynums. It grows on most of the Bahama Islands.

Editor's Note / Yellow-rumped Warbler
(*Dendroica coronata*)

This bird, called by Catesby the yellow rump, was considered by W. L. McAtee (1957) to be unidentifiable; however, there can be little doubt that this plate was intended to represent the very common migrant and winter resident of the Atlantic states, the yellow-rumped warbler or myrtle warbler. These birds are a conspicuous part of the winter avifauna, from October to May, actively feeding in the trees on small insects and also on small berries, especially the waxmyrtle and bayberry. Like tiny flycatchers, they also dart out for flying insects. Yellow-rumped warblers often frequent residential areas and are a common bird at winter feeders. By the middle of May they depart for their breeding grounds in Canada and the northeastern United States.

This is one of Catesby's most unusual plates; the dead yellow-rump hangs from the rosebud orchid (*Cleistes divaricata*) by a thread attached to its foot. Even without the absurd pose, this is a most unlikely association of bird and plant. The plant blooms in May and June. At the bottom of the plate is shown the devil's potato-root or rubber vine (*Echites umbellata*) of the Bahama Islands.

PLATE 83

The Yellow-throated Creeper (62)

Weighs seven penny-weight. The bill is black. The fore part of the head black, having two yellow spots on each side, next the upper mandible. The throat is of a bright yellow, bordered on each side with a black list. The back and hind part of the head are gray. The wings are of a darker gray, inclining to brown, with some of their covert feathers edged with white. The under part of the body white, with black spots on each side, next the wings. The tail black and white. The feet are brown; and, like those of the Certhia, have very long claws, which assist them in creeping about trees in search of insects, on which they feed. There is neither black nor yellow upon the hen. They are frequent in Carolina.

The Red Flowering Maple
(red maple)

These trees grow to a considerable height; but their trunks are not often very large. In February, before the leaves appear, the little red blossoms open, and continue in flower about three weeks; and are then succeeded by the keys, which are also red, and, with the flowers, continue about six weeks, adorning the woods earlier than any other forest trees in Carolina. They endure our English climate as well as they do their native one; as appears by many large ones in the garden of Mr. Bacon at Hoxton.

Editor's Note / Yellow-throated Warbler
(*Dendroica dominica*)

The yellow-throated warbler is a summer bird of the eastern and central United States; it winters from the southern United States (including southeastern South Carolina) south to Costa Rica. Common breeding birds along the coastal plain of Carolina and Virginia, these warblers begin to arrive in March and continue arriving into April. They frequent cypress swamps, residential area, and even old plantations where oak groves and tall pines predominate. The residential areas of Charleston have a large population of this warbler.

In the low country of the coastal plain of South Carolina this species is associated with, perhaps more than anything, Spanish moss, which serves as a nesting site. The birds usually place their nests, composed of grass fibers, woods, and bark, woven with cobwebs or caterpillar silk, in a large clump of moss at heights from near the ground to over fifty feet or higher. Elsewhere, the yellow-throated warbler nests in pines. Catesby's yellow-throated creeper is illustrated with the red maple (*Acer rubrum*).

PLATE 8 4

The Pine-creeper (61)

Weighs eight penny-weight and five grains. The bill is black. The upper part of the body, from the bill to the tail, of a yellowish green. The neck and breast yellow. The belly near the tail, white. The wings brown, with some spots of white. The tail brown; except the two outermost feathers, which are half white. The legs are dusky black. The hen is all over brown. They creep about trees, particularly pine and fir trees; from which they peck insects and feed on them. These, with most of the other creepers and titmice, associate together in small flights, and are mostly seen on leafless trees in winter.

The Purple-berried Bay
(devilwood or "wild-olive")

This tree grows usually sixteen feet high, and the trunk is from six to eight inches in diameter. The leaves are very smooth, and of a brighter green than the common bay tree; otherwise, in shape and manner of growing, it resembles it. In March, from between the leaves, shoot forth spikes, two or three inches in length, consisting of tetrapetalous very small white flowers, growing opposite to each other on footstalks half an inch long. The fruit, which succeeds, are globular berries, about the size of those of the bay, and covered with a purple-colored skin, enclosing a kernel, which divides in the middle.

Editor's Note / Pine Warbler
(*Dendroica pinus*)

Throughout the southern Atlantic states the pine warbler is generally a resident species in pine woods and pine barrens. In South Carolina it is generally found throughout the state where such habitats exist, but further north it becomes more a bird of the piedmont and mountain regions. An influx of winter migrants usually greatly increases the population during the winter months.

This beautiful little warbler is the only one with bright yellow below that is commonly seen foraging for insects in and about pine trees. Pine warblers nest from March through June, raising as many as three broods. The nests are placed thirty to fifty feet up in pine trees, and four or five eggs are the normal clutch. Catesby's pine creeper is illustrated with the devilwood or "wild-olive" (*Osmanthus americanus*), an evergreen shrub that occurs from southeastern Virginia to central Florida. It was named "devilwood" for its wood, which is very hard to split; the fruit resembles the normal cultivated olive, and the plant is in the same family. This plant would have been a most unusual place to find the pine warbler.

PLATE 85

The Red-start (67)

This bird is about the size of, or rather less than, our red-start; and has a slender black bill. The head, neck, back, and wings, are black; except, that five or six of the exterior vanes of the larger wing feathers are partly red. The breast is red; but divided by a gray list; of which color is the belly. The tail is red, except the end, which is black. The legs and feet are black. The hens are brown.

These birds frequent the shady woods of Virginia; and are seen only in summer.

The Black Walnut

Most parts of the northern continent of America, abound with these trees, particularly Virginia and Maryland, towards the heads of the rivers, where, in low rich lands, they grow in great plenty, and to a vast size. The leaves are much narrower and sharper pointed than those of our walnut, and not so smooth. The thickness of the inner shell requires a hammer to break it. The outer shell is very thick and rough on the outside. The kernels are very oily and rank tasted; yet, when laid by some months, are eat by Indians, squirrels, etc. It seems to have taken its name from the color of the wood, which approaches nearer to black than any other wood that affords so large timber. Wherefore it is esteemed for making cabinets, tables, etc.

Editor's Note / American Redstart
(*Setophaga ruticilla*)

Catesby apparently encountered the American redstart in Virginia, where it is at present an uncommon summer resident in the region around Williamsburg. The redstart male is easily recognized, as it is our only predominantly black wood warbler, with orange red patches on the wings and tail. It breeds in the eastern United States and Canada and winters from Mexico to South America. Redstarts are migrants only through most of the coastal region of the Carolinas, although they commonly breed inland.

The redstart is the best "flycatcher" of the warbler family, frequently flying out from its perch to catch insects on the wing. During the breeding season these birds frequent wooded bottomland areas, placing their small, cup-shaped nest some ten feet above the ground. Four eggs are normal, and there is but one brood per season. Catesby's "red start" is shown on the black walnut (*Juglans nigra*), a tree prized both then and now for its wood, which is used extensively for furniture and gunstocks.

PLATE 86
The Hooded Titmouse (60)

This is about the size of a goldfinch. The bill is black. A broad black list encompasses the neck and hind part of the head; resembling a hood; except which, the fore part of the head and all the under part of the body are yellow. The back, wings and tail are of a dirty green. They frequent thickets and shady places in the uninhabited parts of Carolina.

The Water-tupelo

This tree has a large trunk, especially near the ground, and grows very tall. The leaves are broad, irregularly

notched or indented. From the sides of the branches shoot forth its flowers, set on footstalks about three inches long, consisting of several small narrow greenish petals, on the top of an oval body, which is the rudiment of the fruit; at the bottom of which its perianthium divides into four. The fruit, when full grown, is in size, shape and color like a small Spanish olive, containing one hard channeled stone. The grain of the wood is white, soft and spongy. The roots are much more so, approaching near to the consistence of cork, and are used in Carolina for the same purposes as cork, to stop gourds and bottles. These trees always grow in wet places, and usually in the shallow parts of rivers and in swamps.

Editor's Note / Hooded Warbler
(*Wilsonia citrina*)

The hooded warbler is a striking bird in its summer attire, with its black hood completely encircling the yellow face and forehead. The female is olive green above and yellow below and lacks the black hood. These birds are fairly common summer residents of the eastern part of the United States, arriving in numbers by April and then departing on their fall migrations beginning in August for their wintering grounds in the West Indies and Central America. Catesby recorded the habitat correctly as "thickets and shady places," usually in moist deciduous woodlands. Like other wood warblers they are insectivorous and build a small cup nest placed low in shrubs. Catesby's hooded titmouse is illustrated with the water tupelo (*Nyssa aquatica*), a large aquatic tree with a swollen base, which ranges from southeastern Virginia south to northern Florida and west to Texas. Tupelo is a Creek Indian word meaning "swamp tree."

PLATE 87

The Yellow Brested Chat (50)

This is about the size of our sky-lark; the bill black; the head and all the upper part of the back and wings, of a brownish green; the neck and breast yellow. A white streak reaches from the nostrils over the eye; under which is also a white spot. From the lower mandible of the bill, runs a narrow white line. The belly is dusky white; the tail brown; the legs and feet are black. This bird I never saw in the inhabited parts. They frequent the upper parts of the country, 200 and 300 miles distant from the sea. They are very shy birds, and hide themselves so obscurely that after many hours attempt to shoot one, I was at last necessitated to employ an Indian, who did it not without the utmost of his skill. They frequent the banks of great rivers; and their loud chattering noise reverberates from the hollow rocks and deep cane swamps. The figure represents the singular manner of their flying with their legs extended.

[Trillium; Wake Robin]

This plant rises, with a single straight stalk, five or six inches high; from the top of which, spreads forth three broad pointed leaves, placed triangularly, and hanging down. These leaves have each three ribs, and are variegated with dark and lighter green. From between these leaves shoots forth the flower, consisting of three purple petals growing erect; having its perianthium divided in three.

They grow in shady thickets in most parts of Carolina.

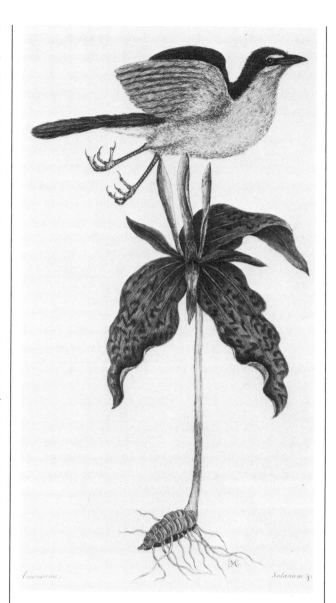

Editor's Note / Yellow-breasted Chat (*Icteria virens*)

Largest of the New World warbler assemblage, the chat is a beautiful yellow-breasted bird, olive green above with a white eye line and white belly. The yellow-breasted chat is a summer resident throughout the eastern United States, but in the Carolinas and Virginia it is encountered most commonly in the low mountains and piedmont, diminishing in numbers toward the coastal plain. Chats arrive from their Central American wintering grounds by mid-April and remain until September.

These are strictly birds of the "brier patch," occurring almost exclusively in old fields grown up in thickets and briers. Although somewhat shy, the chat, as the name implies, is a very noisy bird, with a great reper-toire of whistles and often unbirdlike calls and clucks. It places its nest among briers or even blackberries, and three or four eggs are the normal clutch.

Chats are perhaps best known for their singing courtship flights. The bird flies straight upward with legs dangling, head up, and wings beating, flapping sporadically. Upon reaching the apex of its flight, it utters a series of whistles and other noises and then drops back to its perch. Catesby's bird was no doubt intended to convey some of this drama. It is shown with the wake robin or trillium (*Trillium maculatum*).

Liber Jasmuni floribus

Parus Bahamensis
The Bahama Titmouse.

PLATE 88

The Bahama Titmouse (59)

The bill of this bird is black, and a little bending; the upper part of the head, back and wings is brown. A white line runs from the bill over the eyes to the back

of the head. The breast is yellow, as are the shoulders of the wings. The tail is somewhat long, having the upper part brown, and the under dusky white.

The Seven Years Apple

This shrub grows from six to ten feet high, with a stem seldom bigger than one's wrist, having a wrinkled light-colored bark. The leaves grow in clusters, and are about the bigness of those of our common laurel, hav-ing a wide notch or indenture at the end, which is broadest. These leaves are very thick and stiff; and usually curl up as the figure represents. The flowers grow in bunches; are monopetalous; and in form and size resemble our common jessamine; white in color, with a faint tincture of red. The fruit hangs by a foot-stalk of an inch long, of an oval form, the outside being shaded with green, red, and yellow. When ripe, it is of the consistence of a mellow pear, containing a pulpy matter, in color, substance and taste not unlike the *Cassia fistula*. For nine months I observed a continual succession of flowers and fruit, which ripens in seven or eight months. I know not for what reason the inhabi-tants of the Bahama Islands (where it grows) call it the Seven Years Apple.

Editor's Note / Bananaquit (*Coereba flaveola*)

The bananaquit, or banana bird, is a common species throughout the Bahama Islands and the entire West Indies, as well as much of Central and South America. In fact, it is probably the most common year-round resident in the Bahamas. They are often encountered in settled areas, where they frequent the flowering shrubs of gardens, such as the bougainvillea and hibis-cus. They are also easily attracted to hummingbird feeders. Bananaquits are active foragers, gleaning and probing flowers for nectar and often hanging upside down in their quest for food, which also consists of small insects and fruit. Catesby's Bahama titmouse is shown on the seven-year apple (*Casasia clusiifolia*).

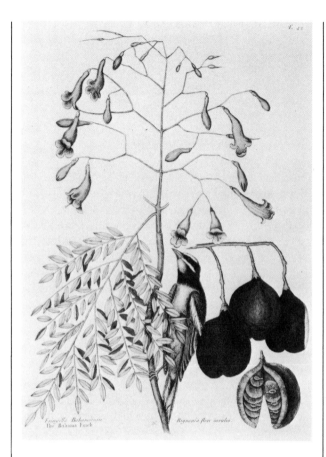

PLATE 89

The Bahama Finch (42)

It weighs fourteen penny-weight. The head is black; except a white line which runs from the bill over the eye, and another under the eye. The throat is black, except a yellow spot, close under the bill. The breast is orange colored; the belly white; the upper part of the neck and the rump, of a dusky red; the back black; the wings and tail brown, with a mixture of white; the legs and feet, lead color. These birds are frequent on many of the Bahama Islands.

The Broad Leafed Guaicum, with Blue Flowers
(boxwood or cancer tree)

This is a tree of a middle-size. The leaves are winged, with many small pointed alternate lobes. In May there proceeds from the ends of its branches several spread-ing footstalks bearing blue flowers, in form not un-like those of the fox-glove, which are succeeded by large flat roundish seed vessels, or pods, commonly two inches over, containing many small flat winged seeds. This tree grows on several of the Bahama Islands, particularly near the town of Nassau on the island of Providence.

Editor's Note / Stripe-headed Tanager (*Spindalis zena*)

This striking tanager of the Bahama Islands and Greater Antilles is easily recognized by its black head with two white stripes and yellow-orange underparts. This species also occurs on Cozumel Island and is a vagrant to Florida from the Bahamas. Stripe-headed tanagers are commonly seen at all seasons in dense bush and also in gardens, where berry bushes provide feeding stations. Catesby's tanager is shown in the box-wood or cancer tree (*Jacaranda caerulea*).

PLATE 90

The Summer Red-bird (56)

This is about the size of a sparrow. It has large black eyes. The bill thick and clumsy, and of a yellowish cast. The whole bird is of a bright red, except the interior vanes of the wing feathers, which are brown, but ap-pear not unless the wings are spread. They are birds of passage, leaving Virginia and Carolina in winter. The hen is brown with a tincture of yellow.

The Western Plane-tree
(sycamore)

This tree usually grows very large and tall. Its leaves are broad, of a light green, and somewhat downy on the backside. Its seed vessels are globular, hanging single and pendant on footstalks of about four or five inches long; the fruit in the texture of it, resembling that of the *Platanus orientalis*. The bark is smooth and usually so variegated with white and green, that they have a fine effect amongst the other trees. In Virginia they are plentifully found in all the lower parts of the country;

and yellow below. The cup-shaped nest is built far out on a horizontal limb usually about twenty feet up, and four eggs are the normal clutch. Catesby's summer redbird is shown in a sycamore (*Platanus occidentalis*).

PLATE 91

The Red Bird (38)

In bigness it equals if not exceeds the sky-lark. The bill is of a pale red, very thick and strong. A black list encompasses the base of it. The head is adorned with a towering crest, which it raises and falls at pleasure. Except the black round the base of the bill, the whole bird is scarlet, though the back and tail have least luster, being darker and of a more cloudy red.

The hen is brown; yet has a tincture of red on her wings, bill and other parts. They often sing in cages as well as the cocks. These birds are common in all parts of America, from New England to the Capes of Florida, and probably much more south. They are seldom seen above three of four together. They have a very great strength with their bill, with which they will

but in Carolina there are but few, except on the hilly parts, particularly on the banks of Savanna River.

Editor's Note / Summer Tanager
(*Piranga rubra*)

The summer tanager, or "summer redbird," is a common summer resident from the central and southern United States to northern Mexico. It arrives in the eastern part of its summer range in mid-April and migrates back south to its wintering grounds, from Mexico to Brazil, beginning in October. These brightly colored birds are a conspicuous part of the summer bird fauna throughout the southern Atlantic states, occurring in open woodlands and wooded residential areas. They move from tree to tree in pursuit of insects, which form the major part of their diet, although they also eat some berries. They have a well-known fondness for bees and wasps, particularly honey bees, and have been known to devastate apiaries. Alexander Wilson recorded that "in several instances I have found the stomach entirely filled with the broken remains of humble bees" (1828, 2:216).

The male of this species is the only summer redbird in the region without a crest; the female is olive above break the hardest grain of maize with much facility. It is a hardy and familiar bird. They are frequently brought from Virginia and other parts of North America for their beauty and agreeable singing, they having some notes not unlike our nightingale, which in England seems to have caused its name of the Virginia-nightingale, though in those countries they call it the red-bird.

The Hickory Tree

This is usually a tall tree, and often grows to a large bulk, the body being from two to three feet in diameter. The leaves are serrated, narrower and sharper pointed than the walnut, but in manner of growing on footstalks, like it. The nuts are enclosed in like manner with the walnut, with an outer and inner shell. In October, at which time they are ripe, the outer shell opens and divides in quarters, disclosing the nut, the shell of which is thick, not easily broken but with a hammer. The kernel is sweet and well tasted, from which the Indians draw a wholesome and pleasant oil, storing them up for their winter provisions. The hogs and many wild animals receive great benefit from them. The wood is course grained; yet of much use for many things belonging to agriculture. Of the saplings or young trees are made the best hoops for tobacco, rice and tar barrels. And for the fire no wood in the northern parts of America is in so much request. The bark is deeply furrowed.

The Pignut

The branches of this tree spread more, are smaller, and the leaves not so broad as the hickory; nor is the bark so wrinkled. The nuts are not above one fourth part so big as those of the hickory, having both the inner and outer shell very thin; so that they may easily be broken with one's fingers. The kernels are sweet; but being small, and covered with a very bitter skin, makes them useless, except for squirrels and other wild creatures.

Another walnut remains to be observed, which I never saw but in Virginia and is there called the white walnut. The tree is usually small; the bark and grain of the wood very white; the nut is about the size or rather less than the black walnut, of an oval form, the outermost shell being rough.

Editor's Note / Northern Cardinal (*Cardinalis cardinalis*)

Catesby's red bird, our cardinal, is one of the best known of North American birds, ranging as a resident species throughout most of the United States (except the western states) and south through parts of Mexico to Belize. Lawson told us that "the red-birds (whose cock is all over of a rich scarlet feather, with a tufted crown on his head, of the same color) are the bigness of a bunting-lark, and very hardy, having a strong thick bill. They will sing very prettily, when taken old, and put in a cage. They are good birds to turn a cage with bells; or if taught, as the bulfinch is, I believe, would prove very docible" (1709, 148). Cardinals were often kept as cage birds in colonial times; Alexander Wilson stated, "This is one of our most common cage birds . . . numbers of them having been carried over both to France and England, in which last country they are usually called Virginia nightingales" (1828, 2:145). Catesby's red bird is pictured in a hickory tree (*Carya alba*), but the smaller fruit is that of the pignut (*Carya cordiformis*).

PLATE 92

The Blew Gross-beak (39)

A narrow black list encompasses the base of the bill and joins to the eyes; the head and whole body, except the tail and part of the wings, of a deep blue. Below the shoulder of the wing are a few red feathers; the lower part of the wing and tail brown, with a mixture of green. The legs and feet are of a dusky black.

The hen is all over dark brown, with a very small mixture of blue. It is a very uncommon and solitary bird, seen only in pairs. They have one single note only, and appear not in winter. I have not seen any of these birds in any parts of America but Carolina.

The Sweet Flowering Bay (sweet bay or swamp magnolia)

This is a small tree, usually growing sixteen foot high; the wood white and spongy, covered with a white bark. The leaves are in shape like those of the common bay,

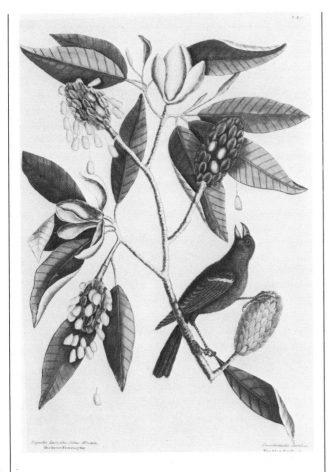

but of a pale green, having their back-sides white. In May they begin to blossom, continuing most part of the summer to perfume the woods with their fragrant flowers, which are white, made up of six petals, having a rough conic stylus, or rudiment of the fruit; which, when the petals fall, increases to the bigness and shape of a large walnut, thick set with knobs or risings; from every of which, when the fruit is ripe, is discharged flat seeds of the bigness of French beans, having a kernel within a thin shell, covered with a red skin. These red seeds, when discharged from their cells, fall not to the ground, but are supported by small white threads of about two inches long. The fruit at first is green; when ripe, red; and when declining, it turns brown. They grow naturally in moist places, and often in shallow water; and what is extraordinary, they being removed on high dry ground, become more regular and handsomer trees, and are more prolific of flowers and fruit. They usually lose their leaves in winter, except it be moderate.

This beautiful flowering tree is a native both of Virginia and Carolina, and is growing at Mr. Fairchild's in Hoxton, and at Mr. Collinson's at Peckham, where it has for some years past produced its fragrant blossoms,

requiring no protection from the cold of our severest winters.

Editor's Note / Blue Grosbeak (*Guiraca caerulea*)

The blue grosbeak is a fairly common summer resident of the southern Atlantic states, from Maryland south, although some individuals may be found to the north. This species is not abundant anywhere in its range, but can be found locally in open fields that are grown up in weeds or other similar situations, where they are always in pursuit of insects and weed seeds and wild fruits of various types. Grosbeaks nest in small trees or shrubs and normally lay four eggs. Catesby's blue grosbeak is drawn in a sweet bay or swamp magnolia (*Magnolia virginiana*); however, in some respects the fruit more closely resembles the southern magnolia (*Magnolia grandiflora*).

PLATE 93

The Blew Linnet (45)

This bird is rather less than a goldfinch, weighing eight penny-weight. The whole bird appears, at a little distance, of an entire blue color. But, upon a nearer view, it is as follows: the bill black and lead color. On the crown of the head the blue is most resplendent and deeper than in any other part. The neck, back and belly of a lighter blue. The large wing feathers are brown, edged with blue. The tail is brown, with a tincture of blue. There are none of these birds within the settlements of Carolina; I never have seen any nearer than 150 miles from the sea; their abode being in the hilly parts of the country only. Their notes are somewhat like those of our linnets.

The Spaniards in Mexico call this bird *Azul lexes*, or the far-fetched blue-bird.

[Catesby's Trillium]

This has a tuberous root; from which shoots forth two or three straight stalks, of about eight inches high; on which are set triangularly three ribbed leaves; from

October, where it can be found in bushy clearings and orchards or along the roadsides sitting on a wire. Its primary foods are insects, seeds, and berries. The nest is a small structure of weeds and grasses placed in small bushes or even in weeds; four eggs are the normal clutch. This bunting is shown on what is now called Catesby's trillium (*Trillium catesbaei*), the beautiful pink trillium of the southeastern piedmont. The male indigo bunting is a beautiful deep blue all over, while the female and young are plain brown.

between which proceeds its flower, of a pale red, composed of six spreading leaves, three large and three smaller, with stamina of unequal lengths. The flower is succeeded by its seed vessel, in form and size of a small hazel-nut, but somewhat channeled, and covered by a perianthium, which divides in three, and turns back. The capsule contains innumerable small seeds, like dust. This plant I found at the sources of great rivers; not having seen any in the inhabited parts of Carolina.

Editor's Note / Indigo Bunting (*Passerina cyanea*)

The beautiful indigo bunting is a common summer resident in Virginia and the Carolinas from April to

PLATE 94

The Painted Finch (44)

This weighs nine penny-weight, and is about the bigness of a canary bird. The head and upper part of the neck, of an ultramarine blue. The throat, breast and belly of a bright red; the back green, inclining to yellow. The wings are composed of green, purple and dusky red feathers; the rump red, the tail dusky red, with mixture of purple. Though a particular description may be required, in order to give the more perfect idea of this bird, yet its colors may be comprised in three; the head and neck are blue; the belly red, and the back green. Its notes are soft; but have not much variety. They breed in Carolina, and affect much to make their nests in orange trees. They do not continue there in winter; nor do they frequent the upper parts of the country. I never saw one fifty miles from the sea. Though the cock is so elegant, the hen is as remarkable for her plain color, which is not unlike that of a hen-sparrow, but with a faint tincture of green.

His excellency, Mr. Johnson, the present Governor of South Carolina, kept four or five of these birds (taken from the nest), in cages two years; in all which time the cocks and hens varied so little in color, that it was not easy to distinguish them. I have likewise caught the cock and hen from their nest, and could see little difference, they being both alike brown. How many years it is before they come to their full color, is uncertain. When they are brought into this cold climate, they lose much of their luster, as appeared by some I brought along with me. The Spaniards call this bird *mariposa pintada*, or the painted butterfly.

The Loblolly Bay

This is a tall and very straight tree, with a regular pyramidal-shaped head. Its leaves are shaped like those of the common bay, but serrated. It begins to blossom in May, and continues bringing forth its flowers the greatest part of the summer. The flowers are fixed to footstalks, four or five inches long; are monopetalous, divided into five segments, encompassing a tuft of stamina, headed with yellow apices; which flowers in November are succeeded by a conic capsule having a divided calyx. The capsule when ripe opens and divides into five sections, disclosing many small half-winged seeds. This tree retains its leaves all the year, and grows only in wet places, and usually in water. The wood is somewhat soft; yet I have seen some beautiful tables made of it.

Editor's Note / Painted Bunting
(*Passerina ciris*)

The painted bunting is a fairly common summer resident along the coastal region of the Carolinas, occurring much more rarely inland, and is only a casual visitor to the north. Catesby no doubt encountered this bird in South Carolina; it is common in the region around Charleston. Like most finches, it places its

nest, a cup of grass, leaves, and so forth, in a tree. These birds were often kept as cage birds during colonial times, and later Alexander Wilson gave a good account of this habit in the area of New Orleans: "I found these birds very commonly domesticated in the houses of the French inhabitants of New Orleans; appearing to be the most common cage bird they have. The negros often bring them to market from the neighboring plantations, for sale; either in cages, taken in traps, or in the nest. A wealthy French planter, who lives on the banks of the Mississippi, a few miles below Bayou Fourche, took me into his garden, which is spacious and magnificent to show me his aviary; where, among many of our common birds, I observed several Nonpareils, two of which had nests, and were then hatching" (1828, 2:201). Painted buntings were known to the French as "le pape," and to the Americans as the "nonpareil." Audubon tells of having seen caged painted buntings for sale in Paris and London. Catesby's nonpareil is pictured in the loblolly-bay (*Gordonia lasianthus*), the bark of which was used locally for tanning.

PLATE 95
The Bahama Sparrow (37)

This is about the size of a canary bird. The head, neck, and breast are black. All the other parts of it of a dirty green color. It is the commonest little bird I observed in the woods of the Bahama Islands. It uses to perch on the top of a bush and sing, repeating one set tune in manner of our chaffinch.

Bignonia
(beef-bush or gunwood)

This shrub usually rises to the height of about ten feet. From the largest branches shoots forth long slender stalks, at the end of every of which are five leaves fixed on footstalks an inch long. Its flower is monopetalous, of a rose color, and somewhat bell shaped, though the margin is deeply divided into five or six sections, to which succeed pods of five inches long, hanging in clusters, and containing within them small brown beans.

Editor's Note / Black-faced Grassquit
(*Tiaris bicolor*)

This small sparrowlike bird is found on all of the Bahama Islands and many of the cays and occurs also throughout most of the West Indies. A seed-eater and one of the commonest birds of the Bahamas, it is often seen perched in a small tree or shrub repeating its monotonous buzzing "tik-zeee" over and over. Catesby drew his Bahama sparrow with the beef-bush or gun-wood (*Tabebuia bahamensis*).

PLATE 96

The Little Black Bullfinch (68)

This is about the size of a canary bird. The whole bird is black, except the shoulders of the wings, and part of the vanes of two of the largest wing feathers, which are white. The bill is thick and short, having a notch in the upper mandible like that of a hawk. This bird is an inhabitant of Mexico; and is called by the Spaniards, *Mariposa nigra*, i.e. black butterfly. Whether this be a cock or hen I know not.

The Fringe Tree
(or "old-man's-beard")

On the banks of rivulets and running streams this shrub is most commonly found. It mounts from six to ten feet high, usually with a crooked irregular small stem. Its leaves are of a light green, and shaped like those of the orange. In May, it produces bunches of white flowers hanging on branched footstalks, of half an inch long. Each flower has four narrow thin petals about two inches long. To these succeed round dark blue berries, of the size of sloes.

Editor's Note / Cuban Bullfinch
(*Melopyrrha nigra*)

Catesby said that this bird was an inhabitant of Mexico, but in reality it is known only from Cuba and the Isle of Pines and Grand Cayman, where it is also known as "negrito." It is a small bird of scrub-covered woodland and is black all over with conspicuous white patches on the wings. Catesby pictured his bird on the fringe tree, or "old-man's-beard" (*Chionanthus virginicus*), a shrub or small tree found in the southeastern United States.

PLATE 97

The Purple Gross-beak (40)

This bird is of the size of a sparrow. Over the eyes, the throat, and at the vent under the tail, are spots of red. All the rest of the body is entirely of a deep purple color.

The hen is all over brown, but has the like red spots as the cock. These birds are natives of many of the Bahama Islands.

The Poison-wood

This is generally but a small tree; and has a light-colored smooth bark. Its leaves are winged, the middle rib seven or eight inches long, with pairs of pinnae one against another on inch-long footstalks. The fruits hang in bunches; are shaped like a pear, of a purple color, covering an oblong hard stone.

From the trunk of this tree distils a liquid black as ink, which the inhabitants say is poison. Birds feed on the berries, particularly this gross-beak, on the mucilage that covers the stone. It grows usually on rocks in Providence, Ilathera, and other of the Bahama Islands.

Editor's Note / Greater Antillean Bullfinch (*Loxigilla violacea*)

Catesby's "purple gross-beak" is the Antillean bull-finch, a chunky, sparrowlike bird with a large bill, about seven inches in length. These are common birds throughout the Bahama Islands and on Hispaniola and Jamaica, where it is a bird of wooded areas and dense bush. Like the grassquit, it is known by its call, a three-note "wichi" followed by a buzzing "scree." Also known in the Bahamas as "Red Spaniard," the males are jet black with red patches above the eyes and on the chin and undertail feathers. Catesby's bird is pictured perched in poison-wood (*Metopium toxiferum*). See the account of the white-crowned pigeon, Plate 42, for more information on the poison-wood.

PLATE 98

The Towhe-bird (34)

This bird is about the size of, or rather bigger than a lark. The bill black and thick; the iris of the eye red;

the head, neck, breast, back, and tail, black; as are the wings, with the larger quill feathers edged with white. The lower part of the breast and belly white; which, on each side, is of a muddy red, extending along its wings. The legs and feet are brown.

The hen is brown, with a tincture of red on her breast. It is a solitary bird; and one seldom sees them but in pairs. They breed and abide all the year in Carolina in the shadiest woods.

The Cowpen Bird (34)

This bird is entirely brown, the back being darkest, and the breast and belly the lightest part of it. In winter they associate with the red-winged starling and purple Jackdaw in flights. They delight much to feed in the pens of cattle, which has given them their name. Not having seen any of them in summer, I believe they are birds of passage. They inhabit Virginia and Carolina.

The Black Poplar of Carolina
(swamp cottonwood or downy poplar)

This tree grows only near rivers, above the inhabited parts of Carolina. They are large and very tall. In April, at which time only I saw them, they had dropped their seeds; which, by the remains, I could only perceive to hang in clusters, with a cotton-like consistence covering them. Upon the large swelling buds of this tree sticks a very odoriferous balsam. The leaves are indented about the edges, and very broad, resembling in shape the black poplar, described by Parkinson.

Editor's Note / Rufous-sided Towhee
(*Pipilo erythrophthalmus*)

The towhee is also commonly known as "joree"; both names are allusions to its call, which it frequently utters from the thickets and underbrush that form its normal habitation. This common permanent resident of Virginia and the Carolinas is certainly one of our more attractive birds; the males is predominantly black with a white breast and beautiful rufous sides; the female is similar but with brown replacing the black. These finches feed on the ground, scratching with both feet to

get to seeds and insects of various kinds. Likewise, they nest on or near the ground, building a small, cup-shaped nest where they deposit two to five eggs. Alexander Wilson commented, "He shows great affection for his young; and the deepest marks of distress on the appearance of their mortal enemy the black snake" (1828, 2:166).

Editor's Note / Brown-headed Cowbird
(*Molothrus ater*)

It is unfortunate that Catesby's name "cowpen bird" has not endured, as it most appropriately describes these birds, who are so often seen feeding in cowpens about the feet of cattle. Common residents of the Atlantic states, both as migrants and summer residents, they are often seen in mixed flocks with blackbirds and grackles. Cowbirds feed on seeds and grain of all kinds as well as insects. They build no nest at all, but are parasitic, laying their eggs in the nests of songbirds such as the towhee and wood thrush. The female cowbird removes an egg from the hosts' nest and then lays her own; the large, aggressive cowbird chick almost always survives at the expense of one or more of the hosts' young. Catesby's cowbird is a female, the male of the species is greenish black with a brown head. Both towhee and cowpen bird are illustrated in a swamp cottonwood, or downy poplar (*Populus heterophylla*).

PLATE 99
The Snow-bird (36)

The bill of this bird is white. The breast and belly are white. All the rest of the body black; but in some places dusky, inclining to lead color. In Virginia and Carolina they appear only in winter; and in snow they appear most. In summer none are seen. Whether they retire and breed in the North (which is most probable) or where they go, when they leave these countries in the spring, is to me unknown.

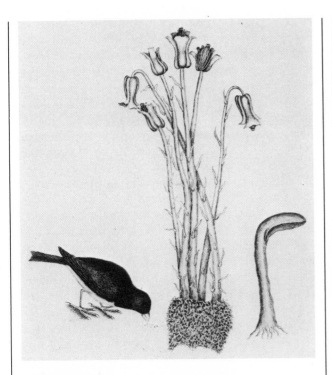

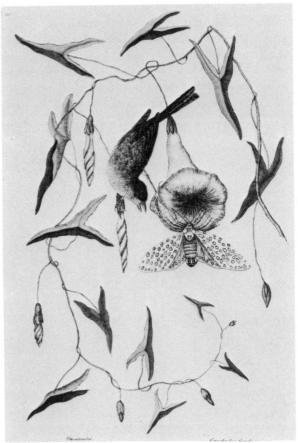

Broom-rape
(Indian pipe)

This plant rises to the height of eight or ten inches; is of a flesh color; the stalks thinly beset with small narrow sharp-pointed leaves. The flowers are monopetalous, but deeply furrowed from the stalk to the top of the flower, where it divides into several sections. Within the flower is an oval chanulated capsule, of the size of a hazel-nut, containing very small seeds like dust. This capsule is surrounded with many yellow stamina.

Editor's Note / Dark-eyed Junco
(*Junco hyemalis*)

Catesby's name for this species, "snow bird," is very descriptive of this winter resident of the Atlantic states. These are birds of the winter and snow and are one of the most abundant species during that period. They are almost always seen in scattered flocks on the ground, scratching for seeds, or in low-lying bushes. The dark-eyed junco is one of the most common birds at feeders during the winter months. They arrive in October and leave in April, and so Catesby's plate of the "snow bird" and the Indian pipe (*Monotropa uniflora*) in bloom is surely contrived.

PLATE 100

The Little Sparrow (35)

This bird is entirely of a brown color; less than our hedge-sparrow, but partaking much of the nature of it. They are not numerous, being usually seen single, hopping under bushes. They feed on insects, and are seen most common near houses in Virginia and Carolina, where they breed and abide the whole year.

The Purple Bind-weed of Carolina
(glades morning glory)

The flower of this convolvulus is of a reddish purple, and of the size and shape of common white bind-weed. They blow in June. The leaves are shaped like the head of an arrow. Col. Moore, a gentleman of good reputation in Carolina, told me, that he has seen an Indian daub himself with the juice of this plant; immediately after which, he handled a rattlesnake with his naked hands without receiving any harm from it, though thought to be the most venomous of the snake-kind. And I have heard several others affirm, that they have seen the Indians use a plant to guard themselves against the venom of this sort of snake; but they were not observers nice enough to inform me what kind it was of.

Editor's Note / Little Sparrow

Catesby's little sparrow is not identifiable. It is illustrated with the glades morning glory (*Ipomoea sagittata*).

PLATE 101

The Rice-bird (14)

In the beginning of September, while the grain of rice is yet soft and milky, innumerable flights of these birds arrive from some remote parts, to the great detriment of the inhabitants. *Anno* 1724, an inhabitant, near Ashley river, had forty acres of rice so devoured by them, that he was in doubt, whether what they had left, was worth the expense of gathering in.

They are esteemed in Carolina the greatest delicacy of all other birds. When they first arrive, they are lean; but, in few days, become so excessive fat, that they fly sluggishly, and with difficulty; and when shot, frequently break with the fall. They continue about three weeks, and retire by that time rice begins to harden.

There is somewhat so singular and extraordinary in this bird, that I cannot pass it over without notice. In September, when they arrive in infinite swarms, to devour the rice, they are all hens, not being accompanied with any cock. Observing them to be all feathered alike, I imagined they were young of both sexes, not perfected in their colors; but by opening some scores prepared for the spit, I found them to be all females. And that I might leave no room for doubt, I repeated the search often on many of them, but could never find a cock at that time of the year.

Early in the spring, both cocks and hens make a transient visit together. At which time I made the like search as before, and both sexes were plainly distinguishable. The hen, which is properly the rice-bird, is about the bigness of a lark, and colored not unlike it on the back; the breast and belly pale yellow; the bill strong and sharp pointed, and shaped like most others of the granivorous kind. This seems to be the bird described by the name of maia, Will. App. p. 386. In September, 1725, lying upon the deck of a sloop in a bay at Andros Island, I and the company with me, heard, three nights successively, flights of these birds (their note being plainly distinguishable from others) passing over our heads northerly, which is their direct way from Cuba to Carolina. From whence I conceive, after partaking of the earlier crop of rice at Cuba, they travel over sea to Carolina for the same intent, the rice there being at that time fit for them.

The cock's bill is lead color; the fore part of the head black; the hind part and the neck, or a reddish yellow; the upper part of the wing white; the back, next the head, black; lower down, gray; the rump white; the greatest part of the wing, and whole tail, black; the legs and feet brown in both sexes.

Editor's Note / Bobolink
(*Dolichonyx oryzivorus*)

Also known as the ricebird or reedbird, the bobolink passes in great numbers through the Atlantic states to and from its breeding grounds in the southern part of Canada to its wintering grounds in southern South America. During the migrations these small, distinctive members of the blackbird family may cause tremendous destruction to crops, particularly rice. During the spring the males are striking in appearance, solid black below and largely white above, with the nape a rich buff color. The female is a dull buff with dark striping on the back and crown. During the spring migration the males arrive several weeks before the females, often in company with other blackbirds. During the return migration, when bobolinks are at their most destructive, the males have lost their brightly colored plumage and closely resemble immature females. Catesby was mistaken in believing that all of the fall birds were female. He had apparently dissected some for eating, but, by pure chance, had found only females.

For a long period the bobolink caused tremendous problems for planters from about the region of the Cape Fear River south through southern Georgia, where rice was cultivated on a large scale. During the migration entire farm families would take to the rice fields and remain from sunrise to sunset, firing shots into the air every few minutes to keep the crop from being destroyed.

Catesby had also encountered the ricebird in his journey to the Bahamas. He gave an account of "lying upon the deck of a sloop at Andros Island" (Sept., 1725) and for three nights listening to the sounds of the ricebirds passing overhead. Catesby's bobolinks are drawn on their favorite plant, rice (*Oryza sativa*).

PLATE 102

The Red Wing'd Starling (13)

A cock weighs between three and four ounces; in shape and size resembling our starling. The whole bird (except the upper part of the wings) is black; and would have little beauty, were it not for the shoulders of the wings, which are bright scarlet. This and the purple-daw are of the same genus; and are most voracious corn-eaters. They seem combined to do all the mis-

chief they are able; and to make themselves most formidable, both kinds unite in one flock, and are always together, except in breeding time; committing their devastations all over the country. When they are shot, there usually falls of both kinds; and before one can load again, there will be in the same place oft-times more than before they were shot at. They are the boldest and most destructive birds in the country.

This seems to be the bird Hernandez calls acolchici, *Will. Orn.* p. 391. They make their nests, in Carolina and Virginia, not on trees, but always over the water, amongst reeds or sedge; the tops of which they interweave very artfully, and under fix their nests; and so secure from wet, that where the tides flow, it is observed never to reach them. They are familiar and active birds, and are taught to talk and sing.

The hens are considerably less than the cocks; of a mixed gray; and the red on their wings is not so bright.

The Broad-leaved Candle-berry Myrtle
(broad-leaved bayberry)

This grows usually not above three feet high; in which, and its having a broader leaf than the tall candle-berry myrtle, it principally differs from it.

Editor's Note / Red-winged Blackbird
(*Agelaius phoeniceus*)

The red-winged blackbird is a common permanent resident throughout the Atlantic states, but the population of these birds is greatly augmented during the winter by migrants from the more northern parts of its range. Few birds are more conspicuous during the spring than these jet black birds, as they sing their gurgling notes from a perch and show off their bright red wing patches. The less conspicuous females are a drab brown above and whitish below, streaked all over with brownish black. These birds usually nest in small groups, placing their nests in small bushes in shallow water. The nest is carefully woven of marsh grasses attached to the branches of the bushes or reeds in which they are constructed, and usually four eggs are deposited. Red-wings feed on a variety of foods, especially insects and seeds of various kinds. Weed seeds are a favorite food, but where rice is grown these birds can be enormously destructive to that crop. During the winter months the sexes segregate into separate flocks, often in association with the purple grackle.

Catesby's red-wing is shown displaying on a broad-leaved bayberry (*Myrica pensylvanica*). Lawson's black-birds are very confusing. He stated that they were the "worst vermin in America. They fly sometimes in such flocks, that they destroy everything before them." He went on to say that both forms built nests in hollow trees, which is of course unlike any blackbird. He then told of one having "part of the head, next to the bill, and the pinions of their wings, are of an orange, and glorious crimson color" (1709, 143). We can guess that he had seen the common grackle and red-wing, but had the biology confused, as well as the exact coloring.

PLATE 103

The Large Lark (33)

This bird weighs three ounces and a quarter. The bill is straight, sharp, and somewhat flat towards the end. Between the eye and the nostril is a yellow spot. The crown of the head is brown, with a dusky white list running from the bill along the middle of it. A black list, of about an inch long, extends downwards from the eye. The sides of the head are light gray. The wings and upper part of the body are of a partridge color. The breast has a large black mark, in form of a horse-shoe; except which, the throat and all the under part of the body is yellow. It has a jetting motion with its tail, sitting on the tops of small trees and bushes in the manner of our bunting; and, in the spring, sings musically, though not many notes. They feed mostly on the ground on the seed of grasses. Their flesh is good meat. They inhabit Carolina, Virginia, and most of the northern continent of America.

The Little Yellow Star-flower
(yellow star grass)

This plant grows usually not above five inches in height, producing many grassy leaves, from which rises a slender stalk bearing a yellow starlike pentapetalous flower. It has five stamina, every leaf of the flower having one growing opposite to it. The flower is suc-ceeded by a small long capsule, containing many little

black seeds. This plant grows plentifully in most of the open pasture lands in Carolina and Virginia, where these larks most frequent and feed on the seed of it.

Editor's Note / Eastern Meadowlark (*Sturnella magna*)

The meadowlark is not a lark at all, but a member of the family of blackbirds (Icteridae). Because it fre-quents meadows, fields, and other grasslands it is sometimes know as the "field lark." Lawson's "lark" was surely this species, as he stated, "The lark with us resorts to the savannas, or natural meads, and green marshes. He is colored and heeled as the lark is; but his breast is of a glittering fair lemon color, and he is as big as a fieldfare, and very fine food" (1709, 148). Meadowlarks are primarily insectivorous and consume large quantities of harmful insects. They place their nests on the ground in tufts of grass, and four to six eggs is the normal clutch. Catesby's meadowlark is shown with the yellow star grass (*Hypoxis* sp.), a plant of dry meadows and open woodlands that occurs all along the Atlantic states.

PLATE 104

The Purple Jack Daw (12)

This is not so big by one third part as the common jack-daw, weighing six ounces; the bill black; the eyes gray; the tail long, the middle feathers longest, the rest gradually shorter. At a distance they seem all black, but at a nearer view, they appear purple, particularly the head and neck has most luster.

The hen is all over brown, the wing, back and tail being darkest. They make their nests on the branches of trees in all parts of the country, but most in remote and unfrequented places; from whence in autumn, after a vast increase, they assemble together, and come amongst the inhabitants in such numbers that they sometimes darken the air, and are seen in continued flights for miles together, making great devastation of grain where they light. In winter they flock to barn doors. They have a rank smell; their flesh is coarse, black, and is seldom eaten.

Editor's Note / Common Grackle (*Quiscalus quiscula*)

This well-known "blackbird" is a common permanent resident through the area of Virginia and the Carolinas, where it is often called the purple grackle. It is easily recognized by its beautiful irridescent purple black colors that shine in the sun, especially in courtship display. These birds are quite gregarious, often feeding on grubs with other "blackbirds" in newly plowed fields or descending in flocks on unripened corn to demolish ear after ear. They also feed on fruits and seeds and small aquatic animals of various sorts. Grackles often nest in groups of ten pairs or so and build large bulky nests in trees at various heights; the normal clutch is four to six. During the winter months these birds gather in huge flocks perhaps numbering a million or more birds that roost communally and undertake long daily flights to feeding grounds.

Brown-headed Cowbird (*Molothrus ater*) *see* p. 124.

PLATE 105

The Yellow and Black Pye (appendix, 5)

This is about the size of a blackbird; the irises of the eyes were yellow, surrounded by a bluish skin; the bill was black, and somewhat more than an inch long; the head was black; the throat had long pointed feathers, hanging loosely down; the upper part of the back, black; as were the wings, with a mixture of white; and under the quill feathers, brown; the neck and under part of the body, with the hind part of the back and rump, of a reddish yellow. They are called in Jamaica, bonano birds, that fruit being a part of their food. They are very sprightly and active birds; and are often kept in cages for their docility and antic gestures.

[Spider Lily]

This plant has a bulbous root, from which rises a thick succulent stalk to the height of seven or eight inches; on the top of which grows a cluster of about eight or ten small green bulbs; from every one of which proceeds a monopetalous, tubulous, white flower. The upper part of the tube divides into six narrow petals, enclosing a cup, with its verge divided into twelve sec-

tions, having a stylus, six stamina, with yellow apices. The whole cluster of flowers is enclosed by a perianthium, which divides in two, and discloses the whole bunch, yet remains hanging to the stalk while the flowers continue; the leaves are of a deep shining green, like those of of the *Lilio-Narcissus flore luteo autumnalis minor.*

These plants I saw growing in a bog near Palluchucula, an Indian town on the Savanna river, within the precinct of Georgia.

[Ichneumon Wasp]

This wasp is about three quarters of an inch in length. A pipe or fistula, of a quarter of an inch long, joins the thorax to the abdomen, all which are of a deep blue. It had six legs. The wings were blended with brown and blue, having each a black spot at their ends.

Mr. Collinson, in the *Philos. Trans. of the Royal Society*, N. 476, p. 363. has described and figured two ichneumon wasps, with their nests, from Pennsylvania;

but as the descriptions of the colors in his and mine does not exactly agree, it cannot be absolutely determined, whether his and mine be the same.

This species of wasp form cylindrical pipes of clay, about the bigness, but twice the length of one's little finger; these they fix horizontally under sheds or penthouses, joining eight, ten, or more of them together, side by side; these tubes are divided by several partitions, forming as many cells, in every one of which they lay an egg, and fill up the vacancy with spiders, and close up the cell securely. It is to be observed, that the wasp cripples the spiders, with an intent not only to disable them from crawling away while she is accumulating a sufficient store of them, but also that they continue alive to serve the nymphs with a supply of fresh food, till it enters into its change; in order for which it spins itself a silken case, in which it lies in its chrysalis state all the winter, and in the spring gnaws its way through the clay structure, and takes its flight. They are silent, but in the very action of plastering and forming their fabrics, which, so soon as they set about, they strike up their odd musical notes, and with surprising dexterity and odd gesticulations cheerfully perform the business they are about; and then cease singing, till they return with a fresh mouthful of moist clay; repeating their labor in this manner till the whole is finished.

N.B. The wasp described at the following 13th page [Plate 71], forms also a nest of clay, but of a different structure from this; though the method of working and singing in both differs little or nothing.

These wasps seem not to affect nor to have anything to do with vegetables, for they subsist on insects only; spiders particularly seem to be their principal food; wherefore they mostly frequent outhouses, cellars, etc. where spiders most abound; these they seize and fly away with in their mouths, though some of them are of equal size with themselves.

Editor's Note / Troupial (*Icterus icterus*)

Catesby's "yellow and black pye" is one of the common orioles that occurs from northern South America up through parts of the West Indies, including Jamaica, where it is a bird of semiarid woodlands and also mangrove swamps. In its coloration it somewhat resembles our own Baltimore oriole, but is larger and the pattern of yellow and black is quite different, with a broad orangish yellow collar across the back of the neck. Like orioles of North America, these birds build a pendant, purse-shaped nest. It is not surprising that Catesby selected this bird, as it has been a favorite cage bird in Columbia and Venezuela, and even during Audubon's time was kept in cages in Charleston. It is illustrated with the spider lily (*Hymenocallis caroliniana*) and an ichneumon wasp.

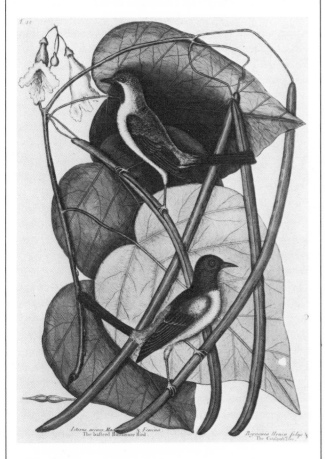

PLATE 106

The Bastard Baltimore (49)

Weighs thirteen penny-weight. The bill is sharp pointed; the throat black; the tail brown; as are its wings, having most of the feathers verged with white. All the rest of the bird is yellow, the breast being brightest.

The hen being as handsomely clothed (though with very different colored feathers) induced me to give the figures of both. Her head and upper part of the back are of a shining black; the breast and belly of a dirty red; as is the lower part of the back and rump. The upper part of the wing red; the lower part dusky black; the tail black; the legs and feet blue in both sexes.

The Catalpa Tree

This is usually a small tree, seldom rising above 20 feet in height; the bark smooth; the wood soft and spongy; the leaves shaped like those of the lilac, but much larger, some being ten inches over. In May it produces spreading bunches of tubulous flowers, like the common fox-glove, white, only variegated with a few reddish purple spots and yellow streaks on the inside. The calyx is of a copper color. These flowers are succeeded by round pods, about the thickness of one's finger, fourteen inches in length; which, when ripe, opens and displays its seeds, which are winged, and lie over each other like the scales of fish. This tree was unknown to the inhabited parts of Carolina till I brought the seeds from the remoter parts of the country. And though the inhabitants are little curious in gardening, yet the uncommon beauty of the tree has induced them to propagate it; and it has become an ornament to many of their gardens, and probably will be the same to ours in England, it being as hardy as most of our American plants; many of them now at Mr. Bacon's at Hoxton, having stood out several winters without any protection except the first year.

Editor's Note / Orchard Oriole
(*Icterus spurius*)

Even as late as the early 1800s there was considerable confusion as to the exact nature of this species. Catesby had given this bird the name "bastard Baltimore bird," surely because its colors could not match that of its fine-feathered cousin. Linnaeus based his species mainly on the bastard Baltimore of Catesby (*Icterus minor*) and, following Catesby, gave it the scientific name *spurius*, which seemed to impart some second-class status. Fortunately the common name has become the perfectly acceptable orchard oriole.

Unlike the Baltimore, the orchard oriole is a summer resident throughout the eastern United States and is one of the common summer birds of Virginia and the Carolinas, particularly in the coastal plain. It is particularly abundant in groves and orchards, where it places a basket-shaped, woven structure of grass in trees usually no more than twenty feet above the ground. Four to six eggs are the normal clutch. Orchard orioles are very beneficial birds, as insects make up about 90 percent of their diet, which also includes some fruits and berries, particularly mulberries.

Much of the confusion concerning this species lies in its variety of plumages. The adult male is black above, with a deep chestnut breast and underparts.

The female and young of the year are a greenish yellow above and yellow below. The first-year male resembles the female, but acquires a black bib, and it is not until the second year that the male acquires his full dress. Catesby apparently confused the sexes, as one can tell from his description. Catesby's bastard Baltimore bird is drawn in the catalpa tree (*Catalpa bignonioides*), a tree also known as the "catawba," or "indian-bean." This tree, a noted shade tree and ornamental with large cigar-shaped seed pods, has been widely introduced across the country, beginning with Catesby's introduction of seeds "from the remoter parts of the country."

PLATE 107

The Baltimore Bird (48)

Is about the size of a sparrow; weighing a little above an ounce. The bill is sharp and tapering; the head and halfway down the back, of a shining black. The wings, except the upper parts (which are yellow) are black, with most of the feathers edged on both sides with white. The rest of the body is of a bright color, between red and yellow. The two uppermost feathers of the tail

are black; the rest yellow. The legs and feet are of a lead color. It disappears in winter. This gold-colored bird I have only seen in Virginia and Maryland; there being none of them in Carolina. It is said to have its name from the Lord Baltimore's Coat of Arms, which are paly of six, topaz and diamond, a bend, coun-rechanged; his Lordship being a proprietor in those countries. It breeds on the branches of tall trees, and usually on the poplar or tulip-tree. Its nest is built in a particular manner, supported only by two twigs fixed to the verge of the nest, and hanging most commonly at the extremity of a bough.

The Tulip Tree
(yellow- or tulip-poplar)

This tree grows to a very large size; some of them being thirty feet in circumference. Its boughs are very unequal and irregular, not straight, but making several bends or elbows; which peculiarly makes this tree distinguishable, at a great distance, from all other trees even when it has lost its leaves. The leaves stand on footstalks, about a finger in length; they somewhat resemble the smaller maple in shape, but are usually five or six inches over, and, instead of being pointed at the end, seem to be cut off with a notch.

The flowers have been always compared to tulips; whence the tree has received its name; though, I think in shape they resemble more the fritillaria. They are composed of seven or eight petals; the upper part being of a pale green, and the lower part shaded with red and a little yellow intermixed. They are at first enclosed by a perianthium, which opens and falls back when the flower blows. These trees are found in most parts of the northern continent of America, from the Cape of Florida to New England. The timber is of great use.

Editor's Note / Northern Oriole
(*Icterus galbula*)

The word *oriole* is from the Latin *aureolus*, meaning yellow or golden; it was first applied to the common golden oriole (*Oriolus oriolus*), which occurs commonly throughout Europe and western Asia. The New World orioles are a group of predominantly tropical birds belonging not to the family of true orioles but to the blackbird family. Only a handful of species live in North America, the most strikingly colored of which is the northern or Baltimore oriole, easily recognized by its black head and wings and golden body. This bird was originally named for its colors, which were those of the coat of arms of Sir George Calvert, the first baron of Baltimore. Lawson commented that "the Baltimore-bird, so called from the Lord Baltimore, Proprietor of all Maryland, in which province many of them are found. They are the bigness of a linnet, with yellow wings, and beautiful in other colors" (1709, 149).

Although Catesby claimed only to have seen the bird in Virginia and Maryland, the Baltimore oriole is also known as a migrant and winter visitor in the Carolinas, and some breed in the mountains of western North Carolina. The Baltimore oriole feeds primarily on various insects and caterpillars and small fruits and berries.

These birds are also noted for their nest, a pendant, purse-shaped structure that is miraculously woven from fibers of various materials and placed in a fork or long limb of a tree. Persons who have a Baltimore oriole nesting in their yards often place old pieces of yarn out for the orioles to use in nest construction. Catesby's Baltimore bird is illustrated in the yellow-poplar or tulip-poplar (*Liriodendron tulipifera*), with a nest shown in the upper part of the plate. This tree, among the tallest of the eastern hardwoods, was introduced into Europe from Virginia by early colonists.

PLATE 108

The Purple Finch (41)

In size and shape this bird differs but little from our chaffinch. The belly is white; the rest of the body is of a dusky purple color; but with a mixture of brown in some parts; particularly, the interior vanes of the wing feathers are brown, as are the tail feathers towards the end. The hen is brown, having her breast spotted like our mavis. When they first appear in Carolina (which is usually in November) they feed on the berries of juniper; and in February they destroy the swelling buds of fruit trees, in like manner as our bull-finches. They associate in small flights, and retire at the approach of winter.

The Tupelo Tree
(black tupelo)

This tree usually grows large and spreading, with an erect trunk and regular head. The leaves are shaped like those of the bay-tree. In autumn its branches are thick set with oval black berries on long footstalks, each berry having a hard channeled flattish stone. These berries have a very sharp and bitter taste, yet are food for many wild animals, particularly raccoons, opossums, bears, etc. The grain of the wood is curled and very tough, and therefore very proper for naves of cart wheels and other country uses. They grow usually in moist places, in Virginia, Maryland and Carolina.

Editor's Note / Purple Finch
(*Carpodacus purpureus*)

The purple finch is fairly common during the winter months in Virginia and the Carolinas, arriving around mid-October and departing in April. Purple finches are usually seen traveling about in small flocks that are often attracted to bird feeders. They are particularly fond of seeds and tree buds. Catesby's purple finch is drawn in the black tupelo (*Nyssa sylvatica*), a widespread tree across the eastern United States. The black tupelo is a beautiful ornamental, as well as a honey plant, and many birds and mammals consume its juicy fruit.

Carduelis Americanus.
The American Goldfinch.   Acacia abrus folis &c.

PLATE 109

The American Goldfinch (43)

This agrees, in size and shape, with our goldfinch. The bill is of a dusky white; the fore part of the head black; the back part of a dirty green. All the under part of the body, from the bill to the vent, and likewise the back, of a bright yellow; the wings black, having some of the smaller feathers edged with dusky white; the legs and feet brown. They feed on lettuce and thistle seed. These birds are not common in Carolina. In Virginia they are more frequent; and at New York they are most numerous; and are there commonly kept in cages.

Acacia
(waterlocust)

This tree grows to a large size and spreading. The leaves are winged, composed of many small pointed lobes, like most others of its tribe. The fruit is somewhat like a bean, contained in an oval capsule, and grows commonly five or six together in a bunch. Many very large sharp thorns are set on its branches and larger limbs. This tree I never saw but at the plantation of Mr. Waring on Ashley River, growing in shallow water.

Editor's Note / American Goldfinch
(*Carduelis tristis*)

The American goldfinch ranges from southern Canada to the southern United States, but is most abundant in the southern Atlantic states during migration and the winter months. Although a breeding bird of the region, it is not normally found toward the coastal plain during the summer months. During the winter these birds, male and female, are a dull yellow olive, but during the spring migration and summer months the males are truly gems of the bird world, with their bright canary yellow bodies and black wings. Goldfinches are quite fond of thistle; their Latin name *Carduus* means "eats seeds of thistle." Catesby's goldfinch is shown in the waterlocust (*Gleditsia aquatica*), a species not known north of South Carolina (see comments in Catesby's text concerning locality).

This concludes the whole number of birds exhibited in both volumes, containing in all 113; and in which are also contained all the land birds I have ever seen, or could discover, in that part of North-America included between the 30th and 45th degrees of latitude. And though more kinds may not improbably remain unknown within those limits, yet north of them I think there cannot reasonably be thought to be many new species, because there are not only but a few birds at the northern limits, but also because animals in general, and particularly birds, diminish in number of species so much the nearer they approach the pole.*

*This remark appeared as an addendum to the appendix, volume 2.

The Text of *The Natural History*
of Carolina, Florida, and the Bahama Islands

THE
NATURAL HISTORY
OF
CAROLINA, FLORIDA *and the* BAHAMA ISLANDS:

Containing the FIGURES of

BIRDS, BEASTS, FISHES, SERPENTS, INSECTS, and PLANTS:

Particularly, the FOREST-TREES, SHRUBS, and other PLANTS, not hitherto defcribed,
or very incorrectly figured by Authors.

Together with their DESCRIPTIONS in *Englifh* and *French*.

To which, are added

OBSERVATIONS on the AIR, SOIL, and WATERS:

With Remarks upon

AGRICULTURE, GRAIN, PULSE, ROOTS, &c.

To the whole,

Is Perfixed a new and correct Map of the Countries Treated of.
BY
MARK CATESBY, F.R.S.

VOL. I.

HISTOIRE NATURELLE
DE
La CAROLINE, la FLORIDE, & les ISLES BAHAMA:

Contenant les DESSEINS

DES OISEAUX, ANIMAUX, POISSONS, SERPENTS, INSECTES, & PLANTES.

Et en particulier,

Des ARBRES des Forets, ARBRISSEAUX, & autres PLANTES, qui n'ont point été decrits,
jufques à prefent par les Auteurs, ou peu exactement deffinés.

Avec leur Defcriptions en François & en Anglois.

A quoi on a adjouté,

Des Obfervations fur l'Air, le Sol, & les Eaux,

Avec des Remarques fur l'Agriculture, les Grains, les Legumes, les Racines, &c.

Le tout eft precedé d'une CARTE nouvelle & exacte des Païs dont ils s'agift.
Par *MARC CATESBY*, de la Societè Royale.

TOME I.

LONDON:

Printed at the Expence of the AUTHOR; and Sold by W. INNYS and R. MANBY, at the Weft End of
St. *Paul*'s, by Mr. HAUKSBEE, at the *Royal Society* Houfe, and by the AUTHOR, at Mr. BACON's
in H xton:

MDCCXXXI.

The Preface

The early inclination I had to search after plants, and other productions in nature, being much suppressed by my residing too far from London, the center of all science, I was deprived of all opportunities and examples to excite me to a stronger pursuit after those things to which I was naturally bent. Yet my curiosity was such, that not being content with contemplating the products of our own country, I soon imbibed a passionate desire of viewing as well the animal as vegetable productions in their native countries; which were strangers to England. Virginia was the place, as I had relations there, which suited most with my convenience to go to, where I arrived the 23rd of April 1712. I thought then so little of prosecuting a design of the nature of this work, that in the seven years I resided in that country (I am ashamed to own it) I chiefly gratified my inclination in observing and admiring the various productions of those countries; only sending from thence some dried specimens of plants and some of the most specious of them in tubs of earth, at the request of some curious friends, amongst whom was Mr. Dale, of Braintree in Essex, a skillful apothecary and botanist; to him, besides specimens of plants, I sent some few observations on the country, which he communicated to the late William Sherard, L.L.D. one of the most celebrated botanists of this age, who favored me with his friendship on my return to England in the year 1719; and by his advice (though conscious of my own inability) I first resolved on this undertaking, so agreeable to my inclination. But as expenses were necessary for carrying the design, I here most gratefully acknowledge the assistance and encouragement I received from several noble persons and gentlemen, whose names are hereunder mentioned.

His Grace the Duke of Chandois.
The Right Honourable the Earl of Oxford.
The Right Honourable Thomas Earl of Macclesfield.
The Right Honourable John Lord Percival,
Sir George Markham, Bart. F.R.S.
Sir Hans Sloane, Bart. President of the Royal Society, and
   of the College of Physicians.
The Honourable Colonel Francis Nicholson, Governor of
   South Carolina.
Richard Mead, M.D. and F.R.S.
Charles Dubois, Esq; F.R.S.
John Knight, Esq; F.R.S.
William Sherard, L.L.D. and F.R.S.

With this intention, I set out again from England, in the year 1722, directly for Carolina; which country, though inhabited by English above an age past, and a country inferior to none in fertility, and abounding in variety of the blessings of nature; yet its productions being very little known except what barely related to commerce, such as rice, pitch and tar; was thought the most proper place to search and describe the productions of: accordingly I arrived in Carolina 23rd of May 1722, after a pleasant though not a short passage. In our voyage we were frequently entertained with diversions not uncommon in crossing the Atlantic Ocean, such as catching of sharks, striking of porpoises, dolphins, bonitos, albacores, and other fish; which three last we regaled on when fortune favored us in catching them; and even the flesh of sharks and porpoises would digest well with the sailors, when long fed on salt meats. The pursuit of dolphins after flying-fish, was another amusement we were often diverted with; the dolphins having raised the flying-fish, by the swiftness of their swimming, keep pace with them, and pursue them so close that the flying-fish being at length tired, and having their wings dried, and being thereby necessitated to drop into the water, often fall into the jaws of their pursuers; at some times neither element affords them safety, for no sooner do they escape their enemies in the water, but they are caught in the air by voracious birds. But what seemed most remarkable of this kind, was, that in the latitude of 26 degrees north, about the midway between the two continents of Africa and America, which I think cannot be less then 600 leagues, an owl appeared hovering over our ship; these birds have short wings, and have been observed not to be capable of long flights, it being a common diversion for boys to run them down after the second or third flight. This owl after some attempts to rest, disappeared; and the same day being the 22nd of March, an hawk with a white head, breast, and belly, appeared in like manner, and the day after some swallows appeared, but none ventured to alight on any part of the ship. No birds seem more able to continue long on their wings, than hawks and swallows; but that an owl should be able to hold out so long a flight, is to me most surprising.

Upon my arrival at Charles Town, I waited on General Nicholson, then Governor of that province, who received me with much kindness, and continued his favors during my stay in that country. Nor could I excuse myself of ingratitude without acknowledging the hospitable and kind entertainment I generally met with amongst the gentlemen of the country, which much contributed to the facilitating the work I went about.

As I arrived at the beginning of the summer I unexpectedly found this country possessed not only with all the animals and vegetables of Virginia, but abounding with even a greater variety. The inhabited parts of Carolina extend west from the sea about sixty miles, and almost the whole length of the coast, being a level, low country. In these parts I continued the first year searching after, collecting and describing the animals and plants. I then went to the upper uninhabited parts of the country, and continued at and about Fort Moore, a small fortress on the banks of the River Savanna, which runs from thence a course of 300 miles down to the sea, and is about the same distance from its source, in the mountains.

I was much delighted to see nature differ in these upper parts, and to find here abundance of things not to be seen in the lower parts of the country. This encouraged me to take several journeys with the Indians higher up the rivers, towards the mountains, which afforded not only a succession of new vegetable appearances, but the most delightful prospects imaginable, besides the diversion of hunting buffalo, bears, panthers, and other wild beasts. In these excursions I employed an Indian to carry my box, in which, besides paper and materials for painting, I put dried specimens of plants, seeds, etc.—as I gathered them. To the hospitality and assistance of these friendly Indians, I am much indebted, for I not only subsisted on what they shot, but their first care was to erect a bark hut, at the approach of rain to keep me and my cargo from wet.

I shall next proceed to an account of the method I have observed in giving the natural history of these countries; to begin therefore with plants, I had principally a regard to forest trees and shrubs, showing their several mechanical and other uses, as in building, joinery, agriculture, food, and medicine. I have likewise taken notice of those plants, that will bear our English climate, which I have experienced from what I have growing at Mr. Bacon's, successor of the late Mr. Fairchild at Hoxton, where many have withstood the rigor of several winters, without protection, while other plants, though from the same country, have perished for want of it.

As there is a greater variety of the feathered kind than of any other animals (at least to be come at) and as they excel in the beauty of their colors, and have a nearer relation to the plants of which they feed on and frequent; I was induced chiefly (so far as I could) to complete an account of them, rather than to describe promiscuously, insects and other animals; by which I must have omitted many of the birds (for I had not time to do all); by which method I believe very few birds have escaped my knowledge, except some water fowl, and some of those which frequent the sea.

Of beasts there are not many species different from those in the Old World: most of these I have figured, except those which do not materially differ from the same species in Europe, and those which have been described by other authors.

Of serpents, very few, I believe, have escaped me, for upon showing my designs of them to several of the most intelligent persons, many of them confessed that they had not seen them all, and none of them pretended to have seen any other kinds.

Of fish, I have described not above five or six from Carolina, deferring that work till my arrival at the Bahama Islands; for as they afford but few quadrupeds and birds, I had more time to describe the fishes, and though I had been often told they were very remarkable, yet I was surprised to find how lavishly nature had adorned them with marks and colors most admirable.

As for insects, these countries abound in numerous kinds, but I was not able to delineate a great number of them for the reasons already assigned. After my continuance almost three years in Carolina and the adjacent parts (which the Spaniards call Florida, particularly that province lately honoured with the name of Georgia) I went to Providence, one of the Bahama Islands; to which place I was invited by his Excellency Charles Phinney, Esq; Governor of those islands, and was entertained by him with much hospitality and kindness. From thence I visited many of the adjacent islands, particularly Ilathera, Andros, Abaco and other neighboring islands. Though these rocky islands produce many fine plants, which I have here described, I had principally a regard to the fish, there being not any, or a very few of them, described by any author. Both in Carolina and on these islands, I made succes-

sive collections of dried plants and seeds, and at these islands more particularly I collected many submarine productions, as shells, corallines, *Frutices marini*, sponges, astroites, etc. These I imparted to my curious friends, more particularly (as I had the greatest obligations) to that great naturalist and promoter of science Sir Hans Sloane, Bart. to whose goodness I attribute much of the success I had in this undertaking.

As I was not bred a painter I hope some faults in perspective, and other niceties, may be more readily excused; for I humbly conceive that plants, and other things done in a flat, though exact manner may serve the purpose of natural history, better in some measure, than in a more bold and painter-like way. In designing the plants, I always did them while fresh and just gathered; and the animals, particularly the bird, I painted while alive (except a very few) and gave them their gestures peculiar to every kind of birds, and where it could be admitted, I have adapted the birds to those plants on which they fed, or have any relation to. Fish, which do not retain their colors when out of their element, I painted at different times, having a succession of them procured while the former lost their colors; I do not pretend to have had this advantage in all, for some kinds I saw not plenty of, and of others I never saw above one or two. Reptiles will live many months without sustenance; so that I had no difficulty in painting them while living.

At my return from America, in the year 1726, I had the satisfaction of having my labors approved of; and was honoured with the advice of several of the above-mentioned gentlemen, most skilled in the learning of nature, who were pleased to think them worth publishing, but that the expense of engraving would make it too burdensome an undertaking. This opinion, from such good judges, discouraged me from attempting it any further; and I altered my design of going to Paris or Amsterdam where I at first proposed to have them done. At length by the kind advice and instructions of that inimitable painter Mr. Joseph Goupy, I undertook, and was initiated in the way of, etching them myself, which I have not done in a graver-like manner, choosing rather to omit their method of cross-hatching, and to follow the humor of the feathers, which is more laborious, and I hope has proved more to the purpose.

The illuminating natural history is so particularly essential to the perfect understanding of it, that I may aver a clearer idea may be conceived from the figures of animals and plants in their proper colors, than from the most exact description without them; wherefore I have been less prolix in the description, judging it unnecessary to tire the reader with describing every feather, yet, I hope I have said enough to distinguish them without confusion.

As to the plants I have given them the English and Indian names they are known by in these countries; and for the Latin names I was beholden to the above-mentioned learned and accurate botanist Dr. Sherard.

Very few of the birds having names assigned them in the country, except some which had Indian names, I have called them after European birds of the same genus, with an additional epithet to distinguish them. As the males of the feathered kind (except a very few) are more elegantly colored than the females, I have throughout exhibited the cocks only, except two or three; and have added a short description of the hens, wherein they differ in color from the cocks, the want of which method has caused great confusion in works of this nature.

Of the paints, particularly greens, used in the illumination of figures, I had principally a regard to those most resembling nature, that were durable and would retain their luster, rejecting others very specious and shining, but of an unnatural color and fading quality. Yet give me leave to observe there is no degree of green, but what some plants are possessed of at different times of the year and the same plant changes its color gradually with its age; for in the spring the woods and all plants in general are more yellow and bright; and as the summer advances, the greens grow deeper, and the nearer their fall are yet of a more dark and dirty color. What I infer from this is, that by comparing a painting with a living plant, the difference of color, if any, may proceed from the above-mentioned cause.

As to the French translation I am obliged to a very ingenious gentleman, a doctor of physic, and a Frenchman born, whose modesty will not permit me to mention his name.

Of Carolina

Carolina was first discovered by Sir Sebastian Cabot, a native of Bristol, in the reign of King Henry the Seventh, about the year 1500; but the settling of it being neglected by the English, a colony of French Protestants, by the encouragement of Gaspar Coligni, admiral of that Kingdom, were transported thither, and named the place of their first settlement Arx Carolina, in honor of their Prince, Charles IX, King of France; but in a short time after, that colony was by the Spaniards cut off and destroyed, and no other attempt made by any European power to resettle it, till the 29th of May 1604, when eight hundred English landed at Cape Fear, and took possession of the country; and in the year 1670, King Charles II, in pursuance of his claim by virtue of the discovery, granted it to certain noble persons, with extraordinary privileges, as appears by the patent of that King unto George Duke of Albemarle, Edward Earl of Clarendon, William Earl of Craven, John Lord Berkley, Anthony Lord Ashley, Sir George Cartwright, Sir William Berkley, and Sir John Collinton, Baronet, who were thereby created true and absolute Lords and Proprietors of the Province of Carolina, to hold the same *in capite* of the Crown of England, to them, their heirs, and assigns, forever.

OF THE AIR OF CAROLINA

Carolina contains the northernmost part of Florida and lies in the northern temperate zone, between the latitude of twenty-nine and thirty-six degrees, thirty minutes north. It is bounded on the east by the Atlantic Ocean, on the west by the Pacific or South Sea, on the north by Virginia, and on the south by the remaining part of Florida. Carolina, thus happily situated in a climate parallel to the best parts of the Old World, enjoys in some measure the like blessings. It is very little incommoded by excess either of heat or cold. June, July and August are part of them sultry, but where the country is opened and cleared of wood, the winds have a freer passage, and thereby the heats are much mitigated, and the air grows daily more healthy. About the middle of August the declining of the heats begins to be perceived by the coolness of the nights, and from September to June following, no country enjoys a more temperate air. The winter months are so moderate, and the air so serene, that it sufficiently compensates for the heats in summer, in which it has the advantage of all our other colonies on the continent; even in Virginia, though joining to Carolina, the winters are so extreme cold, and the frosts so intense, that James River, where it is three miles wide, is sometimes froze over in one night, so as to be passed. The coldest winds in Carolina usually blow from the northwest, which in December and January produce some days of frost, but the sun's elevation soon dissipates and allays the sharpness of the wind, so that the days are moderately warm, though the nights are cold; after three or four days of such weather usually follow warm sunshiny days; thus it continues many days with some intervals of cloudy weather, which is succeeded by moderate soaking showers of rain, continuing not often longer than a day, then the air clears up with a sudden shift of wind from south to northwest, which again usually brings cold days, and so on.

Though in the beginning of February some few trees and smaller plants decorate the woods with their blossoms, yet the spring makes but slow progress till the beginning of April, when it advances suddenly with frequent rains.

In May, June and July, it rains not often but vehemently, with much lightning, and very loud thunder, which produces numerous effects of its vehemence on trees split from top to bottom; but as the country is not populous, the terrible effects of these destructive phenomena happen not very often on the inhabitants.

At the latter end of July or August it rains in great quantities, usually a fortnight or three weeks, overflowing all the savannah and lower ground; at which time there appears wild fowls of various sorts, particularly of the wading kinds, which retire at the fall of the water.

Usually once in about seven years these rains are attended with violent storms and inundations, which commonly happen about the time of the hurricanes that rage so fatally amongst the Sugar Islands—between the Tropics, and seem to be agitated by them, or from the same cause, but are much mitigated in their force by the time they reach Carolina; and though they affect all the coast of Florida, yet the further north they proceed, so much the more they decrease in their fury, Virginia not having often much of it, and north of that still less. Though these hurricanes are seldom so violent as in the more southern parts, yet in September 1713, the winds raged so furiously, that it drove the sea into Charles Town, damaging much the fortifications, whose resistance it was thought preserved the town. Some low situated houses, not far from the sea, were undermined and carried away with the inhabitants; ships were drove from their anchors far within land; particularly a sloop in North Carolina was drove three miles over marshes into the woods. Another in like manner was drove on land, and wedged in between two trees, the hull of which in that situation I saw some years after; and to the best of my memory, the keel was ten or twelve feet above the ground; this last was in Ilathera, one of the Bahama Islands.

In woods of pine trees are frequently seen glades or openings, occasioned by the fall of trees, which lie prostrate one way, by which is formed a strict and regular avenue a hundred feet wide, more or less, and some miles long; these are likewise the effects of violent gusts of wind.

Those parts of Carolina near the sea are not always exempt from fogs; but the upper parts of the country are seldom otherwise than serene.

In February and March the inhabitants have a custom of burning the woods, which causes such a continual smoke, that not knowing the cause, it might be imagined to proceed from fog, or a natural thickness in the air; likewise the smoke of the tar-kilns contribute not a little to deceive strangers, and possesses them with an ill opinion of the air of Carolina; add to these, an annual custom of the Indians in their huntings, of setting the woods on fire many miles in extent.

The northern continent of America is much colder than those parts of Europe which are parallel to it in latitude. This is evident from the mortal effects the frosts have on many plants in Virginia, that grow and stand the winters in England, though 15 degrees more north; and what more confirms this is the violent and sudden freezing of large rivers, as before-mentioned. Admitting from these circumstances, that in the northernmost part of our island the frosts are not more intense than in Virginia, it will then appear that the winters in Virginia, though in the latitude of 37 degrees north, and parallel with the south part of Spain, are as cold as in the north part of Scotland, which is in the latitude of 57, that is 20 degrees more north.

This great disparity of climate holds throughout our northern colonies: Newfoundland, and the south of Hudson's Bay, being not habitable for cold, though in the latitude of the south parts of England.

The frosts of Carolina and Virginia continue not long without intervals of warmer weather, yet by their ill effects cause a deficiency of many useful productions, which countries in the same latitude in Europe are blessed with, such as wine, oil, dates, oranges, and many things impatient of hard frost.

There has indeed of late been some efforts towards the making of wine both in Virginia and Carolina; the success of which, time will discover.

Some oranges there are in Carolina, but in the maritime parts only. I never saw nor heard of one produced ten miles from salt water. Such is the great difference of temperature between the maritime parts, and those lying distant from the sea, as the following instance may serve to illustrate.

Accomack is a narrow slip of land in Virginia, having the sea on one side, and the Bay of Chesapeake on the other. Here I saw fig trees, with trunks of a large size, and of many years standing, without any injury received by hard weather. On the opposite shore were only fig trees of a very small size, occasioned by their being often killed to the ground.

Yet this is not remarkable, as that the same kind of tree will endure the cold of Carolina five miles distant from the sea, so well as Accomack, though five or six degrees north of it.

Many, or most part of the trees and shrubs in Carolina, retain their verdure all winter, though in most of the low and herbacious plants, nature has required a respite; so that the grass, and what appears on the ground, looks withered and rusty, from October to March.

OF THE SOIL OF CAROLINA

The whole coast of Florida, particularly Carolina, is low; defended from the sea by sandbanks, which are generally two or three hundred yards from low-water mark, the sand rising gradually from the sea to the foot of the bank, ascending to the height of fourteen or sixteen feet. These banks are cast up by the sea, and serve as a boundary to keep it within its limits. But in hurricanes, and when strong winds set on the shore, they are then overflowed, raising innumerable hills of loose sand further within land, in the hollows of which, when the water subsides, are frequently left infinite variety of shells, fish, bones, and other refuse of the ocean. The sea on these coasts seldom makes any sudden or remarkable revolution, but gets and loses alternately and gradually.

A grampus cast on the shore of North Edisto River, sixteen feet long, I observed was in less than a month covered with sand. Great winds often blow away the sand two or three feet deep, and expose to view numbers of shells and other things, that has lain buried many months, and sometimes years.

At Sullivans Island, which is on the north side of the entrance of Charles-Town harbor, the sea on the west side has so encroached (though most defended, it being on the contrary side to the ocean) that it has gained in three years time, a quarter of a mile laying prostrate, and swallowing up vast pine and palmetto trees. By such a progress, with the assistance of a few hurricanes, it probably, in some few years, may wash away the whole island, which is about six miles in circumference.

At about half a mile back from the sandbanks before mentioned, the soil begins to mend gradually, producing bays, and other shrubs; yet, till at the distance of some miles, it is very sandy and unfit for tillage, lying in small hills, which appear as if they had been formerly some of those sandhills formed by the sea, though now some miles from it.

Most of the coast of Florida and Carolina, for many miles within land, consists of low islands and extensive marshes, divided also by innumerable creeks, and narrow muddy channels, through which only boats, canoes, and periaguas can pass.

These creeks, or rather gutters, run very intricately through the marshes, by which in many places a communication is necessitated to be cut from one creek to another, to shorten the passage, and avoid those tedious meanders.

These inland passages are of great use to the inhabitants, who without being exposed to the open sea, travel with safety in boats and periaguas; yet are necessitated sometimes to cross some rivers and sounds, eight or ten miles wide, or go far about. The further parts of these marshes from the sea, are confined by higher lands, covered with woods, through which, by intervals, the marsh extends in narrow tracts higher up the country, and contracts gradually as the ground rises; these upper tracts of marshland, by their advantageous situation, might with small expense be drained, and made excellent meadowland, the soil being exceeding good. But so long as such spacious tracts of higher lands lie uncultivated, and continue of no other use than for their cattle to range in, such improvements are like to lie neglected, and the marshes, which is a considerable part of the country, remain of little or no use.

The soil of Carolina is various; but that which is generally cultivated consists principally of three kinds, which are distinguished by the names of rice land, oak and hickory land, and pine barren land. Rice land is most valuable, though only productive of that grain, it being too wet for anything else. The situation of this land is various, but always low, and usually at the head of creeks and rivers, and before they are cleared of wood are called swamps; which being impregnated by the washings from the higher lands, in a series of years are become vastly rich, and deep of soil, consisting of a sandy loam of a dark brown color. These swamps, before they are prepared for rice, are thick, overgrown with underwood and lofty trees of mighty bulk, which by excluding the sun's beams, and preventing the exhalation of these stagnating waters, occasions the land to be always wet, but by cutting down the wood is partly evaporated, and the earth better adapted to the culture of rice; yet great rains, which usually fall at the latter part of the summer, raises the water two or three feet, and frequently cover the rice wholly, which nevertheless, though it usually remains in that state for some weeks, receives no detriment.

The next land in esteem is that called oak and hickory land; those trees, particularly the latter, being observed to grow mostly on good land. This land is of most use, in general producing the best grain, pulse, roots, and herbage, and is not liable to inundations; on it are also found the best kinds of oak for timber, and hickory, an excellent wood for burning. This land is generally light and sandy, with a mixture of loam.

The third and worst kind of land is the pine barren land, the name implying its character. The soil is a light sterile sand, productive of little else but pine trees, from which notwithstanding are drawn beneficial commodities, of absolute use in shipping, and other uses, such as masts, timber, etc. pitch, tar, rosin and turpentine. One third part of the country is, I believe, of this soil.

Though what is already said may suffice for a general description of the inhabited lands of Carolina, and of which the greatest part of the soil consists, yet there are some tracts interspersed of a different nature and quality; particularly pine lands are often intermixed with narrow tracts of low lands, called bay swamps, which are not confined by steep banks, but by their gradual sinking seem little lower than the pine land through which they run. In the middle of these swamps, the water stands two or three feet deep, shallowing gradually on each side. Their breadth is unequal, from a quarter to half a mile, more or less, extending in length several miles. On this wet land grows a variety of evergreen trees and shrubs, most of them aquatics, as the *Akea floridana*, red bay, water tupelo, alaternus, whorts, smilax, *Cistus virg.* or the upright honeysuckle, *Magnotia lauri*, *folio*, etc.

The swamps so filled with a profusion of flagrant and beautiful plants, give a most pleasing entertainment to the senses; therein excelling other parts of the country; and by their closeness and warmth in winter are a recess to many of the wading and waterfowls. This soil is composed of a blackish sandy loam, and proves good rice land; but the trouble of grubbing up, and clearing it of the trees and underwood has been hitherto a discouragement to the culture of it.

Another kind of land may be observed more sterile than that of pine barren land. This land is rejected, and not capable of cultivation, and produces nothing but shrubby oaks, bearing acorns at the height of two feet. I think it is called shrubby oak land.

All the lower (which are the inhabited) parts of Carolina, are a flat sandy country; the land rising imperceptibly to the distance of about an hundred miles from the sea, where loose stones begin to appear, and at length rocks, which at the nearer approach to the mountains, increase in quantity and magnitude, forming gradual hills, which also increase in height, exhibiting extensive and most delightful prospects. Many spacious tracts of meadowland are confined by these rugged hills, burdened with grass six feet high. Other of these valleys are replenished with brooks and rivulets of clear water, whose banks are covered with spacious tracts of canes, which retaining their leaves the year round, are an excellent food for horses and cattle, and are of great benefit particularly to Indian traders, whose caravans travel these uninhabited countries; to these shady thickets of canes (in sultry weather) resort numerous herds of buffalo where solacing in these limpid streams they enjoy a cool and secret retreat. Pine barren, oak, and hickory land, as has been before observed to abound in the lower parts of the country, engross also a considerable share of these upper parts.

The richest soil in the country lies on the banks of those larger rivers, that have their sources in the mountains, from whence in a series of time has been accumulated by inundations such a depth of prolific matter, that the vast burden of mighty trees it bears, and all other productions, demonstrates it to be the deepest and most fertile of any in the country. Yet pity it is that this excellent soil should be liable to annual damage from the same cause that enriched it, for being subject to be overflowed lessens the value of it. In other places on the banks of these rivers extend vast thickets of cane, of a much larger stature than those before mentioned, they being between twenty and thirty feet high, growing so close, that they are hardly penetrable but by bears, panthers, wild cats, and the like. This land, in depth of soil, seems equal to the preceding, and is equally liable to inundations. Though the worst land is generally remote from rivers, yet there are interspersed spacious tracts of rocky ground, covered with a shallow but fertile soil. Many of these valleys are so regularly bounded by steep rocks, that in several of them remain only an isthmus, or narrow neck of land, to enter otherwise would be wholly enclosed. From these rocks gush out plentiful streams of limpid water, refreshing the lower grounds, and in many places are received into spacious basins, formed naturally by the rocks.

At the distance of about halfway between the sea and mountains, ten miles wide of Fort Savannah, there lies, scattered on the earth, irregular pieces of white stone, or alabaster, some very large, but in general they were from the size of a bushel to various degrees less; some lay under the surface, but none seemed to lie deep in the earth. These stones or pieces of rock extended five miles in width, where we crossed them, and, as the traders and Indians affirmed to me, three hundred in length, running in a north-westerly direction.

The Appalachian mountains have their southern beginning near the bay of Mexico, in the latitude of 30, extending northerly on the back of the British colonies, and running parallel with the seacoast, to the latitude of 40. By this parallel situation of the mountains and seacoast, the distances between the mountains and the maritime parts of most of our colonies on the continent, must consequently be pretty near equal in the course of their whole extent; but as the geography of these extensive countries is hitherto imperfect, the western distances between the sea and mountains cannot be ascertained, though they are generally said to be above two hundred miles. The lower parts of the country, to about halfway towards the mountains, by its low and level situation, differ considerably from those parts above them, the latter abounding with blessings, conducing much more to health and pleasure; but as the maritime parts are much more adapted for commerce, and luxury, these delightful countries are as yet left unpeopled, and possessed by wolves, bears, panthers, and other beasts.

A great part of these mountains are covered with rocks, some of which are of a stupendous height and bulk; the soil between them is generally black and sandy, but in some places differently colored, and composed of pieces of broken rock, and spar, of a glittering appearance, which seem to be indications of minerals and ores, if proper search was made after them. Fossil coal fit for fuel hath been discovered on Colonel Byrd's estate in Virginia; chesnuts and small oaks are the trees that principally grow on these mountains, with some Chinapin, and other smaller shrubs; the grass is thin, mixed with vetch and wild peas; on some other tracts of these mountains is very little vegetable appearance.

In this state, with regard to the soil, and apparent productions, the mountains appear at the sources of the Savannah river, continuing so with little variation, as it is thought, some hundred miles north.

In the year 1714 I traveled from the lower part of St. James's river in Virginia to that part of the Appalachian mountains where the sources of that river rise, from which to the head of the Savannah river, is about four degrees distance in latitude. As some remarks I then made may serve to illustrate what I have now said, I hope it may not be amiss to recite so much of them as may serve for that purpose.

At sixty miles from the mountains, the river, which fifty miles below was a mile wide, is here contracted to an eighth part, and very shallow, being fordable in many places, and so full of rocks, that by stepping from one to another it was everywhere passable. Here we killed plenty of a particular kind of wild geese; they were very fat by feeding on fresh water snails, which were in great plenty, sticking to the tops and sides of the rocks. The low lands joining to the rivers were vastly rich, shaded with trees that naturally dislike a barren soil, such as black walnut, plane, and oaks of vast stature. This low land stretched along the river many miles, extending back half a mile more or less, and was bounded by a ridge of steep and very lofty rocks, on the top of which we climbed, and could discern some of the nearer mountains, and beheld most delightful prospects, but the country being an entire forest, the meanders of the rivers, with other beauties, were much obscured by the trees. On the back of this ridge of rocks the land was high, rising in broken hills, alternately good and bad. Some miles further the banks of the river on both sides were formed of high perpendicular rocks, with many lesser ones scattered all over the river, between which innumerable torrents of water were continually rushing.

At the distance of twelve miles from the mountains we left the river, and directed our course to the nearest of them. But first we viewed the river, and crossed it several times, admiring its beauties, as well as those of the circumjacent parts. Ascending the higher grounds we had a large prospect of the mountains, as well as of the river below us, which here divided into narrow rocky channels, and formed many little islands.

So soon as we had left the river, the land grew very rugged and hilly, increasing gradually in height all the way. Arriving at the foot of the first steep hill we pursued a bear, but he climbing the rocks with much more agility than we, he took his leave. Proceeding further up, we found by many beaten tracts, and dung of bears, that the mountains were much frequented by them, for the sake of chesnuts, with which at this time these mountains amounted.

The rocks of these mountains seem to engross one half of the surface; they are most of a light gray color; some are of a coarse grained alabaster, others of a metallic luster, some pieces were in form of slate and brittle, others in lumps and hard; some appeared with spangles, others thick, sprinkled with innumerable small shining specks like silver, which frequently appeared in stratums at the roots of trees when blown down.

These different spars appeared most on the highest and steepest parts of the hills, where was little grass and fewest trees, but the greatest part of the soil between the rocks is generally of a dark-colored sandy mold, and shallow, yet fertile, and productive of good corn, which encourages the Tallipooses, a clan of the Cherokee nation of Indians, to settle amongst them, in the latitude of 34, and are the only Indian nation that has a constant residence upon any part of this whole range of mountains.

Certain places in Virginia, towards the heads of rivers, are very much impregnated with a nitrous salt, which attracts for many miles round numerous herds of cattle, for the sake of licking the earth, which at one place is so wore away into a cave, that a church, which stands near it, has attained the indecent name of Licking hole Church.

OF THE WATER

The larger rivers in Carolina and Virginia have their sources in the Appalachian mountains, generally springing from rocks, and forming cascades and waterfalls in various manners, which being collected in their course, and uniting into single streams, cause abundance of narrow rapid torrents, which falling into the lower grounds, fill innumerable brooks and rivulets, all which contribute to form and supply the large rivers.

All those rivers which have their sources in the mountains, have cataracts about one-third of the distance from the mountains to the sea. These cataracts consist of infinite numbers of various sized rocks, scattered promiscuously in all parts of the river, so close to one another, and in many places so high, that violent torrents and lofty cascades are continually flowing from between and over them. The extent of these cataracts (or falls, as they are commonly called) is usually four or five miles; nor are the rivers destitute of rocks all the way

between them and the mountains; but between these falls and the sea, the rivers are open, and void of rocks, and consequently are navigable so far, and no further, which necessitates the Indians in their passage from the mountains, to drag their canoes some miles by land, till they get below the cataracts, from which they have an open passage down to the sea, except that the rivers in some places are encumbered by trees carried down and lodged by violent torrents from the mountains.

The coasts of Florida, including Carolina and Virginia, with the sounds, inlets, and lower parts of the rivers, have a muddy and soft bottom.

At low water there appears in the rivers and creeks immense beds of oysters, covering the muddy banks many miles together; in some great rivers extending thirty or forty miles from the sea, they do not lie separate, but are closely joined to one another, and appear as a solid rock a foot and a half or two feet in depth, with their edges upwards.

The rivers springing from the mountains are liable to great inundations, occasioned not only from the numerous channels feeding them from the mountains, but the height and steepness of their banks, and obstructions of the rocks.

When great rains fall on the mountains, these rapid torrents are very sudden and violent; an instance of which may give a general idea of them, and their ill consequences.

In September 1722, at Fort Moore, a little fortress on the Savannah river, about midway between the sea and mountains, the waters rose twenty-nine feet in less than forty hours. This proceeded only from what rain fell on the mountains, they at the fort having had none in that space of time.

It came rushing down the river so suddenly, and with that impetuosity that it not only destroyed all their grain, but swept away and drowned the cattle belonging to the garrison. Islands were formed, and others joined to the land. And in some places the course of the river was turned. A large and fertile tract of low land, lying on the south side of the river, opposite to the fort, which was a former settlement of the Savannah Indians, was covered with sand three feet in depth, and made unfit for cultivation. This sterile land was not carried from the higher grounds, but was washed from the steep banks of the river. Panthers, bears and deer were drowned, and found lodged on the limbs of trees. The smaller animals suffered also in this calamity; even reptiles and insects were dislodged from their holes, and violently hurried away, and mixing with harder substances were beat in pieces, and their fragments (after the waters fell) were seen in many places to cover the ground.

There is no part of the globe where the signs of a deluge more evidently appears than in many parts of the northern continent of America; which, though I could illustrate in many instances, let this one suffice. Mr. Woodward, at his plantation in Virginia, above an hundred miles from the sea, towards the sources of Rappahannock river, in digging a well about seventy feet deep, to find a spring, discovered at that depth a bed of the Glossopetrae, one of which was sent me.

All parts of Virginia, at the distance of sixty miles, or more, abound in fossil shells of various kinds, which in stratums lie imbedded a great depth in the earth, in the banks of rivers and other places, among which are frequently found the vertebras, and other bones of sea animals. At a place in Carolina called Stono, was dug out of the earth three or four teeth of a large animal, which, by the concurring opinion of all the Negroes, native Africans, that saw them, were the grinders of an elephant; and in my opinion they could be no other; I having seen some of the like that are brought from Africa.

OF THE ABORIGINES OF AMERICA

Concerning the first peopling of America, there has been various conjectures how that part of the globe became inhabited. The most general opinion is, that it was from the northern parts of Asia. The distance between the western parts of the Old World and America is too well known to suppose a passage that way practicable from one continent to the other. The difference from the eastern most part of the Old World to America not being known, there is a probability that the continent of the northeast part of Asia may be very near, if not contiguous to that of America; or according to the Japanese maps in Sir Hans Sloane's museum, the passage may be very easy from a chain of islands at no great distance from each other there laid down. The great affinity of the Americans with the Eastern Tartars in the resemblances of their features, hair, custom, etc. adds some weight to this conjecture. But, without taking upon me to determine this point, I shall attempt to give some account of these American aborigines as they now exist.

Though the difference between the inhabitants of the various parts of the Old World is such as would startle one's faith, to consider them all as descendants of Adam; in America it is otherwise. The inhabitants there (at least of the Northern Hemisphere, if not from pole to pole) seem to be the same people, or sprung from the same stock; this affinity in the aborigines of America with one another, holds not only in regard to resemblance, in form and features, but their customs, and knowledge of arts are in a manner the same; some little differences may be in the industry of one nation more than others. I am the more persuaded to this opinion, having had many opportunities of seeing and observing the various nations of Indians inhabiting the whole extent of North America from the Equinoctial to Canada, particularly the Charibeans, Muskitos, Mexicans, Floridans, and those extending on the back of all our colonies, the northernmost of which differ no otherwise from the Caribbeans (who inhabit near the Equinoctial) than in being not altogether so swarthy, and generally somewhat of a larger stature.

I have not the like knowledge of the inhabitants of South America; but from what I could ever learn of them, the characters of their persons, customs, etc. differ but little from those of the North.

If the relations of Herrera, Solis, and other Spanish authors could be relied on, they were, I confess, enough to excite in us an high opinion of the knowledge and politeness of the Mexicans, even in the more abstruse arts of sculpture and architecture, the darling sciences of the ancients, and which added such glory to the Greeks and Romans, whose unparalleled fabrics still remain a testimony of their superior knowledge in those arts, though above 2000 years have passed since the finishing of some of them. Yet that all those stupendous buildings which the Spanish authors describe, standing at the time of their conquering the city and territory of Mexico, should be so totally destroyed, that an hundred years after its conquest there should remain not the least fragment of art or magnificence in any of their buildings; hard fate!

For my own part I cannot help my incredulity, suspecting much the truth of the above-mentioned relations, which (agreeable to the humor of that nation) seems calculated to aggrandize their achievements in conquering a formidable people, who in reality were only a numerous herd of defenseless Indians, and still continue as perfect barbarians as any of their neighbors.

OF THE INDIANS OF CAROLINA AND FLORIDA

Mr. Lawson, in his account of Carolina, printed *Anno* 1714, has given a curious sketch of the natural dispositions, customs, etc. of these savages. As I had the same opportunities of attesting that author's account as he had in writing it, I shall take the liberty to select from him what is most material, which otherwise I could not have omitted from my own observation. I cannot but here lament the hard fate of this inquisitive traveler, who though partial in his favorable opinion of these barbarians, died by their bloody hands, for they roasted him alive in revenge for injuries they pretended to have received from him.

Their Persons

The Indians of Carolina are generally tall, and well shaped, with well-proportioned limbs, though their wrists are small, their fingers long and slender; their faces are rather broad, yet have good features and manly aspects; their noses are not flat, nor their lips too thick; their eyes are black, and placed wide from one another; their hair is black, lank, and very coarse, approaching to the substance of horsehair; the color of their skin is tawny, yet would not be so dark did they not daub themselves over with bear's oil continually from their infancy, mixing therewith some vegetable juices, particularly that of the Sanguinaria, figured in *Hort. Elt.* p. 334, Vol. II. The women before marriage are generally finely shaped, and many of them have pretty features. No people have stronger eyes, or see better in the night or day than Indians, though in their houses they live in perpetual smoke; their beards are naturally very thin of hair, which they are continually plucking away by the roots; they never pare their nails but laugh at the Europeans for paring theirs, which they say disarms them of that which Nature designed them for; they have generally good teeth, and a sweet breath. There are few amongst these Americans so robust, and of so athletic a form as is amongst Europeans, nor are they so capable of lifting great burdens, and enduring so hard labor; but in hunting they are indefatigable, and will travel further, and endure more fatigue than a European is capable of. In this employment their women serve instead of packhorses, carrying the skins of the deer they kill, which by much practice they perform with incredible labor and patience. I have often traveled with them 15 and 20 miles a day for many days successively, each woman carrying at least 60, and some above 80 weight at their back.

Running and leaping these savages perform with surpassing agility. They are naturally a very sweet people, their bodies emitting nothing of that rankness that is so remarkable in Negroes; and as in traveling I have been sometimes necessitated to sleep with them, I never perceived any ill smell; and though their cabins are never paved nor swept, and kept with the utmost neglect and slovenliness, yet are void of those stinks or unsavory smells that we meet with in the dwellings of our poor and indolent.

Their Habits

Indians wear no covering on their heads, their hair, being very long is twisted and rolled up in various manners, sometimes in a bunch on each ear, sometimes on one ear only, the hair on the other side hanging at length, or cut off. Others having their hair growing on one side of their head at full length, while the hair of the other side is cut within an inch or two of the roots, standing upright. Some of the modish wear a large bunch of downy feathers thrust through a hole made in one and sometimes both ears; others strow their heads usually with the down of swans.

In summer they go naked, except a piece of cloth between their legs, that is tacked into a belt, and hangs in a flap before and behind. Their ordinary winter dress is a loose open waistcoat without sleeves, which is usually made of a deer skin, wearing the hairy side inwards or outwards in proportion to the cold or warmth of the season; in the coldest weather they clothe themselves with the skins of bears, beavers, raccoons, etc. besides warm and very pretty garments made of feathers. They wear leather buskins on their legs, which they tie below the knee. Their moccasins, or shoes are made of bear or buck skins, without heels, and are made as fit for the feet as a glove to the hand.

The women wear short petticoats of woolen, and some of moss. In summer they generally go naked from the waist upwards, but in winter they wrap themselves in a mantle of skins or woolen cloth, which they purchase of the English. Their hair they manage in a different manner from the men, sometimes rolling it up in a bunch to the crown of their head, others braid it, and bind it with wreaths of peak and ronoack, which are shells ground into regular pieces, with holes bored through them, and strung; this is their money, and both sexes use it for their principal ornaments with which they deck themselves, making of them pendants, bracelets, girdles, garters, etc. Besides which, the military men especially, wear at their breasts a concave shell, cut to the form of, though somewhat less than a gorget; this is an universal decoration with all the Indians of the northern continent; and as all their mechanism, for want of good tools, is performed with great

labor, so these gorgets bear a great price in proportion to their largeness and carving. Their war captains and men of distinction have usually the portrait of a serpent, or other animal, on their naked bodies; this is done by puncture and a black powder conveyed under the skin. These figures are esteemed not only as ornamental, but serve to distinguish the warriors, making them more known and dreaded by their enemies. In their hunting marches, at the entrance of the territories, or hunting grounds of an enemy, the captain, or leader of them chips off the bark from one side of a tree, on which he delineates his own person, with the dreadful hieroglyphic figure before mentioned, which is sometimes a rattlesnake open-mouthed, at a corner of his mouth, twisting in spiral meanders round his neck and body, the hero also holding in his hand a bloody tomahawk. By this menace or challenge is signified, that he whose portrait is there displayed, hunts in these grounds, where if any of his enemies dare intrude, they shall feel the force of his tomahawk.

At their going on enterprises of war, they dress in their greatest gallantry, daubing their hair with bear's fat and the juice of the puckoon root, and another red root, sticking therein the wings and feathers of birds, besides rings of copper, peak and wampum in their ears, at the same time painting their faces in various manner, sometimes red, with a circle of black round one eye, others have one side of their face red and the other black, while others daub their faces with white clay, black lead, and other colors. This they do not only to terrify their enemies, but that they should not be known again; for in all their hostilities against the English, the savages always appeared in this disguise.

Of Their Arms

There are very few Indians (and those very remote) that retain the use of bows and arrows, they being now supplied with guns by the English. Their bows were made of the locust-tree, i.e. pseudo-acacia, it being when old a very tough and pliant wood. Their arrows were reeds headed with pieces of stone, spurs of turkey cocks, and the bones of fish. Besides bows and arrows, tomahawks were the only weapons of war they had. These were of two kinds: one was a staff about three feet long, with a large knob at the end; the others were made of stone ground to an edge, of the form and size of a small hatchet, and fixed to a strong handle; these would cut, and were of most use, as well for war as for hollowing their canoes, and other mechanic uses; with these they fought and worked, but since the introduction of iron hatchets, which they still call tomahawks, they have wholly laid aside their stone ones.

Of Their Food and Cookery

The Indians are a temperate people, not from a principle of virtue, but from an ancient savage and indolent custom, which all the examples of industry and economy can never eradicate. They have a vast country to range in, and the choice of the most delightful and fertile parts of it to inhabit, by which with little labor they might indulge the greatest luxury. Yet so little are they inclined that way, or even make so little use of these blessings, that, by depending wholly on providence, they are sometimes drove to necessity. Except a few hens, which were first brought among them by the Europeans, the Indians breed no tame animals for food, and consequently eat neither beef, mutton, nor pork, yet are fond of these meats, when they get them amongst the English. No animal is of so general use to them as the deer, which supplies them with food and raiment; yet these following animals are also their food, buffaloes, elks, squirrels, bears, panthers, wild-cats, pole-cats, opossums, raccoons, beavers, alligators, terrapins and serpents, besides all sorts of fowls, not rejecting the rapacious kinds. The nymph of wasps they esteem a dainty. Fish of all kinds are a great part of the food of those who inhabit near the sea.

The only grain they cultivate is maize, which, with various kinds of pulse, they had amongst them before the arrival of the Europeans. In summer they feed much on vegetables, particularly maize before it is ripe, and while tender, they roast it in the fire, also pumpkins, gourds, squashes, melons, cucumbers, potatoes; besides peaches, raspberries, and strawberries, which their woods abound in. Indians seldom plant corn enough to last them the year round, yet in some measure they supply that want by their autumn collection of black walnuts, hickory nuts, chinkapins and acorns, which they lay up for winter store; from these they press wholesome oil, particularly from the acorns of the live oak. The kernels also of these nuts and acorns being beat in a mortar to a paste, serve to thicken and enrich their broths.

Besides roasting and boiling, they barbecue most of the flesh of the larger animals, such as buffalo, bear and deer; this performed very gradually, over a slow clear fire, upon a large wooden gridiron, raised two feet above the fire. By this method of curing venison it will keep good five or six weeks, and by its being divested of the bone, and cut into portable pieces, adapts it to their use, for the more easy conveyance of it from their hunting quarters to their habitations. Fish is also thus preserved for the better conveyance of it from the maritime to the inland countries. The manner of their roasting is by thrusting sticks through pieces of meat, sticking them round the fire, and often turning them. At their festivals they make some compound dishes, which, as I have often partook of, the following may serve as a specimen of their cookery. They stew the lean of venison till little liquor remains, which is supplied with marrow out of their deer's bones; to which is added, the milky pulp of maize before it hardens. It is common with some nations at great entertainments, to boil bear, deer, panther, or other animals, together in the same pot; they take out the bones, and serve up the meat by itself, then they stew the bones over again in the same liquor, adding thereto purslane and squashes, and thicken it with the tender grain of maize, this is a luscious soup. A fawn cut out of the deer's belly and boiled in its natural bag, is a dish in great esteem with them. The pigeons, described p. 23, Vol. I, afford them some years great plenty of oil, which they preserve for winter use; this and sometimes bear's fat they eat with bread, with it they also supply the want of fat in wild turkeys, which in some winters become very lean by being deprived of their food, by

the numerous flights of the migratory pigeons devouring the acorns, and other mast. Oil drawn from nuts and acorns have also their peculiar uses in cookery. Indians (as has been before said) are often without corn, (and from the same negligent principle) when they have it, they are often without bread, contenting themselves with eating the grain whole, after being softened by boiling it with their meat. They thicken their broths with *roccahomony*, which is indeed, for that purpose, much preferable to oatmeal or French barley. Peaches they dry in the sun for winter use, and bake them in the form of loaves. Phishimons, whorts, and some other fruit and wild berries they also preserve for winter, using them in their soups and other ways. Indians also eat the earth-nuts, which they call *tuccabo*. Turkeys, hares, squirrels, with other smaller animals, they roast with their guts in their bellies; they use instead of salt, wood ashes; yet I have seen amongst the Chigasaws very sharp salt in chrystalline lumps, which they told me was made of a grass growing on rocks in fresh rivers. Indians eat no raw saleds, and have an aversion to pepper and mustard. Victuals are common throughout the whole kindred, and often to the whole town, especially when they are in hunting quarters, then they all fare alike, whoever of them kills the game.

They have no fence to part one another lots in their corn fields, every man knows his own, and it scarce ever happens that they rob one another of so much as an ear of corn, which if any is found to do, the thief is sentenced by the elders to work or plant for him that was robbed, till he is recompensed for all the damage he has suffered in his corn field; yet they make no scruple to rob the English, having been taught this lesson by the latter. They are very kind and charitable to one another, but more especially to those of their own nation, for if any one of them have suffered loss by fire or otherwise, they make a general collection for him, every one contributing to his loss in proportion to his abilities.

OF THE HABITATIONS OF THE INDIANS

The wigwams, or cabins of the Indians are generally either circular or oval, having but one floor, but of various dimensions, some containing a single family, others four or five families, but of the same kindred. In building their fabrics they stick into the ground at about four or five feet asunder, very long pliant poles, bending their tops, and tying them together with bark; then they brace them together with other poles to strengthen them, afterwards covering them all over, both roof and sides with bark, particularly that of sweet gum, cypress, and cedar, so that they are warm and tight, and will keep firm against all weathers. In the top of the roof is left a hole to let out smoke, under which, in the middle of the cabin, is their fire; in the sides is left a hole or two for light, and a door at one end; round the cabin are fixed to the walls broad benches of split cane, laying thereon mats or skins, on which they sleep. Their state cabins, for the reception of ambassadors, and other public transactions, are built with greater magnificence, being loftier, and of far larger dimensions, the inside being hung with mats of rushes or cane, as is also the wigwam of the king, and some others of prime note.

They have also houses for the summer, which are built more open and airy, which in sultry weather they sleep in. A town of Totero Indians, seated on Meherin river, is built with strong posts or trees drove into the ground close to one another, the interstices being stopped up with moss, and covered with the bark of the sweet gum tree; from two of which trees, being bereaved of their bark, I gathered more than my hat full of the fragrant rosin that trickles from between the bark and the wood, and by the heat of the sun condenses to a resemblance of transparent amber.

OF THEIR ARTS AND MANUFACTURES

Arts amongst the Indians are confined to a very narrow compass, the business of their lives being war and hunting, they trouble themselves with little else, deeming it ignominious for a Coccorous, that is, a war captain, or good hunter, to do mechanic works, except what relates to war or hunting, the rest they leave to the women and sorry hunters. Their canoes are made of pine or tulip trees, which (before they had the use of English tools) they burned hollow, scraping and chipping them with oyster shells and stone hatchets. Their mats are neatly made of rushes, and serve them to lie on and hang their cabins with; they also make very pretty baskets of rushes and silk-grass, dyed of various colors and figures, which are made by the Indians of Virginia, and those inhabiting further north. But the baskets made by the more southern Indians, particularly the Choctaughs and Chigasaws, are exceeding neat and strong, and is one of their masterpieces in mechanics. These are made of cane in different forms and sizes, and beautifully dyed black and red with various figures; many of them are so close wrought that they will hold water, and are frequently used by the Indians for the purposes that bowls and dishes are put to. But that which they are more especially useful for to the English inhabitants is for portmanteaus, which being made in that form are commodious, and will keep out wet as well as any made of leather. The principal of their cloth manufacture is made of the inner bark of the wild mulberry, of which the women make for themselves petticoats and other habits. This cloth, as well as their baskets, is likewise adorned with figures of animals represented in colors; its substance and durableness recommends it for floor and table carpets. Of the hair of buffalo, and sometimes that of raccoons, they make garters and sashes which they dye black and red; the fleshy sides of the deer skins and other skins which they wear, are painted black, red and yellow, which in winter they wear on the outside, the hairy side being next their skins. Those who are not good hunters dress skins, make bowls, dishes, spoons, tobacco pipes, with other domestic implements. The bowls of their tobacco pipes are whimsically though very neatly made and polished, of black, white, green, red, and gray marble, to which they fix a reed of a convenient length. These manufactures are usually transported to some remote nations, who having greater plenty of deer and other game, our neighboring Indians barter these commodities for their raw hides with the hair on, which are brought home and dressed by the sorry hunters. The method of dressing their skins is by soaking them in deer's brains, tempered with water, scraping them with an oyster shell till they become soft and pliable. Maize, when young, and beat to a pulp, will effect the same as the brains; then they cure them with smoke, which is performed by digging a hole in the earth, arching it over with hoop sticks, over which the skin is laid, and under that is kindled a slow fire, which is continued till it is smoked enough.

Of Their Hunting

Before the introduction of firearms amongst the American Indians (though hunting was their principal employment), they made no other use of the skins of deer, and other beasts, than to clothe themselves, their carcasses for food, probably, then being of as much value to them as the skins; but as they now barter the skins to the Europeans for other clothing and utensils they were before unacquainted with, so the use of guns has enabled them to slaughter far greater number of deer and other animals than they did with their primitive bows and arrows. This destruction of deer and other animals being chiefly for the sake of their skins, a small part of the venison they kill suffices them; the remainder is left to rot, or becomes a prey to the wolves, panthers, and other voracious beasts. With these skins they purchase of the English, guns, powder and shot, woolen cloth, hatchets, kettles, porridge pots, knives, vermilion, beads, rum, etc.

Their methods of hunting and fishing differ from ours, particularly in their manner of deceiving deer, by an artificial head of one, by which they the more easily come up with, and kill their game. This is made with the head of a buck, the horns being diminished by scraping them hollow for lightness of carriage; to the head is left the skin of the breast and neck, which is extended with hoops for the arms to enter; the hunter's coat is also a deer's skin; the eyes are well represented by the globular shining seeds of the Pavia, or scarlet flowering horse chesnut. In these habiliments an Indian will approach as near a deer as he pleases, the exact motion or behavior of a deer being so well counterfeited by them, that it has been frequently known for two hunters to come up with stalking heads together, and unknown to each other, so that an Indian has been killed instead of a deer.

Their annual custom of fire hunting is usually in October. At this sport associate some hundreds of Indians, who, spreading themselves in length through a great extent of country, set the woods on fire, which with the assistance of the wind is driven to some peninsula, or neck of land, into which deers, bears, and other animals are drove by the raging fire and smoke, and being hemmed in are destroyed in great numbers by their guns.

Of Their Sagacity

The Indians are generally allowed to have a good capacity, which seems adapted and even confined to their savage way of life. Reading and writing is the highest erudition that I have known or heard any of them attain to; though a great number of them have been, and still continue to be educated at Williamsburg college in Virginia, by the benefaction of the great Mr. Boyle, whose pious design was, that after attaining a due qualification, they should inculcate amongst their brethren true religion and virtue, yet I have never heard of an instance conformable to that worthy intention. And so innate an affection have they to their barbarous customs, that though from their infancy they have been bred, and fared well with the English, yet as they approach towards manhood, it is common for them to elope several hundred miles to their native country, and there to resume their skins, and savage way of life, making no further use of their learning so unworthily bestowed upon them.

But I shall here remark, that although every clan or nation hath a language peculiar to itself, there is one universal language like the lingua franca in the seaports of the Mediterranean, which is understood by all their chiefs and great men through a great part of North America.

Though their disesteem for literature, or their incapacity of attaining it is such, that is in some measure compensated by a sagacity or instinct that Europeans are incapable of, and which is particularly adapted to their conveniency of life. An instance or two is as follows:

When a body of Indians set out on an hunting journey of five hundred miles, more or less, perhaps where none of them ever were, after the imaginary place of rendezvous is agreed on, they then consult what direction it lies in, everyone pointing his finger towards the place; though but little variation appears in their pointings, the preference of judgment is given to the eldest; thus it being concluded on, they set out all singly, and different ways, except the women, who jog on a constant pace, while the men traverse a vast tract of land in hunting on each side, and meet together in small parties at night. Thus they proceed onward their journey, and though they range some hundred miles from one another, they all meet at the place appointed. And if any obstruction happens, they leave certain marks in the way, where they that come after will understand how many have passed and which way they are gone. They are never lost, though at the greatest distance from home; and where they never were before, they will find their way back by a contrary way from that they went.

An Indian boy that was brought up very young to school at Williamsburg, at the age of 9 or 10 years, ran from school, found means (nobody knew how) to pass over James river, and then traveled through the woods to his native home, though the nearest distance was three hundred miles, carrying no provision with him, nor having anything to subsist on in his journey but berries, acorns, and such like as the wood afforded.

They know the north point wherever they are; one guide is by a certain moss that grows most on the north side of trees.

Their sagacity in tracing the footsteps of one another is no less wonderful: on a dry surface, where none but themselves are able to discern the least impression of anything, they often make discoveries; but on moist land that is capable of impression, they will give a near guess, not only of the number of Indians that have passed, but by the make and stitching of their moccasins, will know of what nation they are, and consequently whether friends or enemies. This is a piece of knowledge on which great consequences depend; therefore, they who excel in it are highly esteemed, because these discoveries enable them to ambuscade their enemies, as well as to evade surprises from them; and also to escape from a superior number by a timely discovery of their numerous tracts. One terrible warlike nation gives them more of this speculative trouble than all others: these are the Sennegars, a numerous people seated near the lakes of Canada, who live by depredation and rapine on all other Indians, and whose whole employment is to range in troops all over the northern continent, plundering and murdering all that will not submit; women and children they carry away captive, and incorporate with themselves. By this policy they are numerous and formidable to all the nations of Indians from their northern abodes to the gulf of Florida, except some few who pay them tribute for their safeguard.

If a prisoner attempts to escape, they cut his toes and half his feet off, lapping the skin over the stump, and make a present cure. This commonly disables them from making their escape, they not being so good travelers as before; besides, the impression of their half feet making it easy to trace them.

In their war expeditions they have certain hieroglyphics, whereby each party informs the other of the successes or losses they have met with; all which is so exactly performed by their sylvan marks and characters, that they are never at a loss to understand one another.

Their Drunkenness

The savages are much addicted to drunkenness, a vice they never were acquainted with till the Christians came amongst them. Rum is their beloved liquor, which the English carry amongst them to purchase skins and other commodities with. After taking a dram, they are insatiable till they are quite drunk, and then they quarrel, and often murder one another, though at other times they are the freest from passion of any people in the world. They are very revengeful, and never forget an injury till they have received satisfaction, yet they never call any man to account for what he did when he was drunk; but say it was the drink that caused his misbehavior, therefore he ought to be forgiven.

Their Wars

Indians ground their wars on enmity not interest, as Europeans generally do; for the loss of the meanest person of the nation they will go to war, and lay all at stake, and prosecute their design to the utmost, till the nation they were injured by being wholly destroyed. They are very politic in carrying on their war, by advising with the ancient men of conduct and reason that have been war captains; they have likewise field counsellors, who are accustomed to ambuscades and surprises, in which consists their greatest achievements; for they have no discipline, nor regular troops, nor did I ever hear of a field battle fought amongst them. A body of Indians will travel four or five hundred miles to surprise a town of their enemies, traveling by night only, for some days before they approach the town. Their usual time of attack is at break of day, when, if they are not discovered, they fall on with dreadful slaughter, and scalping, which is to cut off the skins of the crown from the temples, and taking the whole head of hair along with it as if it was a night cap; sometimes they take the top of the skull with it; all which they preserve, and carefully keep by them for a trophy of their conquest. Their caution and temerity is such, that at the least noise, or suspicion of being discovered, though at the point of execution, they will give over the attack, and retreat back again with precipitation.

Part of an enterprise of this kind I chanced to be a witness of which was thus: Some Chigasaws, a nation of Indians inhabiting near the Mississippi River, being at variance with the French, seated themselves under protection of the English near Fort Moor on Savannah River; with five of these Indians and three white men we set out to hunt; after some days continuance with good success, at our returning back, our Indians being loaded with skins, and barbecued buffalo, we espied at a distance a strange Indian, and at length more of them appeared following one another, in the same tract as their manner is; our five Chigasaw Indians perceiving these to be Cherokee Indians and their enemies, being alarmed, squatted, and hid themselves in the bushes, while the rest of us rode up to the Cherokees, who were then increased to above twenty; after some parley, we took our leave of each other, they marching on towards their country, and we homeward; in a short time we overtook our Chigasaws, who had hid their loads, and were painting their faces, and tripping up every little eminence, and preparing themselves against an assault. Though the Cherokees were also our friends, we were not altogether unapprehensive of danger, so we separated from our Indian companions, they shortening their way by crossing swamps and rivers, while we with our horses were necessitated to go further about, with much difficulty, and a long march, for want of our Indian guides. We arrived at the fort before it was quite dark; about an hour after, while we were recruiting our exhausted spirits, we heard repeated reports of guns in the woods, not far from us, by which we concluded that the Cherokees were come up with the Chigasaws, and that they were firing at each other; nor were we undeceived, until the next morning, when we were informed, that our Indians discharged their guns for joy that they were alive, and had escaped their enemies. But had they then known of a greater escape, they would have had more reason to rejoice; for the next morning some men of the garrison found hid in a close cane swamp two large canoes painted red; this discovered the bloody attempt the Cherokees had been upon when we met them, who, with sixty men in these canoes came down the river between two and three hundred miles, to cut off the little town of the Chigasaws; but from some little incident being disheartened, and not daring to proceed, were returning back, by land when we met them. And so great was their dread of us, and our few Chigasaws, that fearing we should follow them, they run precipitately home, leaving some of their guns and baggage behind them,

which some time after were found and taken up by our Chigasaws, when they went for their packs they had hid. It is the custom of Indians, when they go on these bloody designs, to color the paddles of their canoes, and sometimes the canoe, red. No people can set a higher esteem on themselves, than those who pretend to excel in martial deeds, yet their principles of honor, and what they deem glorious, would in other parts of the world be esteemed most base and dishonorable: they never face their enemies in open field (which they say is great folly in the English) but skulk from one covert to another in the most cowardly manner; yet their confidence in, and the opinion they have of the prowess of white men is such, that a party of them being led on by an European or two, have been frequently known to behave with great bravery.

Their savage nature appears in nothing more than their barbarity to their captives, whom they murder gradually with the most exquisite tortures they can invent. At these diabolical ceremonies attend often both sexes, old and young, all of them with great glee and merriment assisting to torture the unhappy wretch, till his death finishes their diversion. However timorous these savages behave in battle, they are quite otherwise when they know they must die, showing then an uncommon fortitude and resolution, and in the height of their misery will sing, dance, revile, and despise their tormentors till their strength and spirits fail.

A warlike crafty Indian, called Brims (who had been an enterprising enemy to the English, as well as to a nation of Indians in alliance with them) was taken prisoner, and delivered up to the English, who, for reasons more political than humane, returned him back again to be put to death by the Indians that took him. He was soon environed by a numerous circle of his tormentors, preparing for him the cruelest torments. Brims, in this miserable state and crisis of his destiny, addresses himself to the multitude, not with complaisance and humility, but with the utmost haughtiness and arrogance, reviling and despising them for their ignorance in not knowing how to torture, telling them that if they would loosen him (for they could not think it possible for him unarmed to escape from such a multitude) he would show them in what manner he would torture them were they in his power. He then demanded the barrel of an old gun, one end of which he put into the fire; while everybody were attentive to know his design, he suddenly snatches up the red hot barrel, furiously brandishing it about, breaks through the astonished multitude who surrounded him, run to the bank of the river, from which he leaped down above 100 feet, and swam over, entered into a thicket of canes, and made his escape. He afterwards made peace with the English, and lived many years after with reputation in his own country.

Indians Healthful

The Indians have healthful constitutions, and are little acquainted with those diseases which are incident to Europeans, as gout, dropsies, stone, asthma, phthisic, calentures, paralytic, apoplexies, smallpox, measles, etc. Although some of them arrive to a great age, yet in general they are not a long-lived people, which in some measure may be imputed to their great negligence of their health by drunkenness, heats and colds, irregular diet and lodging, and infinite other disorders and hardships (that would kill an European) which they daily use. To this happy constitution of body is owing their little use of physic, and their superficial knowledge therein, little is proportionable. No malady is taken in hand without an exorcism to effect the cure; by such necromantic delusions, especially if the patient recovers, these crafty doctors, or conjurers (which are both in one) raise their own credit; insinuating the influence they have with the good spirit to expunge the evil one out of the body of the patient, which was the only cause of their sickness. There are three remedies that are much used by all the Indians of the northern continent of America; these are bagnios, or sweating houses, scarification, and the use of casena or yaupon. The first is used in intermitting fevers, colds, and many other disorders of the body; these bagnios are usually placed on the banks of a river, and are of stone, and some of clay; they are in form and size of a large oven, into which they roll large stones heated very hot; the patient then creeps in, and is closely shut up; in this warm situation he makes lamentable groans, but after about an hour's confinement, out from his oven he comes, all reeking in torrents of sweat, and plunges into the river. However absurd this violent practice may seem to the learned, it may reasonably be supposed that in so long a series of years they have used this method, and still continue so to do, they find the benefit of it.

Amongst the benefits which they receive by this sweating, they say it cures fevers, dissipates pains in the limbs contracted by colds, and rheumatic disorders, creates fresh spirits and agility, enabling them the better to hunt.

When the Indians were first infected by the Europeans with the smallpox, fatal experience taught them that it was a different kind of fever from what they had been ever used to, and not to be treated by this rough method of running into the water in the extremity of the disease, which struck in and destroyed whole towns before they could be convinced of their error. Scarification is used in many distempers, particularly after excessive travel; they cut the calves of their legs in many gashes, from which oftentimes is discharged a quantity of coagulated blood, which gives them present ease, and they say, stops and prevents approaching disorders. The instrument for this operation is one of the deadly fangs of a rattlesnake, first cleansed from its venom by boiling it in water.

As I have (Vol. II, p. 57) figured and described the casena, I shall here only observe, that this medicinal shrub, so universally esteemed by the Indians of North America, is produced but in a small part of the continent, confined by northern and western limit, *viz.* north to lat. 37, and west to the distance of about fifty miles from the ocean; yet the Indian inhabitants of the north and west are supplied with it by the maritime Indians in exchange for other commodities. By the four faces the Indians make in drinking this salubrious liquor, it seems as little agreeable to an Indian as to an European palate, and consequently that the pains and expenses they are at in procuring it from remote distances, does not proceed from luxury (as tea with us from China) but from its virtue, and the benefit they receive by it.

Indians are wholly ignorant in anatomy, and their knowledge in surgery very superficial; amputation and phlebotomy they are strangers to; yet they know many good vulnerary and other plants of virtue, which they apply with good success; the cure of ulcers and dangerous wounds is facilitated by severe abstinence, which they endure with a resolution and patience peculiar to themselves. They knew not the pox in North America, till it was introduced by the Europeans.

Indian Women

Indian women by their field, as well as by domestic employment, acquire a healthy constitution, which contributes no doubt to their easy travail in childbearing, which is often alone in the woods; after two or three days have confirmed their recovery, they follow their usual affairs, as well without as within doors; the first thing they do after the birth of the child, is to dip, and wash it in the nearest spring of cold water, and then daub it all over with bear's oil; the father then prepares a singular kind of cradle, which consists of a flat board about two foot long, and one broad, to which they brace the child close, cutting a hole against the child's breech for its excrements to pass through; a leather strap is tied from one corner of the board to the other, whereby the mother slings her child on her back, with the child's back towards hers; at other times they hang them against the walls of their houses, or to the boughs of trees; by these, and other conveniences, these portable cradles are adapted to the use of Indians; and I can't tell why they may not as well to us, if they were introduced here. They cause a singular erectness in the Indians, nor did I ever see a crooked Indian in my life.

Indians are very peaceable, they never fight with one another, except drunk. The women particularly are the patientest and most inoffensive creatures living; I never saw a scold amongst them, and to their children they are most kind and indulgent.

The Indians (as to this life) seem to be a very happy people, though that happiness is much eclipsed by the intestine feuds and continual wars one nation maintains against another, which sometimes continue some ages, killing and making captive, till they become so weak, that they are forced to make peace for want of recruits to supply their wars. This probably has occasioned the depopulated state of North America at the arrival of the Europeans, who by introducing the vices and the distempers of the old world, have greatly contributed even to extinguish the race of these savages, who it is generally believed were at first four, if not six times as numerous as they now are.

I shall now conclude my account of the Indians, in which I might have been more prolix, but I chose rather to confine myself to what I learned by a personal knowledge of them; and as natural history is the subject of this book, I conceive it impertinent to relate tedious narratives of religious ceremonies, burials, marriages, etc. which are too often the product of invention, or credulity in the relater. Indians being so reserved and averse to reveal their secret mysteries to Europeans, that the relations of the most inquisitive can be but little depended on.

OF THE AGRICULTURE OF CAROLINA

The lands of America from a series of years have accumulated such a coat of prolific soil that tillage is in a manner useless. So soon as the fertility of a field is exhausted by repeated crops, they take down the fence which enclosed it, and let it lie as useless; this fence is removed to another fresh piece of land, some of which yields them plentiful crops twenty years successively without respite, or any other tillage than with an hoe, to raise the earth where the grain is dropped. At a planter's entering on fresh land, he is necessitated first to clear it of a vast burden of large trees and underwood; so much of which as is movable is piled in heaps, and burned, the trunks being left to rot, which is usually effected in six or eight years; in the meantime maize, rice, etc. is sown between the prostrate trees.

The fields are bounded by wooden fences, which are usually made of pine split into rails of about 12 or 14 feet long; the frequent removing of these fences to fresh land, and the necessity of speedy erecting them are partly the reasons why hedges are not hitherto made use of, besides the facility of making wooden fences in a country abounding in trees.

OF THE GRAIN PULSE, ROOTS, FRUIT AND HERBAGE, WITH THEIR CULTIVATION

Indian Corn

This is the native grain of America, from whence other parts of the world were at first supplied. It agrees with all climates from the Equinoctial to the latitude of 45. Yet the climate which best agrees with it, and produces the fairest and largest corn, is that between the degrees of 30 and 40. Of this grain there are reckoned two sorts, differing in stature, largeness of the spike and grain, and different time of ripening, besides accidental variety in the colors of the grain. The largest is cultivated in Virginia and Carolina. It is usually planted in April, and the largest ripens not until October, and is frequently left standing in the field until December before it is gathered in. The smaller grain opening in half the time of the large recommends it to the Indians, who according to their custom do not provide corn for the whole winter; this by its quick ripening affords them early food, and is therefore by them most propagated. This kind is also cultivated in New England, where heat is deficient for ripening the larger kind, and it is also propagated in Languedoc, and in some parts of Italy, and in kindly summers will come to maturity in England, as I myself have experienced. The large kind grows usually nine or ten feet high, and sometimes in strong land, to the height of fourteen feet. The smaller sort grows commonly five or six feet high. In planting this corn, six or

eight grains are dropped in the circumference of about thirty inches, and covered with a hoe; when it appears some inches above ground, the supernumeraries, if any, are pulled up, and three left in a triangle to grow, they are also weeded, and earth raised about them with a hoe, which being repeated three or four times in the summer, raises a hill about them. After the corn is come up some small height, there are dropped into every hill two or three beans called bonavis, which as they shoot up are supported by the stalks of the corn, and are ripe and gathered before the corn. These hills of corn are at the distance of about four feet or under, regularly planted in lines or quincunx order. In June the plants are suckered, i.e. stripping off the superfluous shoots. In August they are topped, and their blades stripped off, and tied in small bundles for winter provender for horses and cattle. About the same time the spikes or ears of corn, that grow erect naturally, are bent down to prevent wet entering the husk that covers the grain, and preserves it from rotting. In October, which is the usual harvest month, the spikes of corn with their husks are cut off from the stalks, and housed, and in that condition is preserved till it is wanted for use. It is then taken out of the husk, and the grain separated from the placenta or core. Then it is made saleable, or fit for use. This grain, in Virginia or Carolina, is of most general use, and is eat not only by the Negro slaves, but by the generality of white people. Its easy culture, great increase, and above all its strong nourishment, adapts it to the use of these countries as the properest food for Negro slaves, some of which, at a time when, by the scarcity of this grain, they were obliged to eat wheat, found themselves so weak that they begged of their master to allow them Indian corn again, or they could not work. This was told me by the Hon. Col. Byrd of Virginia, whose slaves they were, adding, that he found it his interest to comply with their request.

It is prepared various ways, though but three principally; the first is baking it in little round loaves, which is heavy, though very sweet and pleasant, while it is new. This is called pone.

The second is called mush, and is made of the meal, in the manner of hasty-pudding; this is eaten by the Negroes with cider, hog's lard, or molasses.

The third preparation is hominy, which is the grain boiled whole, with a mixture of bonavis, till they are tender, which requires eight or ten hours; to this hominy is usually added milk or butter, and is generally more in esteem than any other preparation of this grain. The spikes of this corn, before they become hard, are the principal food of the Indians during three summer months; they roast them in the embers, or before a fire, and eat the grains whole. The Indians prepare this grain for their long marches by parching and beating it to powder, this they carry in bags, and is always ready, only mixing with it a little water at the next spring.

Rice

This beneficial grain was first planted in Carolina, about the year 1688, by Sir Nathaniel Johnson, then Governor of that province, but it being a small unprofitable kind little progress was made in its increase. In the year 1696 a ship touched there from Madagascar by accident, and brought from thence about half a bushel of a much fairer and larger kind, from which small stock it is increased as at present.

The first kind is bearded, is a small grain, and requires to grow wholly in water. The other is larger, and brighter, of a greater increase, and will grow both in wet and tolerable dry land. Besides these two kinds, there are none in Carolina materially different, except small changes occasioned by different soils, or degeneracy by successive sowing one kind in the same land, which will cause it to turn red.

In March and April it is sown in shallow trenches made by the hoe, and good crops have been made without any further culture than dropping the seeds on the bare ground and covering it with earth, or in little holes made to receive it without any further management. It agrees best with a rich and moist soil, which is usually two feet under water, at least two months in the year. It requires several weedings till it is upward of two feet high, not only with a hoe, but with the assistance of fingers. About the middle of September it is cut down and housed, or made into stacks till it is threshed, with flails, or trod out by horses or cattle; then to get off the outer coat or husk, they use a hand-mill, yet there remains an inner film which clouds the brightness of the grain, to get off which it is beat in large wooden mortars, and pestles of the same, by Negro slaves, which is very laborious and tedious. But as the late Governor Johnson (as he told me) had procured from Spain a machine which facilitates the work with more expedition, the trouble and expense (it is hoped) will be much mitigated by his example.

Wheat

In Virginia they raise wheat not only for their own use, but for exportation. The climate of Carolina is not so agreeable to it, so that few people there think it their advantage to sow it. The generality of the inhabitants are supplied with flour from Pennsylvania and New York.

That which is propagated in Carolina, came first from the Madeira Island, none being found so agreeable to this country, it lying in a parallel latitude. The grain has a thinner coat, and yields more flower than that of England. The upper parts of the country distant from the sea is said to produce it as well as in Virginia; but as there are hitherto but few people settled in those distant parts, little else has been yet planted but Indian corn and rice, for exportation. Wheat is sown in March and reaped in June.

Barley

As Barbary, and the northern parts of Africa, are much adapted to the growth of barley, Carolina lying in about the same latitude, is also very productive of it; yet it is but little cultivated.

The brewing of beer has been sometimes attempted with good success, but the unsteadiness, and alternate hot and cold weather in winter is not only injurious to the making malt here, but has the like ill effects in brewing, which has induced some people to send for malt from England.

Oats

Oats thrive well in Carolina, though they are very rarely propagated; Indian corn supplying its use to better purpose, particularly for horses, one quart of which is found to nourish as much, and go as far as two quarts of oats.

Bunched Guinea Corn

But little of this grain is propagated, and that chiefly by Negroes, who make bread of it, and boil it in like manner of firmety. Its chief use is for feeding fowls, for which the smallness of the grain adapts it. It was at first introduced from Africa by the Negroes.

Spiked Indian Corn

This corn has a smaller grain than the precedent, and is used as the other is, for feeding fowls; these two grains are rarely seen but in plantations of Negroes, who brought it from Guinea, their native country, and are therefore fond of having it.

Kidney-beans

Of the kidney-bean kind there are in Carolina and Virginia eight or ten different sorts, which are natives of America, most of which are said to have been propagated by the Indians before the arrival of the English; amongst them are several of excellent use for the table, and are prepared various ways, as their various properties require. They are also of great use for feeding Negroes, being a strong hearty food.

English beans and peas degenerate after the first or second years sowing, therefore an annual supply of fresh seeds from England is found necessary to have them good.

The American Potato

Potatoes are the most useful root in Virginia and Carolina, and as they are a great support to the Negroes they are no small part of a planter's crop, everyone planting a patch, or enclosed field, in proportion to the number of his slaves. I having been particular in the description of the different kinds and figure of this root, refer my reader to it, Vol. II, p. 60.

The Yam

The culture of this useful root seems confined within the torrid zone, it not affecting any country, north or south, of either tropic; Carolina is the farthest north I have known them to grow, and there more for curiosity than advantage, they increasing so little that few people think them worth propagating. Sir Hans Sloane, in his natural history of Jamaica, has given an accurate account of this root; so I shall only observe, that next to the potato this root is of more general use to mankind than any other in the Old and New World.

Eddoes

This I have described and figured, Vol. II. p. 45.

The Martagon

The Indians boil these martagon-roots, and esteem them dainties.

The Common European Culinary Plants, *viz.*

Carrots, parsnips, turnips, peas, beans, cabbage and cauliflowers, agree well with the climate of Carolina; but after the first or second years sowing, they are apt to degenerate. Therefore an annual supply of fresh seeds from England is found necessary to have them good. Thyme, savory, and all aromatic herbs are more volatile here than in England. All other culinary roots, pulse, and herbaceous sallating are as easily raised, and as good as in England.

In Carolina and Virginia are introduced of all our English fruit trees, though they do not equally agree with the climates of these countries.

The Crab and Apple-tree

Crabs in Carolina are the product of the woods, and differ but little from ours, except in the fragrance of their blossoms, which in March and April perfume the air. Apples were introduced from Europe; they in Carolina are tolerably well tasted, though they keep but a short time, and frequently rot on the trees. In Virginia they are better, and more durable, and great quantities of cider is there made of them; further north the climate is still more agreeable, not only to apples, but to pears, plums, and cherries.

The Pear-tree

Pears in some parts of Carolina are very good and plentiful, particularly on the banks of Santee River.

The Plum and Cherry-tree

Plums, and cherries of Europe have hitherto proved but indifferent which probably may be occasioned for want of artful management; to the same cause may be imputed the imperfection of the other cultivated fruits, in the management of which little else but nature is consulted.

The Peach-tree

Of peaches there are such abundance in Carolina and Virginia, and in all the British continent of America, that, were it not certain that they were at first introduced from Europe, one would be inclined to think them spontaneous, the fields being everywhere scattered with them, and large orchards are planted of them to feed hogs with, which when they are satiated of the fleshy part, crack the shells and eat the kernels only. There are variety of kinds, some of the fruit are exceeding good, but the little care that is taken in their culture causes a degeneracy in most. They bear from the stone in three years, and I have known them do it in two; were they managed with the like art that they are in England it would much improve them. But they only bury the stones in Earth and leave the rest to Nature.

The Nectarine-tree

Nectarines, though so nearly akin to the peach, yet rarely prove good in Carolina and Virginia.

The Apricot-tree

Apricots no more than peaches agree well with this climate, though both these trees arrive to a large stature.

The Gooseberry and Currant-tree

Gooseberries and currants will not bear fruit in Carolina and in Virginia sufficient to encourage their cultivation.

Raspberries and Strawberries

Raspberries are very good, and in great plenty; they were at first brought from England. Strawberries are only of the wood kind, and grow naturally in all parts of the country, except where hogs frequent.

Blackberries

There are three or four kinds of blackberries in the woods, of better flavor than those in England; particularly one kind growing near the mountains, approaching to the delicacy of a raspberry.

The English Mulberry-tree

The common black mulberry produce not so large fruit as they do in England.

The Silk-worm Mulberry-tree

The Italian or silk-worm mulberry, with small white and some red fruit. These were introduced into Virginia by Sir William Berkley, when he was Governor of that province, for feeding silk-worms, and at length were propagated in Carolina.

The Quince-tree

Quinces in Carolina have no more astringency than an apple, and are commonly eat raw. In North Carolina is made a kind of wine of them in much esteem.

The Fig-tree

Figs were first introduced into Carolina from Europe; they will not grow anywhere but near the sea, or salt water, where they bear plentifully; but they are of a small kind, which may be attributed to their want of skillful management. An excellent liquor is made of figs, resembling mum in appearance and taste; this is most practiced at James's Island near Charles-town.

The Orange and Lemon-tree

Carolina being in the climate which produces the best oranges and lemons in the Old World, they might therefore be expected to abound here; but the winters in Carolina being much more severe than in those parts of Europe in the same latitude, these trees are frequently killed to the ground by frost. Yet when they are planted near the sea or salt water, they are less liable to be injured by frosts, and bear successive crops of good fruit.

The Pomegranate-tree

Pomegranates being equally tender with oranges, require the like salt water situation; yet I remember to have seen them in great perfection in the gardens of the Hon. William Byrd, Esq; in the freshes of James River in Virginia.

The Vine

Grapes are not only spontaneous in Carolina, but all the northern parts of America, from the latitude of 25 to 45, the woods are so abundantly replenished with them, that in some places for many miles together they cover the ground, and are an impediment to travelers, by entangling their horses feet with their trailing branches; and lofty trees are overtopped and wholly obscured by their embraces. From which indications one would conclude; that these countries were as much adapted for the culture of the vine, as Spain or Italy, which lie in the same latitude. Yet, by the efforts that have been hitherto made in Virginia and Carolina, it is apparent, that they are not blest with that clemency of climate, or aptitude for making wine, as the parallel parts of Europe, where the seasons are more equal, and the spring not subject, as in Carolina, to the vicissitudes of weather, and alternate changes of warmth and cold, which, by turns, both checks and agitates the rising sap, by which the tender shoots are often cut off. Add to this the ill effects they are liable to by too much wet, which frequently happening at the time of ripening, occasions the rotting and bursting of the fruit. Though the natural causes of these impediments may not presently be accounted for, yet it is to be hoped that time and an assiduous application, will obviate these inclement obstructions of so beneficial a manufacture as the making of wine may prove.

OF PINE-TREES

There are in Carolina four kinds of pine trees, which are there distinguished by the names of

pitch pine
rich-land pine
short-leaved pine
swamp pine

The pitch pine is the largest of all the pine trees, and mounts to a greater height than any of them; its leaves and cones are also larger and longer than those of the other kinds; the wood is yellow, the heart of it is so replete with turpentine. The wood is the most durable, and of more general use than any of the other kinds of pines, particularly for staves, heading, and shingles, i.e. covering for houses; these trees grow generally on the poorest land.

The rich-land pine is not so large a tree, nor are its leaves nor cones so long as those of the pitch pine; besides, the wood contains much less rosin; the grain is of a yellowish white color; the wood of this tree is inferior to that of the pitch pine, though it splits well, and has its peculiar uses; these grow in better land than the pitch pine.

The short-leaved pine is usually a small tree, with short leaves and small cones. It delights in middling land, and usually grows mixed with oaks.

The swamp pine grows on barren wet land; they are generally tall and large; the cones are rather large. These trees afford little rosin, but are useful for masts, yards, and many other necessaries.

There is also in Carolina a fir which is there called spruce-pine.

The numerous species of the fir and pine which our northern colonies abound in, have (till of late) been little known to the curious, of whom no one has contributed more than my indefatigable friend Mr. P. Collinson, who, by procuring from the different parts of America a great variety of seeds, and specimens of various kinds, has a large fund for a complete history of this useful tree.

Besides the trees which are figured, there are in Carolina these following:

Pinus	The Pine-Tree,	} many kinds
Abies	The Fir-Tree,	
Acacia	The Locust-Tree, two kinds	
Tilia	The Lime-Tree	
Pavia	Scarlet-flowering Horse Chesnut	
Siliquastrum	The Fudas-Tree	
Fagus	The Beech-Tree	
Ulmus	The Elm-Tree	
Salix	The Willow-Tree	
Sambucus	The Elder-Tree	
Corylus	The Hazel-Tree	
Carpinus	The Horn-beam-Tree	

THE MANNER OF MAKING TAR AND PITCH

The pitch pine is that from which tar and pitch is made, it yielding much more rosin than any of the other kinds; these trees grow usually by themselves, with very few of any other intermixed. The dead trees only are converted to this use, of which there are infinite numbers standing and lying along, being killed by age, lightning, burning the woods, etc. The dead trunks and limbs of these trees, by virtue of the rosin they contain, remain sound many years after the sap is rotted off, and is the only part from which the tar is drawn. Some trees are rejected for having too little heart; these are first tried with a chop of an ax, whether it be lightwood, which is the name by which wood that is fit to make tar of is called. This lightwood is cut in pieces about four foot long, and as big as ones leg, which with the knots, and limbs, are picked up, and thrown in heaps; after a quantity sufficient to make a kiln is thus gathered in heaps, they are all collected in one heap near their center on a rising ground, that the water may not impede the work. The lightwood being thus brought into one heap, is split again into smaller pieces; then the floor of the tar kiln is made in bigness proportionable to the quantity of the wood; in this manner a circle is drawn thirty foot diameter, more or less, the ground between it being laid declining, from the edges to the center all round about, sixteen inches, more or less, according to the extent of the circle. Then a trench is dug from the center of the circle to the edge or rim, and continued about five or six feet beyond it, at the end of which a hole is dug to receive a barrel. In this trench a wooden pipe is let in of about three inches diameter, one end thereof being laid so as to appear at the center of the circle, the other end declining about two foot, after which the earth is thrown in, and the pipe buried, and so remains till the kiln is built. Then clay is spread all over the circle about three inches thick, and the surface made very smooth; great care is taken to leave the hole of the wooden pipe open at the center, that nothing may obstruct the tar running down from all sides into it; this done they proceed to set the kiln as follows, beginning at the center, they pile up long pieces of lightwood, as close as they can be set end-ways round the hole of the pipe, in a pyramidal form, six feet diameter, and eight or ten feet high, then they lay rows of the four foot split billets from the pyramid all round the floor to the edge, very close one by one, and the little spaces between, are filled up with the split knots before mentioned. In this manner all the wood is laid on the floor, which being made declining to the center, the wood lies so also; thus they proceed, laying the wood higher and higher quite round till it is raised to thirteen or fourteen foot projecting out, so that when finished, the kiln is about four or five foot broader at the top than at the bottom, and is in form of an haystack before the roof is made. Then the short split limbs and knots are thrown into the middle so as to raise it there about two foot higher than the sides, then the kiln is walled round with square earthen turfs about three foot thick, the top being also covered with them, and earth thrown over that. The turfs are supported without by long poles put cross, one end binding on the other in an octangular form, from the bottom to the top, and then the kiln is fit to be set on fire to draw off the tar, which is done in the following manner:

A hole is opened at the top, and lighted wood put therein, which so soon as the fire is well kindled, the hole is closed up again, and other holes are made through the turfs on every side of the kiln, near the top at first, which draws the fire downward, and so by degrees those holes are closed, and more opened lower down, and the long poles taken down gradually, to get at the turfs to open the holes. Great care is taken in burning, to open more holes on the side the wind blows on than on the other, in order to drive the fire down gradually on all sides; in managing this, great skill is required, as well as in not letting it burn too quick, which wastes the tar; and if there is not air enough let in, it will blow, (as they call it) and often hurts the workmen; they are likewise frequently throwing earth on the top, to prevent the fire from blazing out, which also wastes the tar. The second day after firing, the tar begins to run out at the pipe, where a barrel is set to receive it, and so soon as it is full, another is put in its place, and so on till the kiln runs no more, which is usually in about four or five days; after which all the holes in the sides are stopped up, and earth thrown on the top, which puts out the fire, and preserves the wood from being quite consumed, and what remains is charcoal. A kiln of thirty foot diameter, if the wood proves good, and is skillfully worked off, will run about 160 or 180 barrels of tar, each barrel containing 32 gallons. The full barrels are rolled about, every three or four days for about twenty days, to make the water rise to the top, which being drawn off, the barrels are filled again, bunged up, and fit for use.

In making pitch round holes are dug in the earth near the tar kiln, five or six feet over, and about three feet deep; these holes are plastered with clay, which when dry they are filled with tar and set on fire; while it is burning it is kept continually stirring, when it is burned enough (which they often try by dropping it into water) they then cover the hole, which extinguishes the fire, and before it cools it is put into barrels. It wastes in burning about a third part, so that three barrels of tar makes about two of pitch.

No tar is made of green pine trees in Carolina, as is done in Denmark and Sweden.

OF BEASTS

Besides the descriptions of those particular beasts inhabiting the countries here treated of, I shall give an account of the beasts in general of North America.

Which are

The Panther	Monax	Beaver
Wild-Cat	Gray Squirrel	Otter
Bear	Gray Fox Squirrel	Water-Rat
White Bear	Black Squirrel	House-Rat
Wolf	Ground Squirrel	Musk-Rat
Buffalo	Flying Squirrel	House-mouse
Moose Deer	Gray Fox	Field-mouse

Stag	Raccoon	Moles
Fallow Deer	Opossum	Quick-hatch
Greenland Deer	Pole-cat	Porcupine
Rabbit	Weasel	Seal
Bahama Coney	Minx	Morse

These I shall divide into the four following classes.

Beasts of a different Genus from any known in the Old World

The Opossum
Raccoon
Quickhatch

Beasts of the Same Genus, but different in Species from those of Europe, and the Old World

The Panther	Gray Squirrel
Wild-Cat	Gray-Fox Squirrel
Buffalo	Black Squirrel
Moose-Deer	Ground Squirrel
Stag	Flying Squirrel
Fallow Deer	Pole-cat
Gray Fox	Porcupine

Beasts of which the same are in the Old World

The Bear	The House-rat
White Bear	Musk-rat
Wolf	House-mouse
Weasel	Field-mouse
Beaver	Mole
Otter	Seal
Water-rat	Morse

Beasts that were not in America, until they were introduced there from Europe

The Horse	The Goat
Ass	Hog
Cow	Dog
Sheep	Cat

The Panther

The panther at its full growth is three feet high, of a reddish color, like that of a lion, without the spots of a leopard, or the stripes of a tiger, the tail is very long. They prey on deer, hogs, and cattle; the deer they catch by surprise, and sometimes hunt them down. They very rarely attack a man, but fly from him; though this fierce and formidable creature is an overmatch for the largest dog; yet the smaller cur, in company with his master, will make him take a tree, which they will climb to the top of with the greatest agility. The hunter takes this opportunity to shoot him, though with no small danger to himself, if not killed outright; for descending furiously from the tree, he attacks the first in his way, either man or dog, which seldom escape alive. Their flesh is white, well tasted, and is much esteemed by the Indians and white people.

The Wild Cat

This beast is about three times the size of a common cat; it is of a reddish gray color, the tail is three inches and a half long; it much resembles a common cat, but has a fierce and more savage aspect; they climb trees, and prey on all animals they are able to overcome; and though by their smallness they are unable to take deer in the manner that panthers do by running them down, yet lying snug on the low limbs of trees, they leap suddenly on the backs of the deer as they are feeding, fixing so fast with their claws, and sucking them, that the deer by vehement running being spent becomes a victim to the wild cat.

The Bear

The bears in North America are somewhat smaller than those of Europe, otherwise there appears no difference between them. They never attack man, except oppressed by hunger in excessive cold seasons, or wounded by him. Vegetables are their natural food, such as fruit, roots, etc. on which they subsist wholly until cold deprives them of them. It is then only they are compelled by necessity, and for want of such food, to prey on hogs and other animals. So that bears seem with no more reason to be ranked with rapacious carnivorous beasts than jays and magpies do among birds of prey, which in frigid seasons, being deprived of their natural vegetable food, hunger compels to set upon and kill smaller birds. I have seen a chaffinich forced by the like necessity, to feed on putrid carrion; bears as well as all other wild beasts, fly the company of man, their greatest enemy, and as the inhabitants advance in their settlements, bears, etc. retreat further into the woods, yet the remoter plantations suffer not a little by their depredations, they destroying ten times more than they eat of maize or Indian corn. They are so great lovers of potatoes, that when once discovered by them, it is with difficulty they are deterred from getting the greatest share. They have a great command of their fore paws, which by their structure seem as much adapted to the grubbing up roots as the snouts of hogs, and are much more expeditious at it. Nuts, acorns, grain, and roots are their food, several kind of berries by their long hanging are part of their autumn and winter subsistence, the stones and indigested parts appearing in their dung, as those of the cornus, smilax, tupelo, etc. the berries of the tupelo tree are so excessive bitter, that at the season bears feed on them, their flesh receives an ill flavor. In March when herrings run up the creeks, and shallow waters to spawn, bears feed on them, and are very expert at pulling them out of the water with their paws. Their flesh is also very rank and unsavory, but at all other times is wholesome, well tasted, and I think excelled by none; the fat is very sweet, and of the most easy digestion of any other. I have myself, and have often seen others eat much more of it, than possibly we could of any other fat without offending the stomach.

A young bear fed with autumn's plenty, is a most exquisite dish. It is universally granted in America, that no man, either Indian or European ever killed a bear with young. The inhabitants of James River in Virginia in one hard winter killed several hundred bears, amongst which was only two females, which were not with young. This is a fact notoriously known by the inhabitants of that river, from many of whom I had it attested. They are notwithstanding their clumsy appearance, very nimble creatures, and will climb the highest trees with surprising agility, and being wounded will descend breech foremost, with great fury and resentment, to attack the aggressor, who without armed assistance has a bad chance for his life.

The White Bear

The white bear seems to be the most northern quadruped of any other, and is found most numerous within the Arctic Circle, on the continents of both Europe and America. They are never found far within land, but inhabit the shores of frozen seas, and on islands of ice; their chief food is fish, particularly the carcasses of dead whales cast on shore; they also devour seals, and what other animals they can come at; they are very bold and voracious, which oblige the northern voyagers at their whale fishings, to be very vigilant in avoiding being devoured by them. Within these few years there have been exhibited at London two of these animals, one of which, though not above half grown, was as big as two common bears. By the account given of them by northern voyagers they are of a mighty stature at their full growth; a skin of one measured thirteen feet in length. In shape they much resemble the common bear, yet differ from them in the following particulars, *viz.* Their bodies are covered with long thick woolly hair, of a white color, their ears are very small, short, and rounding, their necks very thick, their snouts thicker, and not so sharp as in the common bear.

The Wolf

The wolves in America are like those of Europe in shape and color, but are somewhat smaller; they are more timorous and not so voracious as those of Europe; a drove of them will fly from a single man, yet in very severe weather there has been some instances to the contrary. Wolves were domestic with the Indians, who had no other dogs before those of Europe were introduced, since which the breed of wolves and European dogs are mixed and become prolific. It is remarkable that the European dogs that have no mixture of wolfish blood, have an antipathy to those that have, and worry them whenever they meet, the wolf breed act only defensively, and with his tail between his legs, endeavors to evade the others fury. The wolves in Carolina are very numerous, and more destructive than any other animal; they go in droves by night, and hunt deer like hounds, with dismal yelling cries.

The Buffalo

These creatures, though not so tall, weigh more than our largest oxen; the skin of one is too heavy for the strongest man to lift from the ground; their limbs are short but very large, their heads are broad, their horns are curved, big at their base, and turn inward; on their shoulders is a large prominence or bunch, their chests are broad, their hind parts narrow, with a tail a foot long, bare of hairs, except that at the end is a tuft of long hairs. In winter their whole body is covered with long shagged hair, which in summer falls off, and the skin appears black, and wrinkled, except the head which retains the hair all the year. On the forehead of a bull the hair is a foot long, thick, and frizzled, of a dusky black color the length of this hair hanging over their eyes, impedes their flight, and is frequently the cause of their destruction. But this obstruction of sight is in some measure supplied by their good noses, which is no small safeguard to them. A bull in summer with his body bare, and his head muffled with long hair, makes a very formidable appearance. They frequent the remote parts of the country near the mountains, and are rarely seen within the settlements.

They range in droves, feeding in open savannas morning and evening, and in the sultry time of the day they retire to shady rivulets and streams of clear water, gliding through thickets of tall canes, which though a hidden retreat, yet their heavy bodies, causing a deep impression of their feet in moist land, they are often traced, and shot by the artful Indians; when wounded they are very furious, which cautions the Indians how they attack them in open savannas, where no trees are to screen themselves from their fury. Their hoofs more than their horns are their offensive weapons, and whatever opposes them are in no small danger of being trampled into the earth. Their flesh is very good, of a high flavor, and differs from common beef, as venison from mutton. The bunch on their backs is esteemed the most delicate part of them; they have been known to breed with tame cattle, that were become wild and the calves being so too, were neglected; and though it is the general opinion that if reclaiming these animals is impracticable (of which no trial has been made) to mix the breed with tame cattle, would much improve the breed, yet nobody has had the curiosity, nor have given themselves any trouble about it. Of the skins of these beasts the Indians make their winter moccasins, i.e. shoes, but being too heavy for clothing, are not so often put to that use; they also work the long hairs into garters, aprons, etc. dying them into various colors.

The Moose or Elk

This stately animal is a native of New England, and the more northern parts of America, and are rarely seen south of the latitude of 40, and consequently are never seen in Carolina. I never saw any of these animals, but finding the relations that have been given of their stupendous bulk, and stature, favor so much of hyperbole, I was excited to be the more inquisitive concerning them, which in America I had frequent opportunities of both Indians and white men who had killed them; from which inquiries I could not understand that any of them ever arrive to the height of six feet, which is no more than half the height of what Mr. Fosselin says they are in his account of New England; and though in a later account this lofty animal has been shortened a foot and a half, there still remains four feet and an half, to reduce it to its genuine stature.

A very curious gentleman, and native of New England, informs me that they abound in the remoter parts of that colony, and are very rarely seen in the inhabited parts, and as rarely brought alive into the settlements; it therefore seems probable that the aforesaid exaggerated accounts of this animal was an imposition on the too credulous relaters, who never saw any themselves. The above gentleman further adds, that stag moose is about the bigness of a middle sized ox. The stag of this beast hath palmated horns, not unlike those of the German elk, but differs from them in having branched brow antlers. See a figure of the Horns, *Phil. Transact.* No. 444.

The Stag of America

This beast nearest resembles the European red deer, in color, shape, and form of the horns, though it is a much larger animal, and of a stronger make; their horns are not palmated, but round, a pair of which weighs upwards of thirty pounds; they usually accompany buffalo, with whom they range in droves in the upper and remote parts of Carolina, where as well as in our other colonies, they are improperly called elks. The French in America call this beast the Canada stag. In New England it is known by the name of the gray moose, to distinguish it from the preceding beast, which they call the black moose.

The Fallow Deer

These are the most common deer of America; they differ from the fallow deer in England, in the following particulars, *viz.* They are taller, longer legged, and not so well haunched as those of Europe; their horns are but little palmated, they stand bending forward, as the others do backward, and spread but little. Their tails are longer. In color these deer are little different from the European fallow deer, except that while young their skins are spotted with white. Near the sea they are always lean, and ill tasted, and are subject to botts breeding in their heads and throats, which they frequently discharge at their noses.

The Greenland Deer

In the year 1738, and 1739, Sir Hans Sloane had brought him from Greenland a buck and a doe of this kind of deer. The buck was about the height of a calf of a month old, and at a distance so much resembled one, that at first view it has been taken for a calf, before the horns were grown. These deer have thicker necks, and larger limbs than the fallow deer; the horns are much curved, and stand bending forward, the brow antlers are placed near together, and are palmated. In winter they are warmly clothed, with thick woolly hair, of a dusky white color, which at the approach of spring falls off, and is succeeded by a cooler summer covering of short smooth hair, of a brown color. The does have also horns. The noses of these deer are in a singular manner covered with hair. These seem to be a different species of deer from the reindeer of Lapland.

The Rabbit

The rabbit of Carolina is also common to the other northern parts of America; they are commonly called hares; they differ but little in appearance from our wild rabbit, being of like form and color, as is also the color and taste of the flesh. They do not burrow in the ground, but frequent marshes, hiding in sedgy watery thickets, and when started run for refuge into hollow trees, into which they creep as high as they can, but by kindling a fire, the smoke smothers and compels them to drop down, and so are taken. In autumn these rabbits are subject to large maggots, which are bred between the skin and flesh.

The Monax

This animal is about the bigness of a wild rabbit; and of a brown color, the head also resembles most that of a rabbit, except that the ears are short, like those of a squirrel; the feet are like those of a rat, the tail like that of a squirrel, but much less hairy. It feeds on bread, fruit, and other vegetable diet. At certain times they retire to their subterraneous lodgings, and sleep continually a month or longer together; they are inhabitants of Maryland, Pennsylvania, etc. Their flesh is esteemed good meat.

The Raccoon

The raccoon is somewhat smaller, and has shorter legs than a fox, it has short pointed ears, a sharp nose, and a brush tail, transversely marked with black and gray, the body is gray, with some black on its face and ears. They resemble a fox more than any other creature, both in shape and subtlety, but differ from him in their manner of feeding, which is like that of a squirrel, and in not burrowing in the ground; they are numerous in Virginia and Carolina, and in all the northern parts of America, and are a great nuisance to corn fields and hen roosts; their food is also berries, and all other wild fruit. Near the sea, and large rivers, oysters and crabs are what they very much subsist on; they disable oysters when open, by thrusting in one of their paws, but are often catched by the sudden closing of it, and held so fast (the oyster being immovably fixed to a rock of others) that when the tide comes in they are drowned. They lie all the day in hollow trees, and dark shady swamps; at nights they rove about the woods for prey; their flesh is esteemed good meat, except when they eat fish. Through their penis runs a bone in form of an S.

The Opossum

The opossum is an animal peculiar to America, particularly all the northern continent abound with them as far north as New England, and as Merian has described them at Surinam, it is probable they inhabit as far to the south as they do to the north. This beast being of a distinct genus, has little resemblance to any other creature. It is about the size of a large rabbit, the body is long, having short legs, the feet are formed like those of a rat, as are also its ears, the snout is long, the teeth like those of a dog; its body is covered thinly with long bristly whitish hair, the tail is long, shaped like that of a rat, and void of hair. But what is most remarkable in this creature and differing from others, is its false belly, which is formed by a skin or membrane (enclosing its dugs) which it opens and closes at will. Though contrary to the Laws of Nature, nothing is more believed in America than that these creatures are bred at the teats of their dams. But as it is apparent from the disection of one of them by Dr. Tyson, that their structure is formed for generation like that of other animals, they must necessarily be bred and excluded the usual way of other quadrupeds; yet that which has given cause to the contrary opinion is very wonderful, for I have many times seen the young ones just born, fixed and hanging to the teats of their dams when they were not bigger than mice; in this state all their members were apparent, yet not so distinct and perfectly formed but that they looked more like a fetus than otherwise, and seemed inseparably fixed to the teats, from which no small force was required to pull their mouths, and then being held to the teat, would not fix to it again. By what method the dam after exclusion fixes them to her teats, is a secret yet unknown. See *Phil. Transact.* No. 239 and No. 290. In Brazil it is called cariqueya.

Mr. Le Brun, in his travels through Moscovy, Persia, etc. to the East Indies, Vol. II, p. 347, hath given a figure and imperfect description of an animal somewhat resembling this species of creatures which he saw kept tame near Batavia, in the Island of Java, and was there called Filander.

The Beaver

Beavers inhabit all the northern continent of America, from latitude of 30 to the latitude of 60. They differ nothing in form from the European beaver; they are the most sagacious and provident of all other quadrupeds; their economy and inimitable art in building their houses would puzzle the most skillful architect to perform the like; in short, their performances would almost conclude them reasonable creatures. Their houses they always erect over water, which is a necessary situation, that as they being amphibious, may in the most convenient manner enjoy both elements, and on any emergency plunge into the water. These edifices are usually three stories high, one of them under water, another over that, and a third over both; the uppermost chamber serves as a retreat and a store-room in case of inundations, and though instinct guides them to such places, which by situation are less liable to rapid streams, and that these apartments are built with a strength better able to resist torrents, than human art can perform, with the like materials; yet these artful fabrics are often swept away by impetuous currents, which necessitates them to rebuild in another place. The materials that compose these fabrics are trees, with the limbs of trees, cut into different dimensions fitting their purpose, besides reeds, sedge, mud, etc. The capacity and unanimity of these creatures is in nothing more remarkable than in their cutting down trees with their teeth, and carrying them considerable distances. I have measured a tree thus fallen by them, that was three feet in circumference, and in height proportion-

able, which I was assured by many was much smaller than some they cut down. Their joint concurrence and manner of carrying such vast loads is so extraordinary that it can hardly be imagined but that the seeing this remarkable performance must have been attempted by one or other, yet I never heard it confessed by any white man that he saw it. Whether they perform this work in dark nights only, or that they are endowed with a greater sagacity than other animals to conceal their secret ways, I know not. Some are taken by white men, but it is the more general employment of Indians, who as they have a sharper sight, hear better, and are endowed with an instinct approaching that of beasts, are so much the better enable to circumvent the subtleties of these wary creatures. See a farther account of this animal, and of the use of the castoreum in *Phil. Trans.* No. 430.

The Quickhatch

This animal inhabits the very northern parts of America, and has not been observed by any author, or known in Europe till the year 1737, one was sent to Sir Hans Sloane from Hudson's Bay. It was about fourteen inches high, and in shape most resembled a bear, particularly the head. The legs were short and thick, the feet like those of a bear, the number of toes on each foot were five, with strong claws; it had a brush tail, the whole body was covered with a very thick hairy fur of a dark brown color.

My want of an opportunity of figuring this with the monax, porcupine, and Greenland deer, is amply supplied by Mr. Edwards, Beadle of the Royal College of Physicians, who in a collection of the figures, and descriptions of fifty rare animals, has amongst them figured these with great truth and accuracy.

The Porcupine of North America

This beast is about the size of a beaver, and somewhat resembles it in the form of its body, and head, having also four teeth, placed in like manner with those of the beaver; its ears are small, round, and almost hid by the hairs about them; the legs are short, the fore feet having each four toes, and the hind feet five on each foot, with very long claws; the tail is somewhat long, which with its whole body is covered with long soft fur of a dark brown color, amongst which were thinly interspersed stiff bristly hairs, much longer than the fur. Its quills which are the characteristic of this animal, are largest on the hind part of the back, yet are not above three inches in length, gradually shortening toward the head and belly, the point of every quill is very sharp and jagged, with very small prickles, nor discernible but by a microscope. The nose is remarkably covered with hair. These porcupines are natives of New England, and the more northern parts of America, and are sometimes, though rarely found as far south as Virginia.

The Horse

The horses of Carolina are of the Spanish breed, occasioned by some hundreds of them being drove as plunder from the Spanish settlements about the year ——. They are small, yet hardy, and will endure long journeys, and are not subject to so many maladies as are incident to horses in England. As stallions have been introduced from England, the breed must necessarily be improved, Carolina being in a climate that breeds the finest horses in the world.

The Cow

Cows and oxen in Carolina are of a middling size, cows yield about half the quantity of milk as those of England; in the upper parts of the country the milk is well tasted, but where cows feed in salt marshes, the milk and butter receives an ill flavor. Cattle breed so fast, and are so numerous in Carolina, that many run wild, and without having the owners mark, are anyone's property.

The Sheep

The sheep of Carolina being of English breed, have the like appearance, and are of a middling size; their flesh is tolerably well tasted, and will probably be much better, when they are fed in the hilly parts of the country. The wool is fine, and though they are not so much clothed with it as sheep in the northern parts, yet they have much more than those which inhabit more south. An instance of which I observed in sheep carried from Virginia to Jamaica, which as they approached the south, gradually dropped their fleeces, which by the time they arrived at the island, was all fallen off, and was succeeded by hair, like that of goats. This besides infinite other instances, shows the wise designs of providence in bestowing on these creatures extraordinary clothing so necessary to human life in cold countries, and easing them of that load which otherwise might be insupportable to them in sultry countries, and of little use to man.

The Hog

The hogs of Carolina and Virginia are of a small breed, and a rusty reddish color; their being liable to the attacks of rapacious beasts, seemed to have emboldened, and infused into them a fierceness much more than in our English swine; and when attacked, will with their united force, make a bold stand, and bloody resistance. The great plenty of mast, and fruit, so adapts these countries to them, that they breed innumerably, and run wild in many parts of the country. Their flesh excels any of the kind in Europe, which peaches and other delicates they feed on contribute to. But to such hogs, they design to make bacon of, they give Indian corn to harden the fat.

OF FISH

A list of the common names of the fish of Carolina, exclusive of those before figured and described

SEA FISH			RIVER FISH
Whale	Drum-red	Sheep-head	Pike
Grampus	Angel-fish	Eel	Perch
Shark	Shad	Eel Conger	Trout
Dog-fish	Smelt	Eel Lamprey	Roach
Porpoise	Garr-white	Fat-back	Daice
Thresher	Gar green	Herring	Carp
Bottle-nose	Mullet	Taylor	Cat-fish
Sword-fish	Sole	Breem	
Saw-fish	Plaise	Trout	
Devil-fish	Sting-Ray	Toad-fish	
Cavally	Thornback	Sun-fish	
Blue-fish	Flounder	Black-fish	
Drum-black	Bass	Rock-fish	
	Sea-tench	Crabs, etc	

SOME OBSERVATIONS CONCERNING THE FISH ON THE COASTS OF CAROLINA AND VIRGINIA

Whales

Whales of different species are sometimes cast on shore, as are grampuses in storms and hurricanes.

The Devil-fish

This is a flat fish, and somewhat resembles a skate; on its head are two or more horns; in each jaw is a thick flat bone, which by moving horizontally in the manner of millstones, grinds its food, which is shell fish, etc. A small fish of this kind I once caught in a net, but it unluckily falling overboard, I was deprived of an opportunity of observing it, which I much regretted, not only for its scarcity, but the extraordinary oddness of its structure. It is a large fish, and of great strength, as will appear by the following circumstance. A sloop of 80 tons lying at anchor in the harbor of Charles-Town, was on a sudden observed to move and scud away at a great rate; this being in view of hundreds of spectators, and it being known that nobody was on board it, caused no small consternation. At length it appeared to be one of these fish, which had entangled its horns with the cable, and carried the sloop a course of some leagues before it could disentangle itself from it, which at length it did, and left the sloop at anchor again, not far from the place he moved it from.

The Porpoise

Porpoises are numerous in bays, and creeks, where by their furious pursuit of other fish, they often plunge themselves so far on shore, that for want of a sufficient depth of water to retreat back, they are left on land, and become a prize to the discoverer, they yielding much oil. These fish will not be taken by a bait; they are gregarious, being rarely seen single.

They are straight bodied, but by their undulating motion in swimming, and by their appearing alternately in and out of the water, they seem to be curved and resemble the shape of the dolphin, as they are figured in the sculptures of the ancients.

The Shark

Sharks in Carolina are not so numerous, large and voracious as they are between the tropics, yet the coasts, bays, and larger rivers have plenty of them, as well as of a diminutive kind of shark, called a dog-fish, which are eat.

Black and Red Drum Fish

These fish are about the size of cods, and shaped not unlike them; they are esteemed very good fish, and by their great plenty are no small benefit to the inhabitants, who in April and May resort in their canoes to the bays, and large rivers, and at night by the light of a fire in their canoes, kill great plenty of them, by striking them with harpoons, besides in the day time with hook and line. Many of them are yearly barreled up with salt, and sent to the West Indies.

The Bass

The bass is a fish of equal size, and esteemed very good; they are found both in salt, and in fresh water, in great plenty.

Herrings

Herrings in March leave the salt waters, and run up the rivers and shallow streams of fresh water in such prodigious shoals, that people cast them on shore with shovels. A horse passing these waters, unavoidably tramples them under his feet; their plenty is of great benefit to the inhabitants of many parts of Virginia and Carolina.

But the most extraordinary inundation of fish happens annually a little within the northern cape of Chesapeake Bay in Virginia, where there are cast on shore usually in March, such incredible numbers of fish, that the shore is covered with them a considerable depth, and three miles in length along the shore. At these times the inhabitants from far within land, come down with their carts and carry away what they want of the fish; there remaining to rot on the shore many times more than sufficed them; from the putrefaction that this causes, the place has attained the name of Magotty Bay.

These fish are of various kinds and sizes, and are drove on shore by the pursuit of porpoises and other voracious fish, at the general time of spawning; amongst the fish that are thus drove on shore, is a small fish called a fat-back; it is thick and round, resembling a mullet, but smaller. It is an excellent sweet fish, and so excessive fat that butter is never used in frying, or any other preparation of them. At certain seasons and places there are infinite numbers of these fish caught, and are much esteemed by the inhabitants for their delicacy.

All the sea and river fish that I observed in Carolina, differ from those in Europe of the same kind, except pikes, eels and herrings, though possibly there may be more that escaped my knowledge.

The Sturgeon

At the approach of the spring, sturgeons leave the deep recesses of the sea, and enter the rivers, ascending by slow degrees to the upper parts to cast their spawn; in May, June and July, the rivers abound with them, at which time it is surprising, though very common to see such large fish elated in the air, by their leaping some yards out of the water; this they do in an erect posture, and fall on their sides, which repeated percussions are loudly heard some miles distance in still evenings; it is also by this leaping action that many of them are taken, for as some particular parts of the rivers afford them most food, to those places they resort in greater plenty. Here the inhabitants (as the Indians taught them) place their canoes and boats, that when the sturgeon leap, these boats and canoes may receive them at their fall. It is dangerous passing over these leaping holes, as they are called, many a canoe, and small boat having been overset by the fall of a sturgeon into it.

At the latter end of August, great numbers of these sturgeons approach to the cataracts, and rocky places of the river, where the English and Indians go to strike them, which they do with a cane 14 feet in length, and pointed at the smaller end; with this the striker stands at the head of the canoe, another steering it. The striker when he discovers one lying at the bottom (which they generally do in six or eight feet depth) gently moves the pointed end of the cane to the fish, giving it a sudden thrust between the bony scales into its body, at which the fish scuds away with great swiftness, drawing the cane after it, the great end of which appearing on the surface of the water, directs the striker which way to pursue his chase. The fish being tired, slackens its pace, which gives the striker an opportunity of thrusting another cane into it, then it scuds away as before, but at length by loss of blood falters, and turning its belly upwards, submits to be taken into the canoe.

A she sturgeon contains about a bushel of spawn, and weighs usually three hundred, and some three hundred and fifty pounds, and are about nine feet long; the males are less.

Twenty miles above Savannah Fort, on the Savannah River, where the cataracts begin, three of us in two days killed sixteen, which to my regret were left rotting on the shore, except what we regaled ourselves with at the place, and two we brought to the garrison. Such is the great plenty and little esteem of so excellent a fish, which by proper management might turn to good account, by pickling and sending them to the Sugar Islands.

Speculative knowledge in things merely curious, may be kept secret without much loss to mankind. But the concealing things of real use is derogating from the purposes we were created for, by depriving the public of a benefit designed them by the donor of all things. It is on this motive I here insert a recipe for pickling sturgeon and caviar, which though not a nostrum, is not known to many, especially in America, where it can be of most use.

These recipes I was favored with by his excellency Mr. Johnson, late Governor of South Carolina, which he told me he got translated from the original in High Dutch, which was wrote in gold letters, and fixed in the Town Hall at Hambourg. At the same time and place he procured nets for catching them, with a design of manufacturing this useful fish in his government. But perplexities ensuing not long after, obstructed his design, which otherwise would probably have given a good example to so laudable an undertaking.

To Pickle Sturgeon

Let the fish when taken, cool on the ground, 24, 36, or 48 hours, as the weather requires; then cut in pieces, and throw it into clean water, shifting the water several times; while it is soaking, wash and brush it with hard bushes, till it is very clean, which it will be in two or three hours, and then you may tie it up with bass, and boil it; put the fish in the kettle when the water is cold, and in the boiling, the fat must be taken off very well; put in somewhat more salt then in boiling other fish, and scum it well, and boil it very softly till it be tender, an hour, or an hour and half, or two hours, according to the age of the fish, and then let it cool very well, and put it into pickle; the pickle must be made of five-eighths of beer-vinegar and three-eighths of the broth it was boiled in mixed together, and salt the pickle very well with unbeat salt, somewhat more than will make a fresh egg swim, and that will cure it.

To Make Caviar

As soon as the sturgeon is catched, rip up the belly, and take out the roe, and cut it as near as you can, flake by flake asunder, and salt it with good Spanish salt, extraordinary sharp, putting it into a basket, and there let it lie at least six weeks, and then take it out, and wash off the salt very well; then lay it on boards in the sun, so thin as that it may soon dry on both sides. It must be turned, but care must be taken that it be not too hard dried, but that you may pack it close, and as you pack it, take out all the thick skins, in which you must be very nice, and when it is packed very close, you must then take some heavy weights and lay upon it, that it may be pressed very hard, then it will be as close as a cheese to keep for use.

These rocky parts of the rivers, abound also with many excellent kind of fish, particularly perch of a very large size, and delicate taste, which in August and September become so fat by feeding on grapes, which drop from vines hanging over the rivers, that their abdomens are lined with flakes of fat, as thick as one's fingers; there are besides peculiar to these upper parts of the Savannah River a singular species of river turtle, which by boiling with the shell on, the whole becomes tender and eatable, which shell before it is boiled, seem as hard as those of the other kinds.

SOME REMARKS ON AMERICAN BIRDS

The birds of America generally excel those of Europe in the beauty of their plumage, but are much inferior to them in melodious notes; for except the mockbird, I know of none that merits the name of a song bird, unless the red bird known in England by the name of the Virginian nightingale may be allowed it; this deficiency I have observed to be still greater in birds, of the torrid parts of the world, whose chattering odd cries are little entertaining; this is evidenced in a small tract printed in the year 1667, giving an account of Surinam, then possessed by the English, which says that the birds there, for beauty claim a priority to most in the world, but making no other harmony than in horror, one howling, another skreaking, a third as it were groaning and lamenting, all agreeing in their ill concerted voices.

In America are very few European land birds, but of the water kinds there are many, if not most of those found in Europe, besides the great variety of species peculiar to those parts of the world.

Admitting the world to have been universally replenished with all animals from Noah's Ark after the general deluge, and that those European birds which are in America found their way thither at first from the Old World, the cause of disparity in number of the land, and water kinds, will evidently appear by considering their different structure, and manner of feeding, which enables the water fowl to perform a long voyage, with more facility than those of the land. The European water fowl (though they travel southerly in winter for food) are most of them natives of very northern parts of the world, where they return to and make their principal abode; this their situation probably may have facilitated their passage by the nearness of the two continents to each other at these places of their abode.

In the Island of Bermudas it frequently happens that great flights of water fowl are blown from the continent of America by strong northwest winds, on that island, the distance of which from that part of the continent where such a wind must have drove them is little less than a thousand miles; as there has not been observed any land birds, forced in this manner on that island, it seems evident that they are unable to hold out so long a flight, and consequently those few European land birds that are in America, passed over a narrower strait of sea from the Old to the New World, than that from the continent to Bermudas.

Though the nearness or joining of the two continents be not known we may reasonably conclude it to be within or very near the Arctic Circle, the coasts of the rest of the earth being well known; so that those few European land birds that are in America, must have passed thither from a very frigid part of the Old World, and though these birds inhabit the more temperate parts of Europe, they may also inhabit the very northern parts, and by a firmer texture of body, may be by nature better enabled to endure extreme cold than sparrows, finches, and other English birds, which are with us fifty to one more numerous, but are not found in America.

Though these reasons occur to me, I am not fully satisfied, nor do I conclude that by this method they passed from one continent to the other, the climate and their inability of performing a long flight may reasonably be objected.

To account therefore for this extraordinary circumstance there seems to remain but one more reason for their being found on both continents, which is the nearness of the two parts of the earth to each other heretofore, where now flows the vast Atlantic Ocean.

It is remarkable that these European land birds that are found in America are of the small kinds, particularly the *Regulus Cristatus* is one, and is the very smallest of the European birds.

There are in America, as well as in Europe, many birds of passage; those which abide in Carolina the winter, necessity drives from the frigid parts of the north, in search of food with which the more southern countries abound; but where summer birds of passage go at the approach of winter, is as little known as to where those of Europe go.

The general and most natural conjecture is that they retreat to distant countries, but as no ocular testimonies have been produced, some naturalists may have concluded that for want of such information, these birds absent themselves in a different manner. If the immenseness of the globe be considered, and the vast tracts of land remaining unknown but to its barbarous natives, it is no wonder we are yet unacquainted with the retreats of these itinerant birds.

The reports of their lying torpid in caverns and hollow trees, and of their resting in the same state at the bottom of deep waters, are notions so ill attested and absurd in themselves, that they deserve no farther notice.

If with submission I may offer my own sentiments, I must join in the general opinion, with this additional conjecture, *viz.* that the place to which they retire is probably in the same latitude of the Southern Hemisphere, or where they may enjoy the like temperature of air, as in the country from whence they came; by this change they live in perpetual summer, which seems absolutely necessary for their preservation, because all summer birds of passage subsist on insects only, and have tender bills adapted to it, and consequently are unable to subsist in a cold country, particularly swallows, martins, and a few others that feed only on the wing.

Though the warm parts of the world abound most with animals in general, water fowl may be excepted, there being of them a greater number and variety of species in the northern parts of the world, than between the tropics, yet rigid winters compel them to leave their native frozen country, and retire southward for food, and though they sometimes approach within a few degrees of the northern tropic, very few are ever seen within it, and at the return of the spring, they go back again to the north, and there breed; why water fowl particularly should abound most in cold climates, I can no otherwise attempt to account for, than that as nature has endowed all creatures with a sagacity for their preservation, so these birds to avoid the danger of voracious animals (to which they are more exposed than land birds) choose to inhabit where they least abound; all rivers and watery places in the southern latitudes abound so with ravenous fish, turtles, alligators, serpents, and other destructive creatures, that the extinction of water fowl would probably be in danger,

were they wholly confined to these latitudes; yet there are some species of the duck kind, peculiar to these torrid parts of the world, which perch and roost upon trees for their greater security, of these are the whistling duck. *Hist. Jam.* p. 324, the Ilathera duck, Vol. 1, p. 93, of this work, the summer duck, Vol. 1, p. 97, besides some others observed by Margrave and Hernandes.

Land-birds which breed and abide in Carolina in the summer, and retire in winter

The Cuckow of Carolina	The Blue Linnet
The Goat Sucker	The Painted Finch
The Summer red Bird	The Yellow Titmous
The Tyrant	The Purple Martin
The Red Headed Woodpecker	The Humming Bird
The Blue Grossbeck	The Crested Flycatcher

Land-birds which come from the north, and abide in Virginia and Carolina the winter, and retire again to the north at the approach of spring

The Pigeon of Passage	The Lark
The Fieldfare of Carolina	The Snow Bird
The Chatterer of Carolina	The Purple Finch

European land-birds inhabiting America

The Greater Butcher Bird	The Cole Titmouse
The Sand Martin	The Creeper
The Cross-bill	The Golden Crown Wren

European water-fowls which I have observed to be also inhabitants of America, which though they abide the winter in Carolina, most of them retire north in the spring to breed

The common Wild Duck	Sea-pye
The Teal	The Grey Heron
The Pochard	The Turn-Stone
The Shoveler	The Green Plover
The Shag	The Grey Plover
Penguin	Elk or Wild Swan
Aika Hoieri	Divers
Razor-bill	Sea Gulls
The Woodcock	Godwit
Snipes, both Kinds	Red Shank

The following American sea-fowl also frequent the coast of Virginia and Carolina in winter, and are called

Black Duck	Bullneck
Black Flutterers	Water-Witch
Whistlers	

The black duck is considerably bigger than the common wild duck, and is esteemed preferable to it for the goodness of its flesh, which never tastes fishy.

There remains to be observed that in the winter season there are great variety of different species of sea fowl in numerous flocks feeding promiscuously in open bays and sounds, which being at a great distance from land, is their security, and is the cause that they are seldom shot, and consequently little known; yet have they their enemies in the deep, for voracious fish devouring and maiming them, they are frequently cast disabled on shore, which has given me an opportunity of observing that most of these fowl are such whose plumage consist most of down, as loons, doukers, etc. Nature having provided them with suitable clothing for such bleak exposures.

OF INSECTS

From the influence of the sun's continual heat between the tropics, the numerous species of insects abound more within those limits, than in countries that lie north or south of them, particularly many species that are adapted by nature to live only in those hot climates, not enduring the cold of northern climates; besides the perpetual summer in those hot countries enables them to procreate the year round, which winter countries will not admit of. Notwithstanding these advantages may conduce to supply the torrid zone with the greatest number of insects; yet Carolina and the more northern countries are replenished with innumerable species, which though they lie all the winter in a state of inaction, are in their different changes protected from the cold by such various and wonderful methods, that nothing excites more admiration of the wisdom of our great creator. This I own a sufficient motive to have attempted some progress in describing them, but considering how imperfect bare descriptions would be without figures, which would have been impracticable for me to execute, without omitting subjects I thought of more consequence, I concluded to take notice only of the particular genuses I observed in Carolina, besides those which are figured and interspersed in this work.

The Earth-worm	The Cock-roach
The Leg-worm, or Guinea-worm	The Cricket
The Naked Snail	The Beetle
Chinche, Wall-louse, or Bugs	The Fire-fly
Fleas	The Butterfly
Chego	The Moth
The Louse	The Ant
The Wood-worm	The Bee
The Forty-legs, or Centipes	The Humble-bee
The Wood-louse	The Wasp
The Adder-bolt	The Fly
The Cicada, or Locust	The Mosquito
The Grasshopper	The Sand-fly
The Man Gazer	The Spider

Of the Bahama Islands

The Bahama Islands (called at their first discovery Lucaies or the Lucaian Islands) are a tract of small islands extending from the Gulf of Florida in a southeast direction almost the whole length of Cuba. The most northern of these islands is Grand Bahama, which lies in the 27th degree of north latitude, Crooked Island being the southernmost is in the latitude of 22 north. These islands, according to the map, consist of some hundreds, most of them very small; about a half a score of the largest are from 20 to 50 leagues in compass. These are Grand Bahama, Andros, Abaco, Eleutheria, or Ilathera, Providence, Crooked Island, and Cat Island. The island of Providence lies in the latitude of 25 north, it is eighteen miles long, and about ten broad. On the north side of it stands Nassau, the principal town of these islands, and seat of government; opposite to the town lies Hog Island, which is a narrow slip of land, covered with palmetto and other trees, and is about four miles long, which stretching parallel with the coast of Providence, makes a harbor before the town capable of admitting ships of about four hundred tons. The town has about——houses, most of them built with palmetto leaves, a few being of stone. A quarter of a mile from the town stands the Governor's House, on the top of a steep hill, which on the north side overlooks the town, and commands a prospect of the harbor, and sea, sprinkled with innumerable rocks, and little islands; on the south side of the house also is seen a glimmering sight of the sea cross the island south; at the west end of the town stands a fort.

Grand Bahama is the largest of the Bahama Islands; it is low, wet, and full of bogs. The islands of Andros, and that of Abaco, being very little better, yet they are all of use, and much frequented for hunting, fishing, and the plenty of excellent timber, and other useful woods they abound in. The islands of Exuma, and Crooked Island have many salt ponds, for which they are much frequented. These islands with Cat Island, are said to abound with the most good soil of any of the other, particularly Cat Island, which was formerly called St. Salvador, or Guanabani, and is yet more remarkable for being the first land discovered in America by Christopher Columbus. Between Grand Bahama Island, and the island of Cuba on the Gulf of Florida, lies a knot of small islands called the Biminis, abounding in seals. Hither the Bahamians resort to kill them, carrying proper utensils and vessels for boiling and barreling up the oil drawn from these animals. The islands before mentioned are the principal for extent, and goodness of soil, the rest are generally small, and very rocky, and contain so small a quantity of soil, that they are not worth settling. According to the opinion of the most knowing and intelligent inhabitants, Crooked Island and Cat Island (which are esteemed the two best) contain not above a tenth or an eighth part at most of the land that is plantable, and the greater part of that indifferent, the number of inhabitants on the island of Providence are computed to be somewhat less than three hundred; three hundred more are said to inhabit Ilathera, and three hundred more on Harbor Island, which is a small island near Ilathera. These were the number of inhabitants which in the year 1725 was computed to be on the Bahama Islands, besides about———negro slaves.

Though the Crown of England claims all the Bahama Islands, yet there are no residential inhabitants, except on the three before mentioned. The barrenness of these rocky islands, and the little soil they contain, employs not many hands in its culture; therefore the greater part of the inhabitants get their living other ways, *viz*: the more enterprising in building ships, which they lade with salt at Exuma, and Crooked Island, and carry it to Jamaica, and to the French at Hispaniola. They also supply Carolina with salt, turtle, oranges, lemons, etc. but the greater number of the Bahamians content themselves with fishing, striking of turtle, hunting guanas, cutting brasiletto wood, Ilathera bark, and that of wild cinnamon or winter's bark, for these purposes they are continually roving from one island to another, on which shores they are frequently enriched with lumps of ambergris, which was formerly found more plentiful on the shores of these islands. The principal food on which the Bahamians subsist, is fish, turtle, and guanas, there are a few cattle, and sheep, but they increase not so much here as in more northern countries, especially sheep. Goats agree better with this climate. Their bread is made of maize, or Indian corn, and also of wheat; the first they cultivate, but not sufficient for their consumption. Wheat is imported to them in flower from the northern colonies. There are produced likewise plenty of potatoes and yams, which supply the want of bread, and are so much the better adapted to these rocks, as agreeing well with a barren soil. Besides water, the most general and useful of all liquors, their drink is Madeira wine, rum punch, and other liquors, imported to them.

OF THE AIR OF THE BAHAMA ISLANDS

The Bahama Islands are blessed with a most serene air, and are more healthy than most other countries in the same latitude, they being small, having a dry rock soil, and pretty high land, are void of noxious exhalations, that lower and more luxuriant soils are liable to. This healthiness of the air induces many of the sickly inhabitants of Carolina to retire to them for the recovery of their health; the northernmost of these islands lie as much without the northern tropics, as the southernmost do within it, their extent of latitude being about five degrees; yet that distance, so near the tropics, causes little difference in their temperature; but those islands that lie west, and nearest the coast of Florida, are affected with cold winds, blowing from the northwest over a vast tract of continent, to those which lie east, the winds have a larger tract of sea to pass, which blunts the frigid particles, and allays the sharpness of them. At the island of Providence in December 1725, it was two days so cold, that we were necessitated to make a fire in the Governor's kitchen to warm us, yet no frost nor snow ever appears there, nor even on Grand Bahama, which lies not twenty leagues from the coast of Florida, yet there the winters are attended with frost and snow.

The north side of Cuba also enjoys the benefit of these refreshing winds, particularly that part of the island on which the Havana stands, to this, no doubt, is owing the healthiness of the air and good character of that proud emporium; the conquest of which, by British arms, would put us in possession of a country much more agreeable to British constitutions, than any of the islands between the tropics, and under God, enable them to multiply, and stand their ground, without the necessity of such numerous recruits from their mother country, as has been always found necessary to prevent a total extinction of the inhabitants of our unhealthy Sugar Islands.

I never heard that any of the Bahama Islands are subject to earthquakes, and though thunder and lightning is as frequent in these islands, as in most parts of the world in these latitudes, yet it is less violent than on the continent, where the air is more stagnated. The winds blow three-quarters of the year east, and between the south and the east; in winter the winds are most at north and northwest; August and September are blowing months, and are attended with hurricanes, at which time the winds are very changeable, shifting suddenly to all points of the compass. Though the trees and plants are never deprived of their leaves by long droughts, as at Jamaica, and other of the Sugar Islands, they frequently are; yet it rains not often but so violently, that it supplies the deficiency of more frequent refreshments.

OF THE SOIL

The Bahama Islands may not only be said to be rocky, but are in reality entire rocks, having their surface in some places thinly covered with a light mold, which in a series of time has been reduced to that consistence from rotten trees and other vegetables.

Thus much of the character of these islands being considered, one would expect that they afforded the disagreeable prospect of bare rocks. But on the contrary, they are always covered with a perpetual verdure, and the trees and shrubs grow as close and are as thick clothed with leaves, as in the most luxuriant soil.

Though the productive soil on these rocky islands is small, the plantable land, as it is here called, consists of three kinds, distinguished by their different colors, as, the black, the red, and the white.

The black land is at the declivity of narrow valleys and low places, into which it is washed from the ascents above them; the corruption of vegetable matter, which lie in some places several inches deep, of a dark color, light, and fine grained. This soil is very productive the first two or three years. In these little valleys or gullies have formerly been planted sugarcanes, of which were made rum and molasses; but as the fertility of this land was soon exhausted, obliged the proprietors to desist from cultivating it. The next land in goodness is the red land, which is more of a natural soil than the black; it has no good aspect, yet is more durable than the black, and is tolerably productive.

The white ground is found best for Indian corn, it is light-colored sand, and though it appears little better than that on the sea side, to which it usually joins, yet it produces a small kind of maize, with good increase. In many places, where the rocks are loose, they are broke into portable pieces, and piled in heaps, between which is planted yams, cassadar, potatoes, mellons, etc. which fructify beyond imagination. Cotton grows on these islands without cultivation, in the most barren places, it is here perennial, and is said to produce cotton inferior to none in the world.

There are no plains or considerable hills in Providence or any of the other islands I was on, but the superficies is everywhere covered with rocks of unequal sizes, amongst which the trees and shrubs grow so thick and intricately, that is very difficult, and in some places wholly impracticable to pass through these rocky thickets, without cutting a path. Many of the islands, particularly Providence, abound with deep caverns, containing salt water at their bottoms; these pits being perpendicular from the surface, their mouths are frequently so choked up, and obscured by the fall of trees and rubbish, that great caution is required to avoid falling into these unfathomable pits (as the inhabitants call them) and it is thought, that many men, which never returned from hunting have perished in them. In Providence, and some other islands, are extensive tracts of low level land, or rather spongy rock, through which, at the coming in of the tide, water oozes, by subterraneous passages from the sea, covering it some feet deep with salt water, which at the return of the tide sinks in, and is no more seen, until the return of the tide again, so that there is an alternate appearance of a lake and a meadow at every 12 hours; one of these lakes being visible at the distance of about four miles from the Governor's House, surprised me at its appearing and disappearing several days successively, until I was truly informed of the cause. The caverns before mentioned, I make no doubt of, are supplied with salt water from the sea, in like manner with these lakes, but because of their depth and darkness, the rising and falling of the water may not have been observed; the coast of Providence, and most of the Bahama Islands are environed with rocks in various manners; in some places they seem to be tumbled in heaps confusedly, many of them are forty or fifty feet high, and steep towards the sea. Others are scattered promiscuously along the shore, and some way in the sea; some other parts of the shores are covered with sand, whose banks rise gradually fifty or sixty yards above low water mark, below which, in shallow waters innumerable rocks appear in different shapes, some singly, others in level beds, etc. in short the submarine parts environing these islands as well as the islands themselves, are entirely rock. These rocks are of a light gray color, and chalky consistence, not difficult to break with a hammer, except those on the seashore, which by being exposed to the sea air, are harder, more compact and heavy; the shores and shallows of the sea in other places are covered with beds of honeycomb rock, which by the continual agitation of the sea, are perforated and hollowed in a very extraordinary manner.

About a league from the shores of many of the Bahama Islands, are reef or shelves of this kind of rock, running parallel with the land several leagues together, which being covered at high water, are very dangerous, and have frequently proved fatal to the distressed mariner.

These rocky shores must necessarily be a great impediment to the navigation of these islands; but as the inhabitants are well acquainted with the coasts, and expert in building sloops and boats, adapted to the danger, they do not suffer so much, as the terrible appearance of the rocks seem to threaten.

Though the trees on these rocky islands, grow generally not so large as in Virginia and Carolina, where soil is deep, yet it is amazing to see trees of a very large size grow out of rocks, where no soil is visible, and the rock solid and compact, before the roots found way to separate them, particularly mahogany trees, which are usually the largest trees, these islands afford, and are commonly three, and many of them four foot through. All the nourishment that the trees receive, can be only from the rotten wood, leaves and other vegetables digested into mold, and received into the hollows and chinks of the rocks, where the fibers of the trees insinuate, and as they swell and grow bigger, widen the crevices, which, with the assistance of wind and rain, admits of small but repeated supplies of fresh nourishment; where the rocks are so stubborn, as not to admit of the roots penetration, they keep along the surface, until they find a chink or a crevice to creep into; and it is frequent to see more roots of a tree lie out of the ground, than the whole body, limbs and all, contain.

Though the figures of the most remarkable trees, shrubs, etc. of the Bahama Islands are here exhibited, many things remain undescribed for want of a longer continuance there; particularly four kind of palms, which, as it is a tribe of trees inferior to none, both as to their usefulness and majestic appearance, I regret my not being able to give their figures, or at least a more accurate description of them, especially of the silver-leaf and hog-palms, of which, I think, no notice has been taken.

The Plat Palmetto

This palm grows not only between the tropics, but is found further north than any other. In Bermuda its leaves were formerly manufactured, and made into hats, bonnets, etc. and of the berries were made buttons. This is the slowest grower of all other trees, if credit may be given to the generality of the inhabitants of Bermuda, many of the principal of whom affirmed to me, that with their nicest observations, they could not perceive them to grow an inch in height, nor even to make the least progress in fifty years, yet in the year 1714, I observed all these islands abounding with infinite numbers of them of all sizes. This kind of palm grows also on all the maritime parts of Florida and South Carolina, whose northern limits being in the latitude of 34 north, is also the farthest north, that these palms grow to their usual stature, which is about 40 feet high, yet they continue to grow in a humble manner, as far north as New England, gradually diminishing in size, as they approach the north, being in Virginia not above four feet high, with their leaves only growing from the earth, without a trunk, yet producing branches of berries, like those of the trees. In New England they grow much lower, their leaves spreading on the ground. This remarkable difference in the same plant has been the cause of their being thought different species, though I think they are both the same, and that the smallest of the northern ones, is occasioned by their growing out of their proper climate, which is hot, into a much cooler one, where the heat of the sun is insufficient to raise them to trees.

Most plants as well as animals, north of the tropics, grow in different climates particularly adapted to every species; and there are some instances of other plants besides these palms, whose limits are less confined, and which grow in a greater extent of latitude, from south to north, and the nearer they approach the north, so much less they are in stature.

In South Carolina grows a kind of opuntia, which are frequently three or four feet high, from which I have often picked cochineal in small quantities; both plants and insects were much smaller than those of Mexico, but the latter, in color and appearance the same. In North Carolina the same species of Opuntia rises about two feet high, and in Virginia and further north, their leaves grow but little above the ground, lying flat on it. Alligators, as I have before observed, are much less at their northern abodes, than they are in the more southern regions. Many other instances may be produced of vegetables, and animals of the same species abiding in different climates, that are diminutive in their northern situation.

The Thatch Palmetto

This tree seldom aspires above twelve or fourteen feet, the leaves grow low, and spreading, and are particularly made use of for building houses, they serving both for walls and covering.

The Silver Leaf Palmetto

The usual height of these trees, is about sixteen feet, the leaves somewhat less than the precedent, but thicker set, and of a shining silver color. Of the leaves of these trees are made ropes, baskets, etc. The berries are large and sweet, and yield a good spirit.

The Hog Palmetto

These trees grow to the height of ten or twelve feet, the verges of the leaves are divided by deep sections, resembling the leaves of the *Palma altissima*. The singularity of this tree is remarkable, for as the eatable parts of all plants is in their fruit, roots, or leaves, the trunks alone of these trees is an excellent food for hogs; and many little desert islands, that abound with them, are of great use to the Bahamians for the support of their swine. The exterior bark of the trunks of these trees is somewhat hard, and in appearance like those of the other palmettos, within which is contained that soft and pithy substance of a luscious sweet taste, which the hogs are delighted with.

OF THE SEA, ENCOMPASSING THE BAHAMA ISLANDS, WITH ITS PRODUCTIONS

The sea round these islands is generally very shallow, but deep beneath gradually from the land, to the unfathomable abyss of the ocean. The water is so exceeding clear, that at the depth of twenty fathom, the rocky bottom is plainly seen, and in calm weather I have distinctly and with much pleasure beheld variety of fish sporting amidst groves of corallines and numerous other submarine shrubs, growing from the rocky bottom, amongst infinite variety of beautiful shells, fungus, astroites, etc. Amongst these submarine productions there were at certain places, great plenty of the *Lenticula marina*, growing to the rocks; this plant is remarkable for the great quantities of it, with which the Atlantic Sea is in many places covered.

As usually the clearest waters afford the wholesomest and best fish, consequently it might be expected that at the Bahamas, where the water is so remarkably transparent, the fish there might be at least as wholesome as those on the coast of Florida, where the water is not so limpid, but many of the Bahamians have clearly experienced the contrary, several kinds of their fish being so poisonous that they have direful effects on those who eat them. In some particular places they are poison, yet in other places not a mile distant, they are eat with impunity; but experience has taught them to distinguish the places that afford good and bad. From what cause the poison in these fish is, I never could hear accounted for, or so much as conjectured. Possibly the following observation may give some light to the inquiry. In procuring from the bottom of the sea six or eight fathom deep, some corallines and other sea productions for their extraordinary oddness and beauty; the man that dived for them, happened to rub his belly with his hands, that had gathered slime from the corals he brought up; he immediately felt such uneasiness, that casting himself on the sand, he wallowed in distracted postures, crying out with the excessive torture it put him to, though the sharpness of the pain lasted not longer than a quarter of an hour. This coral grows on the rocky bottom of the sea, some leagues from land, as well as near the shore. While young they are soft and pliant, but harden to the consistence of stone, some of them grow above six feet high, and branch into various forms, some resembling the palmed horns of deer, others round horns, with various other odd forms, one plant producing not more than one of these resemblances, every kind sporting after the manner peculiar to it. All these different formed corals are of like consistence, and are covered alike with the same mucilage, or acrimonious slime, which with much handling and daubing ones fingers with, it causes to swell, with such prickling smart, that it is very painful; in places noted for fish being poisonous, these plants most abound. From the guts of the sea-unicorn, or trumpet fish, and some others that are not esteemed good, I have taken much of this coral in small pieces, some being almost digested. It has a sulphurous and very noxious smell, which it retains after the slime is dried up, and laid in the sun and air several months. At first it is yellow, but being some time exposed to the air, turns white.

Neither Providence, nor any of the Bahama Islands have either rivers or springs, the deficiency of which is supplied with rain water, contained in reservoirs of rock, placed by nature on all or most of the islands; this water is so shaded with trees, and shrubs that it is clear, cool, and is esteemed wholesome.

It is no wonder that such unhospitable rocky islands should be deficient of the numbers and variety of animals that the continent abounds with, for except a few beasts of use that have been introduced there (such as horses, cows, sheep, goats, hogs, and dogs) all that are aborigines are guanas, lizards, land crabs, coneys and rats, which last probably were brought by ships. Of land birds I did not observe above nine or ten sorts, except migratory seabirds, which also frequent other coasts.

The shallow seas encompassing these islands, on the contrary are as remarkable for their abundance and variety of its watery inhabitants, exceeding in number of species, and excelling in the elegance of their colors and marks, but inferior in wholesomeness and goodness of taste to the fish in more northern latitudes. Adequate to this, frequent opportunities has confirmed to me, that as the productions of nature in general are very scanty near the Arctic Circle, there is a graduation of increase at every degree of latitude approaching the tropics, and though the distance of one degree may not be sufficient to perceive it, yet four or five degrees makes it evidently appear, not only by the greater number of species of terrestrial animals, but of fish and vegetables, which by how much nearer the torrid zone, so much the more numerous they are. And I think it is not improbable that the numerous species of creatures that inhabit between the tropics, far exceed in number all the rest of the terrestrial world.

A List of the Common Names of the Fish Frequenting the Bahama Seas, Exclusive of Those Already Figured and Described in this Work

The Sperma Ceti Whale	The Dolphin	The Sea Bream
Grampus	Bonito	Pilot-fish
Shark	Albacore	Hound-fish
Barracuda	Sword-fish	Gar-fish
Jew-fish	Saw-fish	Amber-fish
Spanish Mackerel	Grouper	King-fish
Cavally	Porpoise	Turbot
Sting-ray	Black Rock-fish	Black-fish
Whip-ray	Gray Fin Rock-fish	Hedgehog
Plaice		Yellow-fish
Nuss	Yellow Rock-fish	Coney-fish
Chub		Cow-fish
Gray Snapper	Bone-fish	Lobsters
Mutton Snapper	Whiting	Crabs

Though many of the fish in this list, besides those whose figures are exhibited from some resemblance they bear to those in Europe, have attained the same names, yet I never observed in these seas, nor anywhere between the tropics the same kinds of fish, but were all of different species from any in Europe, a few excepted, which are dolphins, bonitos, albacores, sharks, flying-fish, rudder-fish and remoras; which contrary to all other fish frequent the most distant part of the ocean from land, and are also found on the coasts of the Old World, as well as in America. The universality and numerous shoals of these migratory fish, particularly the three first, are a benefit to mariners in long voyages, affording them comfortable changes of fresh diet, after long feeding on salt meats.

OF SHELLS

Shells, as well as other productions of nature, abound more in number of species, and are more beautiful between the tropics, than in the other parts of the world. At the Bahama Islands are produced most of the kinds of American sea shells, *Frutices marini*, etc. that are found between the northern tropics and the line. The shallow seas of these rocky islands seem more adapted to their propagation, than most other places in those latitudes; the vast profusion that are here found with the more frequent opportunities of collecting them, has caused the cabinets of the curious in England to be more furnished with them from thence, than from any other parts of the world; therefore as few new species can be added to those figured by Dr. Lister, Bonana, and others, I shall only add some observations on shells which I made at the place of their production.

Every species of shell-fish inhabit particular parts of the sea agreeable to their natures. This seems to have some analogy to plants, whose different kinds affect a different soil and aspect. The various position of the rocks, and banks on which shells lie, besides other natural causes, may conduce to their abiding more in one place than in another; therefore these islands do not afford shells alike plentiful. Those which lie west and nearest the Gulf of Florida, particularly Providence, Abaco, Andros, and Grand Bahama, have fewer than the windward, or easternmost islands, particularly those called the French Keys, Turks Islands, Exuma, and Long Island. Some shells which are plentiful on the south shore of an island, are rarely seen on the north side, and other kinds that the north sides abound in, are not on the south. Some shells are very scarce, and are found only at a few particular islands, and parts of those islands, bearing the same aspect, and are rarely found promiscuously scattered with other shells. Most of all the different kinds of shell-fish, abide in a certain depth of water. Some so deep and far out at sea, that they are seldom seen alive, but at the death of the fish, the shell is cast on shore. Others are found less deep. Some in shallow water. Others lying flat on the rocks or sand. Some sticking flat to the sides of rocks. Others sticking to the sides of rocks horizontally. Some confined in the hollows and cavities of rocks. Some buried deep in sand, others in mud. Some lying always half out of the sand. Some kinds of shell-fish which cleave to the sides of rocks abide on the north sides, exposed to the violent rage of the sea. Other kinds not enduring such violence of the waves, shelter themselves in the hollows of rocks, and mostly on the south sides of islands, where they are less exposed. Others are yet less exposed, abiding in deep cisterns of rock within land, supplied with sea water by subterraneous passages, where the water is always calm.

Amongst other shells sticking to the rocks, environing these silent waters, were oysters, which stuck horizontally to the sides of the rocks, that edge next the hinge of the oyster, being the part fixed to the rock.

These following kinds of small shells sticking to rocks, are never found in deep water, but abide where they are covered and uncovered at every flux and reflux of the tide.

Buccinum

These shells stick to rocks a little above low water, and are consequently a short time uncovered by the sea. They yield a purple liquor, like that of the murex, which will not wash out of linen stained with it.

Nerita

These shells lie uncovered three or four hours, from the time of the tides leaving them, until its return.

Cochlea

These shells lie above the flowing of the tide, they stick to shrubs and sedge, and are moistened only by the splashing and spray of the sea.

Buccinum

This kind I observed sticking only to the branches of mangrove trees, which always grow in salt water.

From these few instances it is reasonable to conclude that all other shell-fish that lie in deeper waters, abide in a depth adapted to every species; this I observed in many kinds, but for want of opportunity, and the difficulty of submarine searches, obstructed a perfect discovery of this part of their history; yet as it is not impracticable, it is to be hoped that at some time or other an opportunity may favor the curious in inquiring into the knowledge of this beautiful part of the creation, which hitherto extends little further than the shell or covering of the animal.

ADDENDA

The American Partridge

This partridge is little more than half the size of the *Perdix cinerea*, or common partridge, which it somewhat resembles in color, though differently marked, particularly the head has three black lists, one above and two below the eye, with two intermediate white lines. They covey and roost on the branches of trees. Their flesh is remarkably white, and of a different taste from our common partridge.

Gallo-pav

The wild turkeys of America much excel the European tame breed, in stature, shape, and beauty of their plumage, which is in all the same without those variegations that we see in all domestic birds. It is commonly reported that these turkeys weigh sixty pounds apiece, but of many hundred that I handled, I observed very few to exceed the weight of thirty pounds.

There are in the upper parts of Virginia, what are called pheasants, which I never saw, but by the account I have had of them, they seem to be the *Urogallus minor*, or a kind of *Lagopus*.

There is also in Virginia and Carolina, another bird which I have not had the sight of. It is called Whipper-will, and sometimes Whipper-will's Widow, from their imaginary uttering those words. It is a nocturnal bird, being seldom heard and never seen in the daytime; but at night it is heard with a loud shrill voice, incessantly repeating three, and some of them four notes as above. They lie close all day in shady thickets and low bushes, and are seen only (and that very rarely) at the dusk of the evening. I once shot one of them, but could not find it in the dark.

All the domestic or tame fowl, breed as well, and are as good as they are in England; such as cocks and hens, peafowls, turkeys, geese and ducks.

Bibliography

Allen, E. G. 1937. New Light on Mark Catesby. *Auk* 54: 349–63.

————. 1951. The History of American Ornithology before Audubon. *Transactions of the American Philosophical Society*, n.s. 41 (3): 385–91.

American Ornithologists' Union. 1983. *Check-list of North American Birds*. 6th ed. Lawrence, Kan.: Allen Press.

Audubon, J. J. 1827–38. *Birds of America*. Vols. 1–4. London: published by the author. (Double elephant folio.)

————. 1840–44. *Birds of America*. Vols. 1–7. Published by the author, New York; published by J. B. Chevalier, Philadelphia. (This is the first octavo edition, and citations in the text are from this more accessible edition.)

Bent, A. C. 1919. *Life Histories of North American Diving Birds*. U.S. National Museum Bulletin, no. 107. Washington, D.C.

————. 1921. *Life Histories of North American Gulls and Terns*. U.S. National Museum Bulletin, no. 113. Washington, D.C.

————. 1922. *Life Histories of North American Petrals and Pelicans and Their Allies*. U.S. National Museum Bulletin, no. 121. Washington, D.C.

————. 1923. *Life Histories of North American Wild Fowl*. U.S. National Museum Bulletin, no. 126, pt. 1. Washington, D.C.

————. 1925. *Life Histories of North American Wild Fowl*. U.S. National Museum Bulletin, no. 130, pt. 2. Washington, D.C.

————. 1926. *Life Histories of North American Marsh Birds*. U.S. National Museum Bulletin, no. 135. Washington, D.C.

————. 1927. *Life Histories of North American Shore Birds*. U.S. National Museum Bulletin, no. 142, pt. 1. Washington, D.C.

————. 1929. *Life Histories of North American Shorebirds*. U.S. National Museum Bulletin, no. 146, pt. 2. Washington, D.C.

————. 1932. *Life Histories of North American Gallinaceous Birds*. U.S. National Museum Bulletin, no. 162. Washington, D.C.

————. 1937. *Life Histories of North American Birds of Prey*. U.S. National Museum Bulletin, no. 167, pt. 1. Washington, D.C.

————. 1938. *Life Histories of North American Birds of Prey*. U.S. National Museum Bulletin, no. 170, pt. 2. Washington, D.C.

————. 1939. *Life Histories of North American Woodpeckers*. U.S. National Museum Bulletin, no. 174. Washington, D.C.

————. 1940. *Life Histories of North American Cuckoos, Goatsuckers, Hummingbirds, and Their Allies*. U.S. National Museum Bulletin, no. 176. Washington, D.C.

————. 1942. *Life Histories of North American Flycatchers, Larks, Swallows, and Their Allies*. U.S. National Museum Bulletin, no. 179. Washington, D.C.

————. 1946. *Life Histories of North American Jays, Crows, and Titmice*. U.S. National Museum Bulletin, no. 191. Washington, D.C.

————. 1948. *Life Histories of North American Nuthatches, Wrens, Thrashers, and Their Allies*. U.S. National Museum Bulletin, no. 195. Washington, D.C.

————. 1949. *Life Histories of North American Thrushes, Kinglets, and Their Allies*. U.S. National Museum Bulletin, no. 196. Washington, D.C.

————. 1950. *Life Histories of North American Wagtails, Shrikes, Vireos, and Their Allies*. U.S. National Museum Bulletin, no. 197. Washington, D.C.

————. 1953. *Life Histories of North American Wood Warblers*. U.S. National Museum Bulletin, no. 203. Washington, D.C.

————. 1958. *Life Histories of North American Blackbirds, Orioles, Tanagers, and Their Allies*. U.S. National Museum Bulletin, no. 211. Washington, D.C.

Bent, A.C. et al., comps. 1968. *Life Histories of North American Cardinals, Grosbeaks, Buntings, Towhees, Finches, Sparrows, and Their Allies*, ed. O. L. Austin, Jr. U.S. National Museum Bulletin, no. 237, pts. 1–3. Washington, D.C.

Bond, J. 1974. *Birds of the West Indies*. 45th ed., London: Collins.

Brickell, John. 1737. *The Natural History of North Carolina*. Dublin: James Carson.

Britton, N. L., and C. F. Millspaugh. 1920. *The Bahama Flora*. New York: published by the authors. (Gives identification of Catesby's Bahama flora.)

Byrd, William. 1940. *Natural History of Virginia, or the Newly Discovered Eden*. Richmond: Dietz Press. (Translation from the German *New-gefundenes Eden*, 1737, published by Samuel Jenner).

Campbell, D. G. 1978. *The Ephemeral Islands: A Natural History of the Bahamas*. London: Macmillan.

Cantwell, R. 1960. A Legend Comes to Life: Mark Catesby. *Sports Illustrated*, Oct. 31, pp. 70–80.

Catesby, M. 1731–43 [1729–47]. *The Natural History of Carolina, Florida and the Bahama Islands*. 2 vols. London.

————. 1747. Of Birds of Passage. *Philosophical Transactions* (Royal Society of London) 44 (1747): 435–44.

————. (Facsimile ed.) 1974. *The Natural History of Carolina, Florida and the Bahama Islands*. With an introduction by G. Frick and notes by J. Ewan. (Contains a facsimile of part of Catesby's text, and miniature reproductions of all the plates.) Savannah: Beehive Press.

Correll, D. S., and H. B. Correll. 1982. *Flora of the Bahama Archipelago*. Federal Republic of Germany: J. Cramer.

Coues, E. 1879–80. *American Ornithological Bibliography*. Washington, D.C: Government Printing Office.

Darlington, William, ed. 1849. *Memorials of John Bartram and Humphrey Marshall*. Philadelphia.

Forbush, E. H. 1927. *Birds of Massachusetts and Other New England States*. Vol. 2. Norwood, Mass.: Massachusetts Dept. of Agriculture and Norwood Press.

Frick, G. F. 1960. Mark Catesby: The Discovery of a Naturalist. *Papers of the Bibliographical Society of America* 56: 163–75.

Frick, G. F., and R. P. Stearns. 1961. *Mark Catesby: The Colonial Audubon*. Urbana: University of Illinois Press.

Hariot, Thomas. 1588. *A Briefe and True Report of the New*

Found Land of Virginia. London. (See also Quinn, 1955.)

Hilton, William. 1664. *A Relation of a Discovery Lately Made on the Coast of Florida.* London. (See also Salley, 1911.)

Howard, R. A., and G. W. Staples. 1983. The Modern Names for Catesby's Plants. *Journal of the Arnold Arboretum* 64:511–46.

Hulton, P., and D. B. Quinn. 1964. *The American Drawings of John White, 1577–90.* Chapel Hill: University of North Carolina Press.

Jordan, D. S. 1884. An Identification of the Figures of Fishes in Catesby's Natural History. *Proceedings of the U.S. National Museum* 7:190–99.

Josselyn, J. 1672. *New-England's Rarities Discovered.* London.

Lawson, J. 1709. *A New Voyage to Carolina.* . . . London. Revised edition, 1967, edited by Hugh T. Lefler. Chapel Hill: University of North Carolina Press.

Lefler, H. T., and W. S. Powell. 1973. *Colonial North Carolina: A History.* New York: Scribner.

Little, E. L. 1980. *The Audubon Society Field Guide to North American Trees, Eastern Region.* New York: Knopf (Chanticleer Press).

McAtee, W. L. 1940. Unorthodox Thoughts on Bird Migration. *Auk* 35:135–36.

———. 1945. Catesby's Tropic-Bird. *Auk* 62:137–39.

———. 1946. A Long-standing Error. *Auk* 63:242–43. (Attributes Lawson's name "flusterer" to the Surf Scoter.)

———. 1947. Torpidity in Birds. *Auk* 37:191–206.

———. 1948. Confusion of Eastern Caprimulgidae. *Auk* 65:128–29.

———. 1955–56. The Birds in Lawson's "New Voyage to Carolina," 1709. Raleigh: North Carolina Bird Club.

———. 1957. The North American Birds of Mark Catesby and Eleazar Albin. *Journal of the Society for the Bibliography of Natural History* 3 (pt. 4): 177–94.

McKinley, D. 1979. Historical Review of the Carolina Parakeet in the Carolinas. *Brimleyana* 1:81–98.

Mosby, H. S., and C. O. Handley. 1943. *The Wild Turkey in Virginia.* Richmond: Pittman-Roberson Projects.

Morton, T. 1637. *New English Canaan.* 2nd ed. London.

Newton, A. 1896. *A Dictionary of Birds.* London: Adam and Charles Black.

Niering, W. A., and N. C. Olmstead. 1979. *The Audubon Society Field Guild to North American Wildflowers, Eastern Region.* New York: Knopf (Chanticleer Press).

Patterson, A. 1972. *Birds of the Bahamas.* Brattleboro, Vermont: Durrell Publications.

Pearson, T. G., C. S. Brimley, and H. H. Brimley. 1942. *Birds of North Carolina.* (Revised 1959 by D. L. Wray and H. T. Davis.) Raleigh: North Carolina Department of Agriculture.

Philpott, J. 1977. Botanists in Colonial America. *Eno* 5 (2): 3–21.

Potter, E. F., J. E. Parnell, and R. P. Tuelings. 1980. *Birds of the Carolinas.* Chapel Hill: University of North Carolina Press.

Quinn, D. B., ed. 1955. *The Roanoke Voyages, 1584–1590.* London: Cambridge University Press.

Salley, Alexander S., ed. 1911. *Narratives of Early Carolina, 1650–1708.* New York: Scribner.

Schorger, A. W. 1955. *The Passenger Pigeon.* Madison: University of Wisconsin Press.

Sloane, Hans. 1707–25. *A Voyage to the Islands Madera, Barbados Nieves, St. Christopher's and Jamaica, with the Natural History of the Herbs, Trees, Four-footed Beasts, Fishes, Birds, Insects, Reptiles.* . . . 2 vols. London, print for the author.

Sparks, Jared. 1840. *The Works of Benjamin Franklin.* Vol. 10. Boston.

Sprunt, A., Jr., and E. B. Chamberlain. 1949. *South Carolina Bird Life.* (Revised 1970 by E. M. Burton.) Columbia: University of South Carolina Press.

Stearn, W. T. 1958. Publication of Catesby's Natural History. *Journal of the Society for the Bibliography of Natural History* 3:328.

Stearns, R. P. 1970. *Science in the British Colonies of America.* Urbana: University of Illinois Press.

Stone, W. 1905. Some Early American Ornithologists. I. Mark Catesby. *Bird-lore* 7 (2): 126–29.

———. 1929. Mark Catesby and the Nomenclature of North American Birds. *Auk* 46:447–54.

Terres, J. K. 1980. *The Audubon Society Encyclopedia of North American Birds.* New York: Knopf.

Wilson, A. 1808–14. *American Ornithology or the Natural History of the Birds of the United States.* 9 vols. Philadelphia: Bradford and Inskeep.

———. 1828–29. *American Ornithology or the Natural History of the Birds of the United States.* Vols. 1–3 (vol. 3, 1829). Philadelphia: Collins & Co. Edition of George Ord. (Citations in text are from these more accessible volumes.)

Wilson, D. S. 1978. *In the Presence of Nature.* Amherst: University of Massachusetts Press.

Index of Common and Scientific Names of Birds and Plants